the
kitchen
diaries

Nigel Slater is the author of a collection
of bestselling books including the classics
Real Fast Food and *Real Cooking*, and the
award-winning *Appetite*. He has written a
much-loved column for *The Observer* for over
a decade. His autobiography, *Toast – The
Story of a Boy's Hunger*, won six major awards
including the British Biography of the Year,
the Glenfiddich Award and the André Simon
Memorial Prize.

Also by Nigel Slater:
Real Fast Food
The 30-Minute Cook
Real Cooking
Nigel Slater's Real Food
Appetite
Thirst
Toast – The Story of a Boy's Hunger

the kitchen diaries

a year in the kitchen with

Nigel Slater

Photographs by Jonathan Lovekin

GOTHAM
BOOKS

GOTHAM BOOKS
Published by Penguin Group (USA) Inc.
375 Hudson Street, New York, New York 10014, U.S.A.
Penguin Group (Canada), 90 Eglinton Avenue East, Suite 700, Toronto, Ontario M4P 2Y3,
Canada (a division of Pearson Penguin Canada Inc.); Penguin Books Ltd, 80 Strand, London
WC2R 0RL, England; Penguin Ireland, 25 St Stephen's Green, Dublin 2, Ireland (a division
of Penguin Books Ltd); Penguin Group (Australia), 250 Camberwell Road, Camberwell,
Victoria 3124, Australia (a division of Pearson Australia Group Pty Ltd); Penguin Books
India Pvt Ltd, 11 Community Centre, Panchsheel Park, New Delhi – 110 017, India; Penguin
Group (NZ), cnr Airborne and Rosedale Roads, Albany, Auckland 1310, New Zealand (a
division of Pearson New Zealand Ltd); Penguin Books (South Africa) (Pty) Ltd, 24 Sturdee
Avenue, Rosebank, Johannesburg 2196, South Africa

Penguin Books Ltd., Registered Offices: 80 Strand, London WC2R 0RL, England

First published in Great Britain in 2005 by Fourth Estate.

Published by Gotham Books, a member of Penguin Group (USA) Inc.

First Printing, October 2006
10 9 8 7 6 5 4 3 2 1

Gotham Books and the skyscraper logo are trademarks of Penguin Group (USA) Inc.

LIBRARY OF CONGRESS CATALOGING-IN-PUBLICATION DATA
Slater, Nigel.
    The kitchen diaries : a year in the kitchen with Nigel Slater.
      p.   cm.
    ISBN 1-592-40234-8
    1. Cookery.   I. Title.
  TX714.S58625 2006
  641.5–dc22   2006041157

Printed in the United States of America
Set in Berthold Baskerville
Designed by Sam Blok

To Digger, Magrath and Poppy
And to Louise and Jonnie with love

With thanks to Sam Blok, Araminta Whitley,
Allan Jenkins, Nung Puinongpho,
Jane Middleton, Silvia Crompton, and to
Rohan and Sophie, and everyone at 4th Estate

Right food, right place, right time. It is my belief – and the point of this book – that this is the best recipe of all. A crab sandwich by the sea on a June afternoon; a slice of roast goose with applesauce and roast potatoes on Christmas Day; hot sausages and a chunk of roast pumpkin on a frost-sparkling night in November. These are meals whose success relies not on the expertise of the cook but on the more basic premise that this is the food of the moment – something eaten at a time when it is most appropriate, when the ingredients are at their peak of perfection, when the food, the cook and the time of year are at one with each other.

There is something deeply, unshakeably right about eating food in season: fresh scarlet runner beans in July, grilled sardines on a blisteringly hot August evening, a bowl of gently aromatic stew on a rainy day in February. Yes, it is about the quality of the ingredients too, their provenance and the way they are cooked, but the very best eating is also about the feeling that the time is right.

I do believe, for instance, that a cold Saturday in January is a good time to make gingerbread. It is when I made it and we had a good time with it. It felt right. So I offer it to you as a suggestion, just as I offer a cheesecake at Easter, a curry for a cold night in April and a pale gooseberry fool for a June afternoon. It is about seasonality, certainly, but also about going with the flow, cooking with the natural rhythm of the earth.

Learning to eat with the ebb and flow of the seasons is the single thing that has made my eating more enjoyable. Our culinary seasons have been blurred by commerce, and in particular by the supermarkets' much vaunted idea that consumers want all things to be available all year round. I don't believe this is true. I have honestly never met anyone who wants to eat a slice of watermelon on a cold March evening, or a plate of asparagus in January. It is a myth put about by the giant supermarkets. I worry that today it is all too easy to lose sight of food's natural timing and, worse, to miss it when it is at its sublime best. Hence my attempt at writing a book about rebuilding a cook's relationship with nature.

The diary

I wanted to know exactly when I might find something at its glorious, juicy, sweetly flavored peak. If something is to be truly, remarkably good to eat, then isn't it worth knowing precisely when that moment might be? 'Spring' or 'autumn' has always been too vague for me. There is a vast difference between winter-spring and summer-spring. Even labeling raw ingredients by the month in which they are due to ripen is a bit hit and miss (I missed the damson and greengage plums one year relying on that premise). Anyone who has gone to a farmers' market in the first week of May and again in the last week will know where I am coming from. It is like two completely different months.

That said, this is not a book whose dates are to be followed like a mantra. It is simply a book of suggestions for when you might, should you care to look, find gooseberries, Brussels sprouts, damsons etc. at their best. It is a guide to what is and isn't worth eating and when. And I like to think that there are few things more worth knowing than that. It is not some tyrannical culinary calendar but a book to dip in and out of throughout the year and the years to come, a reminder to keep an eye out for something, a gentle – and, I hope, delicious – aide-mémoire.

The photographs

The photography has been done in 'real time'. So when it says October 2nd or April 9th, then that is when the picture was shot. After I have cooked each meal and it has been photographed, we sit down and eat it while it is still hot. Then I wash up. The pictures are taken at home, so if you recognize plates and pans from my books *Real Food* or *Appetite*, then that is because they are things that I have come to love and cherish. Whether it's a vegetable peeler or a palette knife, it works for me and has become part of my life.

The food

For the most part I shop at small local shops, farmers' markets, good butchers, fish markets, delicatessens and cheese shops rather than all at once on a weekly trip to a supermarket. I have honestly never set foot inside a branch of Tesco. This book is very much a gentle plea to buy something, however small, each day, to take time to shop, to treat it as a pleasure rather than a chore. This doesn't mean I spend my life shopping, far from it. It simply means that I stock up on dry goods, such as rice, pasta and the like, once a week, then manage to find half an hour a day (sometimes less) to buy just one or two fresh things from someone who sells them with a passion and a specialist interest – easier than ever now that shops tend to stay open later.

A weekly trip to the farmers' market forms the backbone of my fresh food shopping, plus I have a weekly 'organic box' delivered to my door. I love to see those tables laid out under striped awnings with food that is being sold by the people who made or picked it. Shopping at the farmers' market means that you can buy your cream from the person who churned it, your potatoes directly from the people who dug them from the ground, your salad leaves from the guy who planted the seeds. Food with a story you can follow from seed packet to table, picked that day. This, to me, is as good as food shopping gets.

I feel that buying ingredients as fresh, as honest as this is a chance to cook them as simply as possible, to let the food taste of itself, to allow it to be what it is.

The kitchen

My kitchen is not large, but a trio of skylights and the fact that the doors open up to the garden make it a hugely pleasurable place in which to cook. It has no fancy cookers, no battery of expensive equipment, yet it has been thoughtfully and intelligently designed. The space works perfectly. Good kitchens are not about size, they are about ergonomics and light.

My garden is a tiny urban space, yet it has been crucial to this book. **The garden** Leading down from the kitchen doors are steps on which rest pots of thyme and single marigolds, dark red geraniums and Italian eggplants. There is an old stone terrace where we eat in summer round a zinc-topped table set under a fig tree. The terrace makes way for a small, rather amateurish kitchen garden, with six little beds filled to over-flowing. Two for pot-herbs, roses and old-fashioned scented pinks, one each for raspberries and currants, another for tomatoes and zucchini and one for runner beans, fava beans, artichokes and rhubarb. In amongst the chaos grow sweet peas, dahlias, nasturtiums and opium poppies.

Beyond that is a miniscule wooded patch, no deeper than twelve feet, with a tangle of plum, damson, hazelnut and quince trees, plus wild strawberries and, in winter, snowdrops growing underfoot. What I should emphasize is just how small this garden is. So when I refer to the 'kitchen garden', I am talking about a diminutive patch probably about the same size as the average yard. I make no attempt to be self-sufficient, I simply haven't the space. It is just that by growing some-thing myself, from seed or a small plant, I feel closer to understanding how and when a pear, a crab apple, a fava bean or a raspberry is at its best.

Anyone who has ever grown anything for themselves, or simply has an old apple tree in the garden, will know that you often end up with a glut – too much of the same ingredient at the same time. I was keen to reflect this in *The Kitchen Diaries*, so there are months where there may be a bounty of tomato recipes, others where almost every week seems to feature raspberries in some form or another. If you make the most of the good prices that go hand in hand with a glut at the market, or you want to use every bit of the ripe fruit and vegetables in your gar-den, then you will welcome this. Personally, I think of it as something of a glorious seasonal feast.

Roast rhubarb on a January morning; 'pick-your-own' strawberries in June; a piece of chicken on the grill on an August evening; a braised pigeon on a damp October afternoon; a pork feast in November. This is more than just something to eat, it is food to be celebrated, food that is somehow in tune with the rhythm of nature. Quite simply, the right food at the right time.

january

Dal and pumpkin soup

A salad of fennel, winter
leaves and Parmesan

Stew

A frosted marmalade cake

Frozen yogurt with
roast rhubarb

Double ginger cake

Onion soup without tears

Cheese-smothered potatoes

A velvety soup for a
clear, cold day

Bulgur wheat with eggplant
and mint

A really good spaghetti
Bolognese

Chicken broth with noodles,
lemon and mint

Spiced breaded mackerel
with smoked paprika

An herb butter for grilled
chops

A pot-roasted pheasant with
celery and sage

A clear, hot mussel soup

Sausages with salami
and lentils

A lime tart

New Year's Day. A day of hope and hot soup

There is a single rose out in the garden, a faded bundle of cream and magenta petals struggling against gray boards. A handful of snowdrops peeps out from the ivy that has taken hold amongst the fruit trees. The raspberry canes are bare, save the odd dried berry I have left for the birds, and the bean stems stand brown and dry around their frames. A withered verbena's lemon-scented leaves stand crisp against a clear, gray sky. January 1st is the day I prune back the tangle of dried sticks in the kitchen garden, chuck out anything over its sell-by date from the cupboards, flick through seed catalogues and make lists of what I want to grow and eat in the year to come. I have always loved the first day of the year. A day ringing with promise.

I bought little between Christmas and New Year, just salad and a few herbs, preferring to make do with pantry stuff: white beans and yellow lentils, parsnips and a forgotten pumpkin, cans of baked beans, dried apricots and hard, chewy figs. There is still a crumbling wedge of Christmas cake, some crystallized orange and lemon slices, a few brazils to which I cannot gain entry and a handful of tight-skinned clementines. A feast of sorts, but what I need is a hot meal.

There is juice for breakfast, blood orange, the dull fruit brushed with scarlet and still sporting its glossy green leaves. It's a bracing way to start a new year. I make a resolution to eat less but better food this year: to eat only food whose provenance I know at least a little of; to patronize artisan food producers; to increase my organic food consumption; and to shop even less at supermarkets than I do now. This should be the year in which I think carefully about everything I put in my mouth. 'Where has this come from, what effect will this have on me, my well-being and that of the environment?' Ten years ago this would all have sounded distinctly worthy, but today it just sounds like a blueprint for intelligent eating.

I have a tradition of making soup on New Year's Day, too: green lentil, potato and Parmesan, noodle broth and this year red lentil and pumpkin. It is a warm ochre soup, soothing, yet capable of releasing a slow build-up of heat from its base notes of garlic, chili and ginger; a bowl of soup that both whips and kisses.

Dal and pumpkin soup

a small onion
garlic – 2 cloves
ginger – a walnut-sized knob
split red lentils – 1 cup plus 2 tablespoons
ground turmeric – $1\frac{1}{4}$ teaspoons
chili powder – $1\frac{1}{4}$ teaspoons
pumpkin – 2 cups
cilantro – a small bunch, roughly chopped

For the onion topping:
onions – 2 medium
peanut oil – 2 generous tablespoons
chili peppers – 2 small hot ones
garlic – 2 cloves

Peel the onion and chop it roughly. Peel and crush the garlic and put it with the onion into a medium-sized, heavy-based saucepan. Peel the ginger, cut it into thin shreds and stir that in too. Add the lentils and pour in 6 cups of water. Bring to a boil, then turn the heat down to an enthusiastic simmer. Stir in the ground turmeric and chili powder, season and leave to simmer, covered, for twenty minutes.

While the soup is cooking, bring a medium-sized pan of water to a boil. Peel the pumpkin and scoop out the seeds and pulp, then cut the flesh into fat chunks. Boil the pumpkin pieces for ten minutes, until they are tender enough to pierce with a skewer without much pressure. Drain them and set them aside.

To make the onion topping, peel the onions and cut them into thin rings. Cook them in the oil in a shallow pan until they start to color. Cut the chili peppers in half, scrape out the seeds and slice the flesh finely. Peel and finely slice the garlic and add it with the peppers to the onions. Continue cooking until the onions are a deep golden brown. Set aside.

Remove the lid from the lentils and turn up the heat, boiling hard for five minutes. Remove the pan from the heat, then add the drained pumpkin. Puree the soup in a blender (for safety, a little at a time) until smooth, then pour it into a bowl. Stir in the roughly chopped cilantro and check the seasoning. I find this soup likes a more generous than usual amount of salt.

Serve in deep bowls with a spoonful of the spiced onions on top.
Makes 4 good-sized bowls

A salad of fennel, winter leaves and Parmesan

tarragon vinegar – a generous tablespoon
Dijon mustard – 1¼ teaspoons
an egg yolk
olive oil – ⅓ cup
grated Parmesan – 3 generous tablespoons
lemon juice – 2½ teaspoons
thick slices of white bread – 2
olive oil for frying the bread
1 medium fennel bulb
small, spicy salad leaves such as arugula and watercress –
4 double handfuls
a block of Parmesan for shaving

Make the dressing by whisking the vinegar, mustard, egg yolk and olive oil together with a little salt and black pepper, then beating in the grated cheese. Squeeze in the lemon juice, stir and set aside for a few minutes.

Cut the bread into small squares and fry in shallow oil till golden on all sides. Drain on paper towels. Slice the fennel finely; it should be almost fine enough to see through. Toss it with the salad leaves and the dressing. Pile the salad on to two plates, then shave pieces of Parmesan over with a vegetable peeler. I usually do at least eight per salad, depending on my dexterity with the peeler. Tip the hot croutons over the salad and eat straight away whilst all is fresh and crunchy.
Enough for 2

January 4
A salad of
winter
cabbage and
bacon

We have the first porridge of the year, made with thick-cut oatmeal and water and drizzled with heather honey and several spoonfuls of blueberries. Supper is a tightwad affair of shredded winter cabbage, steamed till just bright and almost tender, tossed with shredded bacon slices and their hot fat spiked with a dash of white wine vinegar. What lifts this from the mundane is the fact that I keep the cabbage jewel bright and use the best, lightly smoked bacon in generous amounts. A few caraway seeds add a nutty, almost musky flavor. Not the sort of thing to serve to guests but fine for a weekday supper.

Afterwards we eat slices of lemon tart from the bakery.

January 6

Grilled mushrooms tonight, slathered with some of that garlicky French cream cheese from the cheese shop and stuffed inside a soft burger bun. A TV dinner of the first order, especially the bit where the cream cheese melts into the cut sides of the toasted bun.

January 7
Frugal, pure
and basic
food for a
rainy night

I try to prune the raspberry patch whilst being buffeted by high winds; sacks, buckets and even the watering can being blown across the garden. It is this annual task, and that of pruning the fruit trees in the thicket at the end of the garden, that is the turning point in the year for me. Seeing the neatly trimmed canes and the newly shorn branches of the young quince, crab apple and mulberry trees is what rings in the new year for me rather than the bells, whoops and popping corks of New Year's Eve. Anyway, Auld Lang Syne always makes me want to burst into tears.

Pruning holds no fears for me. It is a job I look forward to almost more than any other. The crisp snap of shears slicing through young rose-pink and walnut-colored wood brings the possibility that this year I might actually manage to control this downright wayward kitchen garden. A garden where dahlias poke through blackcurrant bushes and dark purple clematis rambles through damson plum trees. Pruning makes me think, however briefly, that I am in charge.

But I give up after an hour or two, the wind thrashing the swaying and heavily thorned raspberry canes across my face just once too often. I go in and toast crumpets, then make a stew and an orange-scented cake.

Stew

Scotch barley – 4oz
onions – 3 medium
celery – 2 large stalks
a large parsnip
carrots – 2
potatoes – 4–5 medium
rack of lamb chops – 8 thick ones
a few sprigs of thyme and a couple of bay leaves
white pepper
water or stock to cover
parsley – a small handful

Boil the Scotch barley in unsalted water for a good twenty-five minutes, then drain it.

Get the oven hot. It needs to be at 325°F. Peel the onions and slice them into thick rings. Cut the celery into short lengths. Peel the parsnip, carrots and potatoes and cut them into fat chunks. That's 1-inch if you are measuring. Pile the vegetables into a large, deep pot, then tuck in the chops, thyme and bay leaves. Season with a little white pepper, no salt, then pour in the drained barley and enough water or stock to cover the meat and vegetables completely. Bring it slowly to a boil.

Skim off the worst of the froth that has accumulated on the surface, easily done with a slotted spoon. Cover the top of the stew with a sheet of parchment paper, then with a lid. Transfer the pot to the oven and leave it there, untouched or fiddled with, for a good two hours.

Remove the lid. The liquor should be thin, thickened only slightly by the potatoes. Chop the parsley and mix it in carefully, so as not to smash the vegetables, then season with salt and black pepper.

Leave overnight. Next day, skim the fat from the top, then reheat slowly on the stove till the meat is thoroughly hot and the broth gently bubbling. Check the seasoning – be generous – and serve piping hot. Enough for 4

A frosted marmalade cake

I don't, as a rule, like icing. Yet on a homemade cake, drizzled over so that it sets wafer thin, it adds a welcome contrast to the soft sponge cake. You could use water to mix the icing but I prefer to use fruit

juice, occasionally adding a hint of orange blossom water to perfume each slice of cake.

butter – ¾ cup
superfine sugar – ¾ cup plus 2 tablespoons
a large orange, well scrubbed
eggs – 3 large
orange marmalade – ¼ cup
self-rising flour – 1¾ cups

For the frosting:
confectioners' sugar – 4oz
orange juice – 2 generous tablespoons

Set the oven at 350°F. Line a loaf pan about 10 x 4in and 3in deep with greased parchment. Put the butter and sugar in a food mixer and beat till pale and fluffy. Finely grate the zest of the orange, then squeeze the juice from it and set aside. Break the eggs into a small bowl and beat them lightly with a fork. With the machine set at moderate speed, pour in the beaten egg a little at a time, beating thoroughly between each addition. Beat in the marmalade and the grated orange zest.

Remove the bowl and fold in the flour with a large metal spoon. Do this slowly, firmly but carefully, till there is no sign of any flour. Lastly, gently stir in the juice of half the orange. Spoon the mixture into the pan, lightly smoothing the top. Bake for forty minutes, checking it after thirty-five with a metal skewer. Leave to cool in the pan – it will sink slightly – then remove and cool completely on a wire rack.

Sift the confectioners' sugar and mix it to a smooth, slightly runny consistency with as much of the remaining orange juice as it takes – probably just under two tablespoons. Drizzle the icing over the cake, letting it run down the sides, and leave to set.
Enough for 8

**January 8
The first
rhubarb**

The first rhubarb appears with impeccable timing. Just as you want a fresh start to the year, along come the pale pink stems of the most tart and clean-tasting fruit to cleanse and invigorate. I no longer cut the stems into chunks and dip each piece raw into the sugar bowl like I did when I was a kid, but I do poach it only very lightly, so that the stems retain their shape, then I eat it first thing in the morning, slurping up spoonfuls of its limpid pink juice.

Frozen yogurt with roast rhubarb
Warm, rudely pink rhubarb and snow-white frozen yogurt has a smart, bright flavor and is breathtakingly pretty on a cold winter's day. The frozen yogurt is simply a bought vanilla smoothie chucked into an

ice-cream machine; the baked fruit just rhubarb bunged in a dish with a spoonful of runny honey and the juice of an orange.

thick vanilla yogurt smoothies – 3 x 8oz
young, pink rhubarb – 5 cups
an orange
mild honey – a generous tablespoon

To make the frozen yogurt, pour the smoothies into the drum of your ice-cream machine and churn till almost frozen. Scoop out and into a plastic freezer box, then keep in the freezer till you need it.

Cut the rhubarb into short lengths about the size of a wine cork. Lay them in a shallow stainless steel or glass baking dish, squeeze over the orange juice and drizzle with the honey. Bake for twenty-five minutes at 400°F, occasionally spooning the juices over the fruit. The rhubarb is done when the stalks are tender enough to crush between your fingers. Leave to cool a little.

Divide the warm rhubarb between four dishes, then place a couple of scoops of frozen yogurt on each, though it looks rather elegant served in separate bowls.
Enough for 4

Note
To make the frozen yogurt without a machine, pour the smoothies into a plastic box and freeze for a couple of hours till a thick layer of ice crystals forms around the edge. Whisk the frozen edges into the middle of the mixture, then freeze again for an hour or so. Repeat, again beating the edges into the middle. Now leave the mixture to freeze. The whole process will take about four hours, depending on the temperature of your freezer. Try to catch the ice just before it freezes solid. The texture will be less smooth than if you use a machine.

January 9
Rain and an old-fashioned cake

This is the gray, endless drizzle that Britain is regularly accused of having, yet in truth we rarely see, even in the depths of winter. It's the sort of day on which to light the fire, turn on the radio and bake a cake. Once the smell of baking fills the house, I find the rain suddenly matters a good deal less, if at all. I make a decent ginger cake, a love of which seems to run in our family. My dad adored them, along with Battenburg, or 'window cake' as he called it, which I leave to the experts. I take mine in the afternoon with a pot of green tea.

Double ginger cake
I am rather proud of this cake. Lightly crisp on top and with a good, open texture, it is light, moist and delicately gingery. It will keep for a week or so wrapped in wax paper and foil.

self-rising flour – 2½ cups
ground ginger – 2½ teaspoons
ground cinnamon – ¾ teaspoon
baking soda – 1¼ teaspoons
a pinch of salt
golden syrup* – ⅔ cup
syrup from the ginger jar – 2½ tablespoons
butter – ½ cup
stem ginger in syrup* – 3 lumps, about 2oz
golden raisins – 2 generous tablespoons
dark brown sugar – ½ cup plus 2 tablespoons
large eggs – 2
whole milk – 1 cup

You will need a square cake pan measuring approximately 8in, lined on the bottom with baking parchment.

Set the oven at 350°F. Sift the flour with the ground ginger, cinnamon, baking soda and salt. Put the golden and ginger syrups and the butter into a small saucepan and warm over a low heat. Dice the ginger finely, then add it to the pan with the raisins and brown sugar. Let the mixture bubble gently for a minute, giving it the occasional stir to stop the fruit sticking on the bottom.

Break the eggs into a bowl, pour in the milk and beat gently to break up the egg and mix it into the milk. Remove the butter and sugar mixture from the heat and pour into the flour, stirring smoothly and firmly with a large metal spoon. Mix in the milk and eggs. The mixture should be sloppy, with no trace of flour.

Scoop the mixture into the lined cake pan and bake for thirty-five or forty minutes, until a skewer inserted in the center of the cake comes out clean. Unless you are serving it warm, leave the cake in its pan to cool, then tip it out onto a sheet of wax paper. Wrap it up in foil and, if you can, leave it to mature for a day or two before eating.
Enough for 8

January 11
Onion soup
without
tears

I do love the classic onion soup, simmered for hours in a deep iron pot, but if I'm honest I hate making it. Onions make me cry at the best of times, but slicing enough for an entire pan of soup is more than I can handle, so this method where you roast the halved onions first solves all that. But there is more to this soup than convenience for those easily brought to tears; the roasting of the onions gives a sweet, caramel depth to the broth and the onions turn silky, slithery and soft. I could also add that the smell of onions baking in butter is a rather more attractive option than the pong of boiled onions wafting through the house.

Available in some supermarkets and speciality shops.

onions – 4 medium
butter – 3 tablespoons
a glass of white wine – about 4oz
vegetable stock – 6 cups
a small French loaf
grated Gruyère, Emmental or other good melting cheese – 1½ cups

Set the oven at 400°F. Peel the onions and cut them in half from tip to root, then lay them in a roasting pan and add the butter, salt and some pepper. Roast until they are tender and soft, and toasted dark brown here and there. You might have to turn them now and again.

Cut the onions into thick segments. Put them in a saucepan with the wine and bring to a boil. Let the wine bubble until it almost disappears (you just want the flavor, not the alcohol), then pour in the stock. Bring to a boil and simmer for about twenty minutes.

Just before you want to serve the soup, make the cheese croutons. Cut the bread into thin slices and toast lightly on one side under a hot broiler. Turn them over and sprinkle with the grated cheese. Get the soup hot, ladle it into heatproof bowls and float the cheese croutons on top. Place the bowls under a hot broiler and leave until the cheese melts. Eat immediately, whilst the cheese is still stringy and molten. Enough for 4

**January 12
Potatoes
and cheese
for a cold
night**

I rather like those dishes that can be eaten as either a side dish or a main course depending on what else you might be eating. They slot neatly into my 'very useful' category. This potato recipe is one of those. If we were having a few slices of cold roast beef or pork, or maybe some chicken left over from Sunday, then this is what I would want to eat with it at this time of year when the weather is so cold. Yet today two of us sit down each with a plate of these potatoes as a main course, with just a bowl of crisp winter salad of chicory, frisée and roughly chopped walnuts. Whichever way you look at it, it's a rough-looking dish of cheese melting over the lightly fried potatoes.

It is not essential to stick to my choice of cheese. Anything that melts easily will do but both Fontina and Taleggio will melt superbly.

Cheese-smothered potatoes

waxy potatoes (such as Eastern or red-skinned) – 1lb
olive oil – 2 generous tablespoons
butter – 4 tablespoons
a medium-sized onion, sliced
garlic – 2 large cloves, finely sliced
fresh thyme leaves – 1 generous tablespoon, chopped
easy melting cheese such as Taleggio or Fontina – 1¼ cups

Rinse the potatoes. There is no need to peel them unless the skins are very tough. Slice them thinly – about $\frac{1}{8}$in thick. The thinner you slice them, the quicker they will cook.

Put the olive oil and butter in a shallow pan about 10in in diameter and cook the onion and garlic in it for about five minutes, until they start to soften. Add the potatoes, some pepper and salt and the thyme to the pan and toss gently in the cooking fat. Cover with a lid and cook over a low heat for twenty-five minutes, turning once.

Test the cooked potatoes for tenderness. If the point of a knife slices into them easily, they are done. Slice the cheese thinly and lay it over the top of the potatoes. Cover the pan once more and continue cooking for a couple of minutes until the cheese has melted. Serve immediately, while the cheese is still soft and oozing.
Enough for 2

January 13 A velvety soup for a clear, cold day

Crisp, clear, and the sky looks like Sweden. One of those days when you get tricked by the bright, crystal sky and go out with one layer too few, then come home freezing cold. I had every intention of bringing back something for supper but, after eating Turkish mezze at lunch, come home empty-handed and end up scouring the fridge and cupboards for something to eat.

I never throw away Parmesan rinds. No matter how dry and cracked they get, the craggy ends are full of intense, cheesy flavor. A more organized cook would freeze theirs; mine tend to collect in one of the little plastic drawers in the fridge door, the one you are supposed to keep eggs in. To get the full, soothingly velvet texture of this soup, you will need a couple of large hunks of rind, about 2in long. If the fridge is bare, then ask at your local deli. They may let you have them for little or nothing.

good-sized leeks – 3
butter – a thick slice, about 3 tablespoons
potatoes – 3 medium-sized
Parmesan rinds
light stock or water – 6 cups
parsley – a handful
grated Parmesan – $\frac{1}{2}$ cup

Trim the leeks, slice them into thick rings, then wash thoroughly under cold running water. Melt the butter in a heavy-based pan (I use a cast-iron casserole), then dump in the washed leeks and let them soften slowly, covered with a lid, over a low to moderate heat. After about twenty minutes and with some occasional stirring they should be silkily tender.

While they are softening, peel the potatoes and cut them into chunks. Add them to the leeks when they are soft and let them cook for five minutes or so, before dropping in the cheese rinds and pouring in the stock or water. Season with salt and black pepper, then partially cover and leave to simmer for a good forty minutes.

Remove and discard the undissolved cheese rinds, scraping back into the soup any cheesy goo from them as you go. Add the leaves of the parsley and process the soup in a blender. Check the seasoning – it may need a surprisingly generous amount of salt and pepper – then bring briefly to a boil. Serve piping hot, with the grated Parmesan. Enough for 6

I buy oysters today, *fines de claire* from the fish shop on Marylebone High Street, six apiece. They smell clean and slightly salty. The heavy-gauge oyster opener I bought five years ago has proved a sound investment, firmer and safer than its predecessor, which was, with hindsight, too flimsy to do the job. Opening oysters requires a no-messing attitude. Not exactly gung-ho, but with a certain amount of (mock) confidence. Even then I have to fish out bits of broken shell from the tender flesh and not-to-be-wasted juices. The shellfish was quite expensive, so I strike a balance with a cheap cupboard recipe to follow. **January 15**

Bulgur wheat with eggplant and mint
Bulgur is one of those mild, warming grains that soothes and satisfies. I value it for its knobbly texture and nutty flavor. This, to me, is supper, but others may like to use it beside something else, such as grilled chicken or a gravy-rich stew.

olive oil – ½ cup
a small onion
a bay leaf
eggplant – 2 small ones
garlic – 2 large cloves, chopped
bulgur wheat – 1 cup
vegetable stock – 2 cups
tomatoes – 4 medium
pine nuts – 3 generous tablespoons, toasted
mint – 15–20 leaves, chopped
lemon juice to taste

Warm the olive oil in a shallow pan, peel and finely slice the onion and let it cook slowly in the oil with the bay leaf. When the onion is soft and pale gold, add the eggplant, cut into 1-in pieces, and the chopped garlic. Let the eggplant cook, adding more oil if necessary, until they are golden and soft.

Pour in the bulgur wheat and the vegetable stock. Bring to a boil,

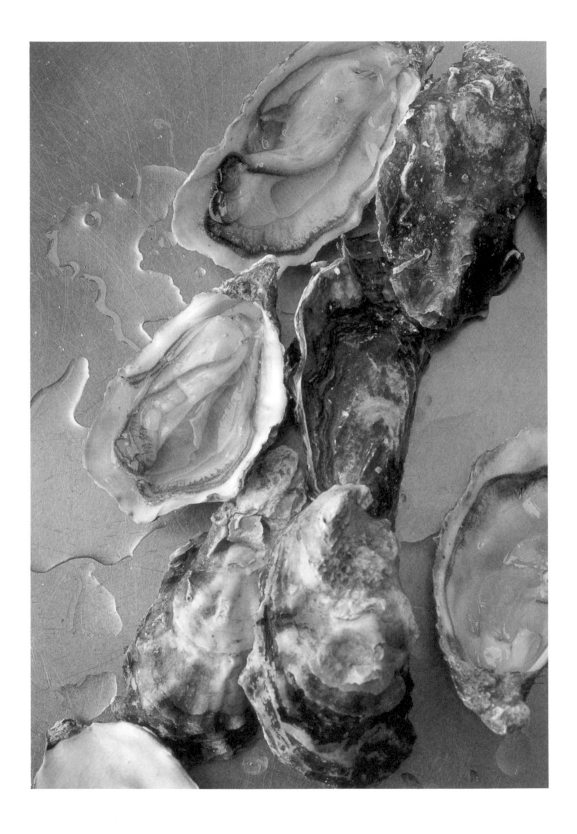

then leave to simmer gently for fifteen to twenty minutes, till the wheat is tender and almost dry. Halfway through cooking, roughly chop the tomatoes and add them. Once the wheat is cooked (it should still be nutty and have some bite), stir in the toasted pine nuts and chopped mint leaves. Check the seasoning; it will need lemon juice, salt and pepper.
Enough for 2, with seconds

No sooner is lunch over (supermarket sushi brought to life with enough wasabi to make my sinuses sting) than it starts to rain. The butcher has fresh chopped meat, which looks straight from the grinder, the sight of which is enough to stir me into making a proper Bolognese. By which I mean one that has been left to blip and putter slowly on the stove, so that the flavors have a chance to mellow and deepen.

A really good spaghetti Bolognese

butter – 4 tablespoons
cubed pancetta – 3oz
a medium onion
garlic – 2 fat cloves
a carrot
celery – 2 stalks
flat mushrooms such as portobello – 2 large, about 4oz
bay leaves – 2
chopped beef or lamb – 1lb
crushed tomatoes or passata – 1 cup
red wine – ¾ cup
stock – ¾ cup
a nutmeg
half and-half or cream – ¾ cup

To serve:
spaghetti or tagliatelle for 4
grated Parmesan

Melt the butter in a heavy-based pan – I use a cast-iron one about 10in in diameter – then stir in the pancetta and let it cook for five minutes or so, without coloring much. Meanwhile peel and finely chop the onion and garlic and stir them into the pancetta. Peel and finely chop the carrot and celery and stir them in, too. Lastly, finely chop the mushrooms and add to the pan, then tuck in the bay leaves and leave to cook for ten minutes over a moderate heat, stirring frequently.

Turn up the heat and tip in the meat, breaking it up well with a fork.

Now leave to cook without stirring for a good three or four minutes, then, as the meat on the bottom is starting to brown, stir again, breaking up the meat where necessary, and leave to color.

Mix in the tomatoes, red wine, stock, a grating of nutmeg and some salt and black pepper, letting it come to the boil. Turn the heat down so that everything barely bubbles. There should be movement, but one that is gentle, not quite a simmer. Partially cover the pan with a lid and leave to putter away for an hour to an hour and a half, stirring from time to time and checking the liquid levels. You don't want it to be dry.

Pour in the half-and-half or cream a bit at a time, stir and continue cooking for twenty minutes. Check the seasoning, then serve with the pasta and grated Parmesan.
Enough for 4

January 19 Sometimes I make my own chicken stock and sometimes I buy it ready-made. Today I take the lazy route, picking up a large tub from the butcher's, idle, good-for-nothing guy that I am. The outcome is another ten-minute supper, which turns out to be more appreciated than any supermarket cook-chill dinner, at once warming (the broth), uplifting (lemon, mint) and satisfying (the noodles).

Chicken broth with noodles, lemon and mint

dried egg noodles – ¾ cup
very good chicken broth – 4 cups
cooked chicken (leftover roast is fine) – 1½ cups
chopped mint leaves – 2 heaped tablespoons
roughly chopped cilantro leaves – 2 heaped tablespoons
the juice of a lemon

Drop the noodles into a deep pan of boiling, salted water and cook for two to three minutes, until tender. Drain them, rinse under cold running water, then leave to cool in a bowl of cold water until you need them.

Bring the chicken broth to a boil, then turn the heat down to a simmer. Shred the chicken with a sharp knife and add it to the simmering broth with the mint, cilantro and lemon juice. Add the noodles, leave for one minute, then serve steaming hot in big bowls.
Enough for 2 as a main dish

January 21
A cheap fish
supper
I sometimes feel as if I am on a one-man mission to make the world eat more mackerel. This recipe, spiced with smoked paprika and rings of soft, golden onions, is one of the best I have come up with for this underrated fish. I am not sure you need anything more with it than some steamed spinach or spinach salad.

Spiced breaded mackerel with smoked paprika

mackerel – 4, filleted
onion – 1 medium to large
olive oil
parsley – a handful
garlic – 3 small cloves
smoked hot paprika – ¾ teaspoon
fresh breadcrumbs – 2 cups
a lemon

Rinse and dry the mackerel fillets and lay them skin-side down in a lightly oiled dish. Season them lightly with salt and pepper. Set the oven at 350°F.

Peel the onion and slice it into very thin rings, then let it cook over a moderate heat in a couple of tablespoons of olive oil until it starts to soften. Chop the parsley, not too finely, then peel and crush the garlic and stir into the onion with the paprika, a seasoning of black pepper and salt and the breadcrumbs. Pour in three tablespoons of olive oil.

Spoon the spiced breadcrumbs evenly over the fish and bake for twenty minutes. It is ready when the crumbs are golden and the fish is opaque and tender. Lift on to plates using a thin spatula, then squeeze the lemon over each one.
Enough for 4

January 25
An herb butter for grilled chops

I make a quick herb butter with equal amounts of blue cheese and butter (I use ½ cup of each), mashed with a tablespoon each of fresh thyme leaves and Dijon mustard, then stir in a couple of tablespoons of heavy cream and a grinding of black pepper. It sits in the fridge till supper, when I lay thick slices of it on grilled pork steaks. The cheese butter melts over the charred edges of the chops, making an impromptu sauce to mop up with craggy lumps of sourdough bread.

No matter how beautiful its carmine and orange stalks, the sight of a bunch of chard in my organic bag always makes my heart sink. This is unfair. It's a useful vegetable, with lush, heavily veined green leaves and enough color to liven up even the grayest of winter days.

You can cook chard in a modicum of water, like spinach; it needs just enough to cover the stalks. I then drain it while the colors are still bright, say after six minutes or so, and drizzle it with olive oil, squeeze over masses of lemon juice and toss in a few green or black olives.
Picture on previous page

January 27

Cauliflower is something I can live without, but it surprises me today in a salad, lightly cooked, then drained and tossed with warmed canned chickpeas, plenty of lemon juice, good olive oil and cilantro leaves. The crisp florets get a scattering of sesame seeds and a few pitted green olives. A pile of warm pita bread finishes it off. Clean, lemony and fresh, this might prove a sound way to win other cauliflower haters round.

On gray January days we must make our own fun. Today is a flat day that only seems to come to life when I go shopping, returning with bags of Italian lemons complete with their bottle-green leaves, craggy lumps of Crockhamdale and snow-white Ticklemore cheeses from Neal's Yard Dairy and a cheap pheasant from Borough Market. There's only two to feed, so a pheasant does nicely here. People get down about this time of year, but even today there were fat little partridges, clementines heavy with juice, and bunches of narcissi to cheer us up. There is good stuff if you are prepared to go and find it.

A pot-roasted pheasant with celery and sage
The pheasant's lack of fat means that we need to find ways of keeping its flesh moist during cooking. The time-honored way is to wrap the bird in fatty bacon. Fine. But I don't always want the intrusion of that particular flavor. Another way is to let the pheasant cook in its own steam. In other words, a pot roast. What you get is plenty of juicy meat that tastes of itself and plenty of clear, savory juices.

a pheasant – plump and oven-ready
butter – 2 thick slices (7 tablespoons)
garlic – 4 large, juicy cloves
celery – 3 large stalks and a few leaves
new potatoes – 12 smallish
sage – 6 decent-sized leaves
white vermouth such as Noilly Prat – 1 cup

Set the oven at 350°F. Wipe the pheasant and remove any stray feathers, then season it thoroughly with salt and pepper.
    Melt half the butter in a deep casserole, one to which you have a lid. You want it hot enough to brown the bird but not so hot that it burns too quickly. Put the bird in the hot butter, letting it color heartily on all sides. When the skin is a rich gold, remove the bird, pour away the butter and wipe the pan with paper towel (the trick is to wipe away any burned butter but to leave any sticky goo stuck to the pan).
    Whilst the bird is coloring in the butter, you can peel the garlic, trim the celery and cut it into short (1-in) lengths, wash the potatoes and either halve them or slice them thickly, depending on their size.
    Melt the remaining butter in the pan and add the potatoes, letting them color lightly. Then introduce the garlic, celery pieces and the sage and celery leaves and season with salt and pepper. Pour over the

vermouth, bring to a boil, letting it bubble for a minute or two, then return the bird and any escaped juices to the pan. Cover with a lid and transfer to the oven for thirty-five to forty minutes.

Remove the pan from the oven, take off the lid and gently split the bird's legs away from its body, nicking the skin with a knife as you go. Return the bird, legs akimbo and without the lid, to the oven for five minutes.

Remove the legs, then remove each breast in one piece. Put a leg and a breast on each of two warm plates, then divide up the potatoes, celery and their juices.
Enough for 2

**January 29
A hot salad
from the
leftovers
and a clear,
aromatic
soup**

There are a few slices of pheasant left, scraps actually. They will do two for supper with some hot onion chutney I found in the cupboard and a plate of boiled potatoes, sliced and fried in hot olive oil. At the last minute I decide to toss the cold cuts with the hot fried potatoes, a couple of spoonfuls of the chutney and a bunch of watercress. It looks a bit of a jumble on the plate, but eats well enough.

A clear, hot mussel soup
The point is that this is a clean-tasting broth, hot and aromatic. If you wish to add fish sauce or even soy sauce, then do, but I suspect the recipe will lose its pure, simple flavors. The cilantro is essential.

mussels in their shells – 2lbs
light chicken or vegetable stock – 3 cups
a small, hot, red chili pepper
the juice of 2 limes
a little sea salt and sugar
a handful of cilantro leaves

Scrub the mussels thoroughly, tug out any of the fibrous 'beards' that may be hanging from their shells and discard any that are broken or open. I always squeeze each mussel hard, pushing the shells together tightly to check they have some life in them. Any that refuse to close when squeezed or tapped on the side of the sink, or any that seem light for their size, should be discarded.

Tip the mussels into a large, heavy pot over a high flame and add a splash of water. Cover them tightly with a lid and let them steam for a minute or two, till their shells are just open and the mussels are quivering and juicy. Remove them from the heat the second they are ready.

Bring the stock to the boil. Cut the pepper in half, remove its seeds and chop the flesh very finely, then put it in with the stock, together with the lime juice, a pinch of salt and the same of sugar. Turn the stock down to a simmer.

Remove the mussels from their cooking liquor, pull the flesh from the shells and drop it into the pan of stock, with a little of the mussel juices. Roughly chop the cilantro leaves and stir them into the hot soup.
Enough for 2

The air is again clear and cold, and there are paper-white narcissi in a bowl on the table, filling the kitchen with their gentle, vanilla smell. Winter at its purest. This is the sort of day on which I like to bake – a cake, a pie, a tart perhaps. I enjoy making pastry, though rarely do, each time adding as much butter as I dare, just to see how crisp and fragile I can get the crust. Today I want something fresh, with a clean bite to it, a dessert to make everyone smack their lips. I decide on a lime custard tart in the style of a *tarte au citron*. The lime zest cuts through the cool air. The warm smell of baking pastry wafts into the rest of the house. Heaven. Halfway through baking, I check the tart's progress, only to find the pastry shell empty and the citrus filling forming a lemon-colored pool on the baking sheet. I pile the whole damn failure into a bowl (and later eat it in secret after everyone has gone home) and start again. This time I make absolutely certain the pastry shell has not the faintest hole or crack in it before I pour in the filling.

Sausages with salami and lentils
A rough-edged casserole that gives the impression of having been cooked for hours but is pretty much ready to eat in forty-five minutes. You could put it in the oven if you prefer, in which case you should let it cook for about an hour at moderate heat. This is the sort of food I like to put on the table at Saturday lunch, with a bowl of arugula salad by the side. Then you can swoosh the salad leaves around your plate to mop up the last bits of tomatoey lentil sauce.

onions – 2 medium
olive oil – 2 generous tablespoons
garlic – 2 cloves
a small salami – about 6–7oz
fresh sausages – ¾lb
crushed tomatoes or tomato passata – 1¾ cups
green or brown lentils – ¾ cup
bay leaves – 3

Peel the onions and cut each one in half from tip to root, then cut each half into four or five pieces. Warm the oil in a heavy-based casserole, add the onions and let them cook over a moderate heat until tender. Meanwhile, peel the garlic, slice it thinly and add it to the onions. You'll need to stir them regularly.

Peel the thin skin from the salami and cut the inside into fat match-sticks. Add this to the softening onions and leave for a couple of minutes, during which time the salami will darken slightly.

Start cooking the sausages in a non-stick pan. You want them to color on the outside; they will do most of their cooking once they are in the sauce. Tip the crushed tomatoes into the onions, add the washed lentils and stir in 2 cups water. Bring to a boil. Remove the sausages from their pan and tuck them into the casserole with the bay leaves. Cover the pot with a lid and leave to simmer gently for about half an hour, until the lentils are tender. Stir the lentils and season with black pepper. You may find it needs little or no salt.
Enough for 2, with seconds

A lime tart

Not difficult this, but do make absolutely certain there are no holes or cracks in the pastry case, otherwise the filling will escape, I guarantee.

limes – 5–7
large eggs – 6
superfine sugar – 1¼ cups
heavy cream – ¾ cup

For the pastry:
all-purpose flour – 1¾ cups
golden confectioners' sugar* – ⅓ cup
cold butter – ½ cup
large egg yolks – 2
cold water – a generous tablespoon

To make the pastry, put the flour and confectioner's sugar into a food processor, add the butter, cut into chunks, and process for a few seconds. Stop when the mixture resembles fine breadcrumbs. Mix in the egg yolks and water. Tip into a mixing bowl and bring the dough together into a thick log with your hands. Wrap it in wax paper and refrigerate for a good half hour. Warning: skipping this bit will make your pastry shrink.

Cut thin, round slices from the log of pastry, then press them into a loose-bottomed 10-in tart pan with high sides (1½in), pressing the pastry gently up the sides and over the base (this pastry is too fragile to roll). Make certain that there are absolutely no holes, otherwise the filling will leak through. Prick lightly with a fork and refrigerate for half an hour.

Set the oven at 400°F. Place a sheet of parchment paper in the tart

White confectioner's sugar can be used as a substitute.

shell and fill it with baking beans (I use old dried beans but you can buy ceramic or metal beans especially for the job from cookware shops). Bake the tart shell for ten minutes, then remove the parchment paper and beans and bake for a further five minutes, until the pastry is dry to the touch.

Turn the oven down to 300°F. Finely grate the zest from two of the limes. Squeeze enough limes to give ¾ cup juice; this could be anything from five to seven limes, depending on their ripeness. Mix the eggs and sugar together, beating lightly for a few seconds – you don't want it to be frothy – then stir in the lime juice and cream. Pour the mixture through a sieve and stir in the lime zest. Pour into the baked tart pan and bake for forty-five to fifty minutes. Remove whilst the filling is still a little wobbly and leave to cool.

Enough for 8

January 31

A ploughman's lunch is something to be kept away from the whims of an imaginative cook. The most tinkering I will tolerate is the occasional oatcake in lieu of bread and the odd radish or pickled onion as a crunchy distraction. If the cheese is firm and British then I'll willingly take an apple too. Today I slice a Cox's apple and let it color in a little butter in a non-stick frying pan. I put a jagged piece of Mrs Appleby's Cheshire cheese and a slice of warm, tender apple on to each oatcake and eat them whilst the apple is still hot. Yes, a mucked-about ploughman's but surprisingly none the worse for it.

february

Chicken patties with
rosemary and pancetta

An herb and barley broth
to bring you back to health

Spiced roast potatoes with
yogurt and mint

Lamb shanks with mustard
and mashed potatoes

Smoked haddock with
flageolet beans and mustard

Roast pumpkin, spicy
tomato sauce

Smoked fish patties, dill
mayonnaise

Pork chops, mustard sauce

Linguine alla vongole

Hot chocolate puddings

Sausage and blood sausage
with baked parsnips

Braised lamb with leeks
and navy beans

Spiced pumpkin soup
with bacon

Slow-roasted lamb with
chickpea mash

Braised oxtail with mustard
and mashed potatoes

Molasses tart

Warm pickled mackerel

February 1   The thought of shopping for home-grown fruit and vegetables in February makes my heart sink. There is only so much enthusiasm you can muster for kohlrabi and potatoes, floury apples and crates of stinky old Brussels sprouts.

As I turn the corner by the farmers' market, I am greeted by a stall almost hidden by tin buckets of daffodils, the traditional variety with large trumpets, the sort that look so cheerful in a jug by the kitchen sink. Beyond them is David Deme's apple stall with bright boxes of Cox's as crisp as shattered ice, russets still in fine nick and plump Comice and Conference pears. There is much pleasure to be found in a pear on a cold winter's day, with its crisp flesh and sweet, nutty juice.

Iridescent, candy-striped beets I have only ever seen in a seed catalogue, boxes of curly, red and Russian kale, fat carrots for juicing and tight little Brussels on the stem are in A1 condition. One grower is showing a wooden crate of the perkiest celeriac I have ever seen, each root with a neat tuft of green leaves looking as if they were dug only an hour ago.

I stop at the stall selling cartons of Hurdlebrook Guernsey cream from Olive Farm in Somerset and proper untreated milk. Dairy produce doesn't come better than this. It is not just about richness, it is about flavor. This is cream worth waiting all week for, a world away from the thin white stuff in the 'super'markets. I buy heavy cream and then rhubarb for a fool. The shopping trip I almost abandoned as a bad idea has come good, and I walk home with a heavy basket.

February 2
Succulent
little patties
for four

It is the deep, salty stickiness of food that intrigues me more than any other quality. The sheer savor of it. The Marmite-like goo that adheres to the skin of anything roasted; the crust where something – usually a potato or a parsnip – has stuck to the roasting pan; the underside of a piece of meat that has been left long enough in the pan to form a gooey crust. This is partly why I cook rather than buying my supper ready-made. This you will probably know, unless of course this is your first Nigel Slater book.

Meatballs, left to cook without constant prodding and poking, will form a satisfyingly savory outer coating that presses all the right buzzers for me. In many ways they are the ultimate casual supper for friends. I say this because of their ability to wait patiently when people are late, to cook quickly so you are not away from your guests for long and, the real clincher, because of the fact that they have a down-to-earth friendliness to them. A meatball never says, 'Look at me, aren't I clever?' It just says, 'Eat me.' No matter how fancy you get in terms of seasoning and sauces, you can't show off with them. Best of all, they are one of the few recipes you can easily multiply for a large number without having to rejig everything. You just double or quadruple as you need. This is of particular resonance today. There are four of us for supper tonight and I know two of them will almost certainly be late. They always are.

Chicken patties with rosemary and pancetta

I put these on the table with fat wedges of lemon and a spinach salad.

a medium onion
garlic – 2 cloves
a thick slice of butter (3–4 tablespoons)
cubed pancetta – ½ cup
rosemary – 3 bushy sprigs
minced chicken – 3½ cups
a little peanut oil for frying
chicken stock – 1 cup

Peel the onion and garlic and chop them finely, then let them soften in the butter over a moderate heat (a non-stick frying pan is best for this, then you can use it to fry the patties in later) until they are lightly honey-colored. Stir in the small cubes of pancetta. Strip the rosemary leaves from their stalks, chop them finely, then add them to the onions, letting them cook for a few minutes till browned. Let the mixture cool a little.

Mix the minced chicken into the onion, seasoning it generously with black pepper and a little salt (the pancetta will contribute to the seasoning).

Set the oven at 375°F. Now, to make the simple patties, shape the mixture into six little burgers about 2in in diameter, then leave to settle for half an hour.

Wipe the onion pan clean and get it hot. Add a little peanut oil and brown the patties on both sides – that's a matter of three minutes per side – then transfer them to an oven-safe dish. Pour in the stock and bake for twenty-five to thirty minutes, till the patties are sizzling and the stock is bubbling. Serve two to three per person and spoon over some of the hot chicken stock.
Enough for 2–3. Picture overleaf

Note
If you want something richer, make stuffed patties. Take a heaped tablespoon of the chicken mixture and push a hollow in it with your thumb. Take a heaped teaspoon of Gorgonzola cheese (you will need 3oz for this amount of chicken) and push it into the hollow, then cover it with a second tablespoon of chicken mixture. Squash gently to form a patty and place on a baking sheet. Continue with this till you have used up the mixture – you will have about six – then refrigerate them for twenty to thirty minutes before cooking.

I try planting some late crocus bulbs in the garden, which I had forgotten about and which now appear to have started sprouting. There's a freezing wind and my fingers are numb even through the fleece-lined luxury of leather gardening gloves. Another of those days when you feel you are going to get snow but all that appears is sleet, which has neither the romance of snow nor the refreshing quality of rain. The ice-cold needles prickle your skin, your cheeks start to lose all feeling. I battle on till I think my nose might be running, but my face is so cold I am not sure. I call it a day and make a big pot of chicken broth, as much out of defiance as anything else.

A herb and barley broth to bring you back to health
The herbs are essential and I don't suggest goose fat just to be annoying; it contains a certain magic.

Scotch barley – ½ cup
carrots – 3 large
leeks – 3, trimmed and rinsed to remove any grit
celery – 3 medium-sized stalks
onions – 2 small
garlic – 4 large cloves
drippings, goose fat or olive oil – 3 tablespoons
enough good chicken stock to cover
a few bay leaves
thyme – 3 or 4 sprigs
sage leaves – 6
potatoes – 4 small to medium
parsley – a small bunch

Simmer the rinsed barley in salted water for about twenty minutes till it feels reasonably tender, then drain it. Set the oven at 350°F.

Peel the carrots and cut them into large chunks, then cut the leeks and celery into short lengths. I think it is important to keep the vegetables in fat, juicy pieces for this. Peel the onions, cut them in half and then into large segments. Peel and finely slice the garlic. Warm the fat in a large, deep casserole. Turn the vegetables and garlic in the hot fat and let them soften a little, but don't allow them to color. Bring the stock to a boil in a separate pan.

Now add the barley to the vegetables, pouring over the hot stock and tucking in all the herbs except the parsley as you go. Slice the potatoes ⅛in thick and lay them over the top of the vegetables – some will inevitably sink; others will sit on top, the stock just lapping at their edges.

Cover with a lid and place in the oven for an hour and a half, by which time the vegetables will be meltingly tender. Remove the lid (the smell is part of the healing process), turn the heat up to 400°F and leave for thirty minutes for the potatoes to color here and there. Remove very carefully from the oven – the pan will be full and very hot – chop the parsley and sink it into the broth.

Spoon the vegetables, barley and plenty of broth into shallow bowls with flakes of sea salt and several firm grinds of the pepper mill.
Enough for 4

February 6
Cold meat,
hot potatoes

There is cold meat to eat up from yesterday's roast but it needs something warming to sit alongside. So potatoes it is, spiced with onions and chili peppers, all cooked to a crisp. To be honest, I let it cook for longer than I intend, with the result that the onions are crisp and slightly singed. A plate of big, mouth-popping flavors that I cool by drizzling yogurt over at the table.

Spiced roast potatoes with yogurt and mint
When Indian cooks bake potatoes, they tend to add spices and some sort of liquid, such as water or yogurt, but I see no reason why you cannot add the yogurt afterwards, which has the advantage of allowing the potatoes to crisp nicely. A moderate heat is needed here to stop the spices from burning in the oven.

potatoes – 4 medium
onions – 2 medium
vegetable or peanut oil
red chili peppers, as hot as you like – 2, chopped
garlic – 2 cloves, crushed
cumin seeds – ¾ teaspoon
ground turmeric – ¾ teaspoon

To finish:
plain yogurt – 5 tablespoons
a little mild chili powder
young mint leaves – a palmful, chopped

Peel the potatoes, cut them into the sort of pieces you would for normal roasting, then bring them to a boil in deep water. Add salt to the pot and simmer for ten to fifteen minutes, until the potatoes are approaching tenderness. You should be able to slide a knifepoint through them with almost no pressure. Drain the potatoes thoroughly, then very gently shake them in their pan so the edges fluff and 'bruise'. Set the oven at 350°F.

Peel the onions and slice them finely. Heat enough oil in a roasting pan to make a thin film over the bottom. The thicker the base, the less likelihood there is of the spices burning. As the oil warms, add the

sliced onions and let them soften, then stir in the chopped chili peppers, garlic and cumin and let them warm through, stirring (and watching like a hawk) so that they do not burn. Add the potatoes to the hot oil, add the turmeric, then slowly stir and toss the potatoes so that they are covered with the seasoned oil.

Roast the potatoes in the preheated oven until they have started to crisp. Thirty to thirty-five minutes or so should do it. You don't want them to be as brown as classic roast potatoes. They should be golden and flecked with spice.

As the potatoes come from the oven, grind over a seasoning of salt, then spoon over the yogurt, sprinkle with a very little mild ground chili powder and scatter with the chopped mint leaves.
Enough for 4 as a side dish

**February 7
Lamb
shanks to
warm the
soul**

A chill day, the sky the color of wet aluminum. I need the sort of meal that ends with everyone squishing their potatoes into the meaty, oniony sauce on their plate. A sauce that is warm rather than spicy, enriched with the goodness of meat cooked on the bone.

The butcher suggests lamb shanks, cheaper now they are not so trendy. I buy nothing else; there is wine, bay leaf, rosemary, garlic and grain mustard in the kitchen already. The preparation will take ten minutes, the cooking an hour and a half on a low heat. A supper of melting tenderness.

Lamb shanks with mustard and mashed potatoes

olive oil
lamb shanks – 2 small
onions – 4 small to medium
bay leaves – 3
sprigs of rosemary – 2 or 3
vegetable or meat stock – 1 cup
red wine – 1 cup
garlic – 3 cloves
grain mustard – 1 heaped tablespoon

To serve:
mashed potato and a bit more mustard

Set the oven at 300°F. Warm a couple of tablespoons of olive oil in a roasting pan large enough to take the meat snugly, then sear the lamb on all sides in the hot oil. The fat and the cut end of the meat should take on a little color.

Peel the onions, slice them in half from root to tip, then each half into quarters. Add them to the lamb with the bay leaves and the leaves from the rosemary sprigs. Pour in the stock and red wine. Peel the garlic cloves and squash them flat with the blade of a heavy knife. Drop them into the roasting pan with a grinding of salt and some coarse black pepper. Cover the dish with foil, place in the oven and bake for an hour and a half.

Halfway through cooking, uncover the dish and stir in the mustard, turning the lamb as you do so. Cover once more and return to the oven. Serve with mashed potato and a bit more mustard.
Enough for 2

There is something old-fashioned about a supper of smoked haddock, something redolent of the 1950s, when women wore an apron when they cooked and would get a meal on the table at the same time each day, year in, year out. I like my smoked haddock baked with a little cream, as I do almost anything smoked, but until recently was never sure what to eat with it. Mashed potatoes never seemed right, buttered toast never substantial enough, rice too reminiscent of kedgeree. It was out of curiosity that I turned to beans, pale ones from a can, their texture a pleasing contrast. Now it is one of my favorite light dinners, though not the prettiest.

Smoked haddock with flageolet beans and mustard
The parsley is important here and should be vivid emerald green and full of life. I see no reason why you can't use equally mealy cannellini beans if that is what you have, though I have used butter beans before now and they were good, too. This is a mild, gently flavored dish, consoling even, for a cold night.

smoked haddock – 14oz
butter
milk – 1 cup, plus a little more for later
bay leaves
flageolet beans – two 14 oz cans
heavy cream – 1¼ cups
parsley leaves – a good fistful
grain mustard – 1 heaped tablespoon
steamed spinach, to serve

Remove the skin from the smoked haddock and place the fish in a lightly buttered baking dish. Pour over the milk, then add enough water almost to cover the fish. Tuck in a couple of bay leaves and grind over some black pepper. Bake at 400°F for about fifteen to twenty minutes or until you can pull one of the large, fat flakes of flesh out with ease. Drain and discard the milk.

Rinse and re-butter the baking dish – you don't want any bits of

skin from the milk left behind. Rinse the beans in a sieve under running water, then empty them into a mixing bowl. Pour in the cream and a couple of tablespoons of milk, then chop the parsley and add it together with the mustard, a grinding of black pepper and a little salt. Go easy on the salt; smoked fish is saltier than fresh.

Spoon the beans into the dish and lay the fish on top, spooning some of the creamy beans over the top to keep it moist. Turn the oven down to 350°F and bake for about forty minutes, until the cream is bubbling and the sauce has thickened around the beans. Serve with spinach.
Enough for 2

A pumpkin has been languishing in the vegetable rack for longer than **February 9** I care to remember. To use it now would be more than a great satisfaction; it would be a relief.

Roast pumpkin, spicy tomato sauce
Deep red and gold, a cheering supper if ever there was one. This simple dish of roast vegetables stands or falls by the timing. I like to roast the pumpkin till it is soft but not quite collapsing, deep golden in color, the edges slightly caramelized and sticky. Undercook it at your peril. The sauce is chunky and has a certain bitter-sweetness from the lightly blackened tomato skins. You may want to cook some brown rice to go with this, especially if you are having nothing to follow.

tomatoes – 2lbs
garlic – 2 cloves
chili peppers – 2 small hot ones
olive oil
pumpkin or squash – 2¼lbs

Set the oven at 400°F. Cut the tomatoes in half and place them cut-side up on a baking sheet or in a roasting pan. Peel and finely slice the garlic, finely chop the chilis. Drizzle the tomatoes with oil, then season with salt and pepper and the garlic and chilis. Roast for forty-five to fifty minutes, till the tomatoes are soft and flecked with black.

Meanwhile, halve and peel the pumpkin. Cut into thick, melon-like slices and scoop out the seeds with a spoon. Place on a baking sheet, toss in a little olive oil and season with salt and black pepper. Roast for forty minutes, turning it over after twenty minutes or so. It is done when it is fully tender to the point of a knife and nice and sticky on the cut edges.

Roughly chop the tomatoes to give a coarse 'sauce'. Serve alongside the roasted pumpkin, with brown rice if you wish.
Enough for 2 as a main dish

February 11 Dinner is a couple of cans of Heinz baked beans, tarted up with finely chopped chili peppers, several shakes of Tabasco and mushroom ketchup, and a tablespoon of black molasses. It will do.

There is no set time for eating in our house, there never has been. One day lunch will be at twelve noon, the next four in the afternoon. Supper can be as early as six and as late as midnight. Neither is our eating always leisurely. Sometimes it is just a question of getting food inside you.

Many is the time supper has been sausage sandwiches all round, either with a jar of mustard on the table, or, if I can be bothered, a pot of wasabi mayonnaise, made by beating the jade green spice-paste from its tube into some commercial mayonnaise. The sausages will be hot and sticky and the mayo shockingly spicy. The general heat is tempered by soft bread cut thick and bottles of cold beer. Other times it may be pepperoni pizzas delivered by bike or sushi or sashimi from town. Just occasionally supper will come out of a bottle.

But there are also occasions when supper is nothing at all. From a health perspective this is probably not to be recommended, but frankly that is sometimes just what I need. A lot of water will pass my lips, but no food.

For the most part, I eat one decent meal a day and then some other stuff. Under which you can file beans on toast, bacon sandwiches, fish-sticks, cheese on toast, more cheese on toast and shop-bought sushi. Sourdough bread dunked into olive oil has been dinner on more than one occasion, as have slices of rye bread with a bit of smoked salmon. Other times I just stand at the fridge eating up the remains of meals past. Cold risotto is quite nice after the initial shock, though not as much fun as cold apple pie.

But I will tell you the best trick for making your bacon sandwich, cold sausage or bit of day-old fridge-rice take on an instant appeal. Have it with a glass of wine, better still a glass of Champagne. Yes, a scavenged supper can be made to sing with pickles or fresh, rough-textured chutney, but nothing works quite as well as a glass of wine.

February 12
Another
smoked fish
supper
At the far end of the fish market's slab are the smoked goods: the primrose-colored haddock and golden mackerel; the elegantly proportioned trout, and the brick-colored lumps of cod roe. There are also smoked fish, their skin shining silver, gold and black. Sometimes I buy one to cook for a lone supper, a slice of butter melting on its mahogany flesh. Other times, with more to feed, I make fish cakes, plump ones the size of a yo-yo.

Smoked fish patties, dill mayonnaise
I make these little golden fish cakes as a change from the more traditional haddock version, usually in the winter when smoky flavors

seem particularly appropriate. Parsley sauce isn't right with the smoked fish, so I make a dill-flavored mayonnaise instead, or sometimes have them with nothing more than a big squeeze of lemon and a generous helping of greens.

mealy potatoes – 1¼lbs (like Russet)
butter – a thick slice
smoked fish fillets – 1lb
dill – a small handful, chopped
flour for dusting
peanut oil for frying

For the sauce:
chopped dill – 2 heaped tablespoons
a crushed clove of garlic
mayonnaise – 7 heaped tablespoons

Peel the potatoes, cut them into quarters, then boil them in salted water till tender. Drain the potatoes, tip them into a food mixer and beat with the butter to make a smooth but firm consistency.

Put the fish fillets in a heatproof bowl and pour a kettle of boiling water over them. Leave them for ten minutes, till they have softened, then drain and flake the flesh. I tend to leave it in short pieces the size of a postage stamp rather than finely mashed.

Fold the fish into the warm potato, together with the chopped dill and a generous seasoning of salt and black pepper. Leave the mixture to cool a little, then shape it into rough patties. I make twelve of them the size of large golf balls, then flatten them slightly. Leave them to cool and firm up.

Dust the patties lightly with flour, then fry in shallow hot oil for five minutes or so.

To make the sauce, simply mix the chopped dill with the crushed garlic and mayo
Enough for 4

The cold and the wet have resulted in a week of 'proper' food; stuff to **February 13** fill hollow tummies and make your ears glow with warmth. No dinky bowls of clear soup and noodles or plates of greens with shaved Parmesan and olive oil on the table this week. Rarely has our eating been so unapologetically old-fashioned. Today is no exception, and I fancy a chop, a big one with a margin of golden fat and a bone on which to gnaw. Twice this week I have used cream in the main course – a rare occurrence, but I need an iota of luxury right now to make me feel better about this endlessly gray month.

Pork chops, mustard sauce

pork spare rib or chump chops – 2 large, about ½in thick
butter – 2 tablespoons
olive oil – 1¼ tablespoons
garlic – 2 large unpeeled cloves, squashed flat
a glass of white wine
double or whipping cream – ⅔ cup
grain mustard – a generous tablespoon
smooth Dijon mustard – a generous tablespoon
cornichons – 8, or half as many larger gherkins

Rub the chops all over with salt and pepper. Put the butter and oil in a shallow pan set over a moderate to high heat and, when they start to froth a little, add the flattened garlic and the seasoned chops. Leave to brown, then turn and brown the other side. Lower the heat and continue cooking, turning once, until the chops are no longer pink when cut into.

Lift out the chops, transfer to a warm serving dish and keep warm. Pour off most of the oil from the pan, leaving the sediment behind, then turn up the heat and pour in the wine. Let it boil for a minute or so, scraping at the sticky sediment in the pan and letting it dissolve. Pour in the cream, swirl the pan about a bit, then leave it to bubble up a little before adding the mustards and the chopped cornichons.

Taste for seasoning; you may need a little salt and possibly black pepper. The sauce should be piquant and creamy. If you want, you can finish the sauce with a few drops of liquor from the cornichon jar to sharpen it up. Pour the sauce over the chops and serve.
Enough for 2 with mashed or unbuttered new potatoes

I won't eat out on Valentine's Day, every restaurant filled with couples talking in whispers, the usual buzz and clatter reduced to a muffled sigh. Home is the place to be. More than that, there is something about cooking a special meal for someone you love that seems to mean more than simply sliding your credit card to a waiter.

I can find no reason not to go over the top on this night of the year: candles, Champagne, a chocolate pudding. St Valentine's is rather like Christmas, in that if you ignore it you always end up regretting it, feeling mean and cynical. Yes, it is more than a bit cheesy, but I think we have to go with it.

**February 14
St Valentine's
Day**

Linguine alla vongole

small clams in their shells – 1lb
a glass of white wine or vermouth
linguine or spaghettini – ⅔lb
garlic – 2 cloves
olive oil – 3 generous tablespoons
dried pepper flakes – a good pinch
flat-leaf parsley – a small bunch

Scrub the clams, throwing away any that are chipped or wide open. Leave them to soak in cold water for half an hour or so. This will clear some of their inherent grit.

Put a large pan of water on to boil. Drain the clams and tip them into a medium-sized pan set over a moderate heat. Pour in the white wine or vermouth and cover them tightly with a lid. After two minutes, no longer, lift the lid and check their progress. If most of the shells are open, turn off the heat. If not, give them a minute or so longer.

Generously salt the boiling water and lower in the pasta. Lift the clams from their liquor and pick out each morsel of clam flesh. Discard the shells, but not the cooking liquor.

Peel the garlic and slice it thinly, then let it soften in a tablespoon or so of the olive oil over a low heat. It must not color. Stir in the dried pepper flakes, then roughly chop the parsley leaves and add them. Let them cook briefly, then strain in the cooking liquor from the clams and let it bubble down for a minute.

Test the pasta for doneness; you want it to be tender but on the tacky side. About nine minutes should do it. Drain the pasta, tip it in with the clam liquor, then stir in the shelled clam meat. Grind over a little black pepper and pour in the remaining olive oil, then toss gently and serve in warm, shallow bowls.
Enough for 2, with seconds

Hot chocolate puddings
It is strange that, despite having a long and passionate love affair with the stuff, I so rarely cook with chocolate. I attempt to redress the balance with these little chocolate puddings – fluffy outside and molten within, a cross between a soufflé and a sponge pudding. I make them with the best chocolate I can get my hands on. Usually Valrhona's Manjari or something from the Chocolate Society. The hazelnut spread, such as Nutella or Green & Black's, sounds an odd addition, an intrusion perhaps, but in fact lends a lingering, nutty depth. If you feel the need to offer cream (and well you might), make it a jug of pouring cream. This recipe is too fiddly to do for two, so I make enough for four and eat the extra two cold the next day, with a drizzle of cream.

dark, fine-quality chocolate – 7oz
superfine sugar – ½ cup
large eggs – 3
butter – 5 tablespoons
chocolate hazelnut spread – 2 heaped tablespoons

Set the oven at 400°F. Lightly butter 4 small ramekins or ovenproof cups.

Break the chocolate into rough pieces and put it in a bowl suspended over a pan of gently simmering water. Let it melt without stirring, occasionally poking any unmelted chocolate down into the liquid chocolate.

Put the sugar into a food mixer, separate the eggs and add the yolks to the sugar. Beat till thick and creamy. In a separate bowl, whisk the egg whites till airy and almost stiff.

Stir the butter into the chocolate and leave to melt, then gently stir in the chocolate hazelnut spread. Fold the chocolate mixture into the egg and sugar, then carefully fold in the beaten egg whites with a metal spoon. Take care not to overmix. Just firmly, calmly mix the egg white into the chocolate, making certain there are no floating drifts of egg white.

Scoop into the four buttered dishes and place on a baking sheet. Bake for twelve to fifteen minutes, till risen. The tops should be cracked and the centers still slightly wobbly. Should you open one too early, it can go back in the oven without coming to as much harm as you might think.
Enough for 4

Miso soup, made with a couple of tablespoons of yellow miso paste to 5 cups of boiling water, is something to have on days when you really cannot be bothered to cook. It manages to be both sustaining and light at the same time, and will take anything else you care to throw at it, by which I mean mushrooms, noodles, Chinese greens or crisp French beans. Tonight I have it just as it is, a meal that stretches the notion of minimal eating to its limit. Dessert is pineapple, cold from the fridge.
Picture overleaf

February 15
A minimal supper

I fall for some exquisitely delicate pâtisserie from a flashy new shop in Soho. Tiny pastries like jewels, and precious in the extreme. They sit awkwardly with tonight's supper and its rough edges and big flavors. Charming though they are, the little cakes would have been much better with last night's miso soup, proving that it is not just what you eat but how you eat it.

February 16

Sausage and blood sausage with baked parsnips

onions – 2 medium
peanut oil
medium parsnips – 4, or 2 very large
pork sausage – 4
blood sausage – 9oz
the leaves from a few sprigs of thyme
chicken stock – 1 cup

Set the oven at 375°F. Peel the onions and slice them in half from root to tip, then cut each half into about six or eight pieces. Soften them slowly in a tablespoon or so of oil in a flameproof baking dish or roasting tin set over a moderate heat. While they are softening, peel the parsnips and cut them into short, thick chunks. Add them to the onions and leave to color, turning up the heat a little if need be.

Cut each sausage into three and add to the pan. Cut the blood sausage into thick slices, then cook them with everything else till they are golden on the outside. It is important that everything is a good color before you proceed. Stir in the thyme and the chicken stock. Bring to a boil, then put in the oven for thirty to forty minutes, until the parsnips are truly tender and the stock has reduced to a syrupy glaze. Enough for 2

Friends and I are debating the merits of bland food, dishes such as squash in white sauce, cauliflower with cheese, porridge and, of course, risotto. My position is that there are times when you want something spicy, bright and hot, and others when you want something less taxing on the taste-buds. Occasionally the mouth and body need calming rather than stimulating. With this in mind, I make a beige casserole of tender lamb and soft leeks. There could be no better example.

**February 18
A mild and
creamy
casserole**

Braised lamb with leeks and navy beans

dried navy beans – 1 cup
olive oil – 3 generous tablespoons
lamb neck fillet – 1lb, trimmed and cut into 2-in cubes
large leeks – 4, trimmed, halved lengthways and rinsed
garlic – 2 cloves, finely chopped
chopped thyme leaves – a generous tablespoon
bay leaves – 2
all-purpose flour – a generous tablespoon
heavy cream – ⅔ cup
a handful of parsley, chopped
a handful of mint leaves

Soak the beans overnight in cold water. I use mineral water for this. The next day, drain them, put them into a deep saucepan and cover with fresh water. Bring to a boil, skim off the froth and simmer for about forty minutes, or until tender. Turn off the heat and leave them in the cooking water.

Warm the oil in a flameproof casserole and add the meat. It should sizzle when it hits the oil. Let the meat brown slightly all over. You may have to do this in two batches, depending on the size of your casserole. Remove the meat from the casserole and set aside.

Set the oven to 300°F. Cut the leeks into 2-in pieces, then put them in the casserole, with a little more oil if need be. Leave them to cook till soft and silky. You will have to give them an occasional stir to ensure they do not color. Stir in the garlic, thyme and bay leaves. Sprinkle the flour over the top and continue cooking for three or four minutes, stirring occasionally.

Pour in 2¼ cups water and return the meat and any juices to the pan. Drain the beans and add them too. Then bring everything to a boil. As soon as the liquid boils, cover the casserole with a lid and put it in the oven for an hour, until the lamb is completely tender. Remove from the oven, stir in the cream, parsley and mint and warm through gently on the burner before serving.

Enough for 4

February 19
A bento
box dinner

Tonight it's bento boxes all round from a Japanese place in town – crystal noodles with cilantro, red chili pepper and sesame seeds with tubs of crisp green edamame. I love these bright green beans and cannot stop popping them out of their pods straight into my mouth. There are crab rolls too with dipping sauce and crunchy matchsticks of cucumber.

February 20
Red soup
and a
crunchy
salad

It has taken me years to figure out that when it rains I invariably make (or think about making) soup. I never noticed this till I started to write everything down.

Spiced pumpkin soup with bacon

a medium onion
garlic – 2 plump cloves
butter – 4 tablespoons
pumpkin – 2lbs
coriander seeds – a generous tablespoon
cumin seeds – 2½ teaspoons
small dried chili peppers – 2
chicken or vegetable stock – 5 cups
smoked bacon – 4 slices
light cream – ⅓ cup

Peel and roughly chop the onion. Peel and slice the garlic. Melt the butter in a large, heavy-based saucepan and cook the onion and garlic until soft and translucent. Meanwhile, peel the pumpkin, remove the stringy bits and seeds and discard them with the peel. You will probably have about 1½lbs of orangey-yellow flesh. Chop into rough cubes and add to the onion. Cook until the pumpkin is golden brown at the edges.

Toast the coriander and cumin seeds in a small pan over a low heat for about two minutes, until they start to smell warm and nutty. Keep the pan to one side for later. Grind the roasted spices in a coffee mill or with a mortar and pestle. Add them and the crumbled chili peppers to the onion and pumpkin. Cook for a minute or so, then add the stock. Leave to simmer for twenty minutes or until the pumpkin is tender.

Fry the bacon in the pan in which you toasted the spices. It should be crisp. Cool a little, then cut up into small pieces with scissors. Process the soup in a blender or food processor till smooth. Pour in the cream and taste for seasoning, adding salt and pepper as necessary. Return to the pan, bring almost to a boil and then serve, piping hot, with the bacon bits scattered on top.
Enough to serve 4 generously

I also make a salad dressing tonight with 4 tablespoons of sake, 4 tablespoons miso paste, 2 generous tablespoons of peanut oil and a couple of teaspoons of sugar. I use it to dress a salad made from the following raw crunchy things: a couple of big handfuls of bean sprouts, a handful of mint leaves and another of cilantro, half a cucumber and a couple of carrots, shredded into matchsticks, four shredded scallions and three red chili peppers, seeded and chopped. I toast 1 cup peanuts till they smell warm and nutty, chop them roughly, then toss the nuts, salad and miso dressing together. It makes a great, scrunchy, nutty, knobbly salad for two of us.

February 21
A slow roast
for a snowy
night

There is something romantic about falling snow. This is the first decent fall we have had this year, in two hours covering the box hedges and settling on the gray branches of the plum trees. By midafternoon, with a single trail of fox prints to the kitchen door, the garden looks like a Christmas card. The cats, huddled together round the Aga, look as if they are not amused: 'Oh, that stuff again.'

Every sound is muffled, the grass across the road sparkles in the streetlights, not a soul passes the front door. It is as if everyone is asleep. It takes something magical to make this stretch of road look as it does now, like a scene from a fairy tale. There is a leg of lamb in the fridge that I intended to roast as usual, with mint sauce and roast potatoes. With each windowpane edged in snow, I now want something more suited to a world white over. I put the leg into a deep cast-iron

casserole with a rub of ground cumin, salt and thyme and let it bake slowly, occasionally basting its fat, as it turns a deep, glowing amber.

Slow-roasted lamb with chickpea mash

a leg of lamb, about 5lbs

For the spice rub:
garlic – 2 cloves
sea salt flakes – a generous tablespoon
a pinch of sweet paprika
cumin seeds – a generous tablespoon
fresh thyme leaves – 2 generous tablespoons
olive oil – 2 generous tablespoons
butter – a thick slice

Set the oven at 325°F. Make the spice rub: peel the garlic cloves, then lightly crush them with the salt, using a pestle and mortar. Mix in the sweet paprika, cumin seeds and thyme leaves. Gradually add the olive oil so that you end up with a thickish paste. Melt the butter in a small pan and stir it into the spice paste.

Put the lamb into a casserole or roasting tin and rub it all over with the spice paste, either with the back of a spoon or with your hands. Put it in the oven and leave for thirty-five minutes. Pour in 1 cup of water and baste the lamb with the liquid, then continue roasting for three hours, basting the meat every hour with the juices that have collected in the bottom of the pan.

Remove the pan from the oven and pour off the top layer of oil, leaving the cloudy, herbal sediment in place. Cover the pan with a lid and set aside for ten minutes or so.

Carve the lamb, serving with the mashed chickpeas below, spooning the pan juices over both as you go.

Chickpea mash:
chickpeas – two 14-oz cans
a small onion
olive oil – 4 tablespoons
hot paprika

Drain the chickpeas and put them into a pan of lightly salted water. Bring to a boil, then turn down to a light simmer. You are doing this to warm the chickpeas rather than cook them any further. Peel and finely slice the onion, then let it soften with the olive oil in a pan over a moderate heat. This will seem like too much oil but bear with me. Let the onion color a little, then stir in a pinch of hot paprika. Drain the chickpeas, then either mash them with a potato masher or, better I think, in a food processor. Mix in enough olive oil from the cooked onion to give a smooth and luxurious purée. Stir in the onion and serve with the roast lamb above.

Enough for 6. Picture on page 65

Cold lamb, sliced thinly and tossed into a salad of tiny spinach leaves, Little Gem lettuce and baby red chard leaves. The whole thing looks pretty pedestrian until I add chopped fresh mint leaves to the olive oil and lemon dressing. Suddenly everything lights up. We eat it with bought focaccia and follow it with slices of commercial gingerbread spread with lemon curd.

There is still snow but it has turned to slush, the odd bit of ice taking you by surprise on your way to the shops. In ten minutes I manage to pick up an oxtail for tomorrow from the butcher, a bottle of wine, a few carrots and some mushrooms and even stop to pay the newspaper bill, which somehow I have let run into three figures. I feel as if I am eating too much meat this month, but squishy snow and ice means just one thing to me: gravy. Rich and thick with onions, gravy to fork into mounds of mashed potato, gravy to soothe and heal, to warm and satisfy. Gravy as your best friend.

Braised oxtail with mustard and mashed potatoes

This is not a liquid stew, but one where the lumps of meat and bone are coated in a sticky, glossy gravy. Piles of creamy mashed potato, made on the sloppy side with the addition of hot milk, are an essential part of this.

a large oxtail, cut into joints
a little flour for dusting
chili powder – $1\frac{1}{4}$ teaspoons
dry mustard powder – a heaped teaspoon
butter – a thick slice
a little oil, fat or drippings
onions – 2 large
thick carrots – 2 large
celery – 2 stalks
garlic – 4 large cloves
mushrooms – 5 large
tomato purée – $2\frac{1}{2}$ teaspoons
bay leaves – 4
thyme – a few bushy sprigs
a bottle of ballsy red wine, such as a Rioja
grain mustard – a generous tablespoon

smooth Dijon mustard – a generous tablespoon
a little parsley
creamy mashed potatoes, to serve

Set the oven at 300°F. Put the oxtail in a plastic or ziploc bag with the flour, chili powder, dry mustard powder and a good grinding of black pepper. Seal it and shake it gently until the oxtail is covered.

Warm the butter and a little oil, fat or drippings in a heavy-based casserole. Lower in the pieces of oxtail and let them bronze on each side, turning them as they take on a nice, tasty bronze color. Whilst the meat is browning, peel the onions and carrots and roughly chop them, then cut the celery into similar-sized pieces. Lift out the meat and set aside, then put the vegetables in the pot and let them color lightly. Peel the garlic, slice it thinly, then add it to the vegetables, along with the mushrooms, each cut into six or eight pieces. Squeeze in the tomato purée. Continue cooking until the mushrooms have softened and lost some of their bulk.

Return the oxtail and any escaped juices to the pan, tuck in the bay and thyme, then pour in the red wine. Bring briefly to a boil, season lightly with salt and cover with a tight lid. Transfer the dish to the oven. You can now leave the whole thing alone for a good two hours. I'm not sure you even need to give it a stir, though I inevitably do halfway through cooking. After an hour, check the meat for tenderness. I don't think it should be actually falling off the bones but it certainly should come away from the bone easily when tugged. Depending on the oxtail, it could take as long as two or three hours in total. Set the oxtail aside to cool, then refrigerate, preferably overnight.

The next day, scrape off the fat that has set on the surface, then reheat the casserole slowly on the hot plate, stirring from time to time. Stir in the mustards. Once they are in, you should cook the stew for no longer than fifteen minutes, otherwise it will lose its edge. Stir in the parsley and serve with creamy mashed potatoes.

Molasses tart

You could call this a basic domestic version of molasses tart, but that would be to undersell it. No frills, none of the oozing unctuousness of a restaurant version, just a pleasingly frugal tart with crisp pastry and a thick golden filling. I do think cream in some form or another is essential here, and by the generous jugful too. You will need an old-fashioned shallow pie plate with sloping sides about 8-in diameter (across the base).

fresh, white bread – ½lb
golden syrup – 8 heaped tablespoons
the juice of half a lemon

For the crust:
all-purpose flour – 1¾ cups
butter – 7 tablespoons
water – 2 generous tablespoons

Put the flour into a food processor with the cold butter cut into cubes and process until they resemble fine breadcrumbs. Pour in the cold water, process briefly, then tip the wet crumbs into a bowl. Bring the mixture together with your hands to form a ball. It will seem dry at first, but once you have squeezed and rolled the dough for a minute with your hands it will soften. Roll out on a lightly floured board to fit the tart pan.

Very lightly butter the pan, then lay the pastry over and push it carefully into the pan. Trim any overhanging pastry, then prick the base gently with a fork and put in the fridge to rest. Set the oven to 400°F.

After twenty minutes' resting (the pastry that is, not you), remove the pastry from the fridge, place a piece of parchment paper over it, then cover it with baking beans or a similar-sized tart pan to stop it bubbling up. Bake for ten minutes. Remove the paper and beans and return the pan to the oven for ten minutes, until the surface of the pastry is dry to the touch.

While the shell bakes, process the bread in a food processor till it is in fine crumbs, then tip them into the empty pastry bowl. Mix in the golden syrup and the lemon juice. Pour the mixture into the pastry shell, turn the oven down to 350°F and bake for thirty minutes. When it comes from the oven, leave the tart to rest for a good ten minutes, then serve with cream.
Enough for 6

**February 25
Grey skies
and piquant
flavors**

After a row of rib-sticking suppers, I need something clean-tasting and sharp. Something to wake us up rather than make me nod off in front of the TV.

Anything cooked with vinegar, onions and northern European spices has always excited me. Juniper is something I can never get enough of, its clean 'gin and tonic' scent instantly invigorating a gray February soul.

Warm pickled mackerel
Piquancy is something I value in a fish recipe, especially when that fish is one of the oily varieties, such as tuna, herring or my favorite

mackerel. It may sound a little strange but I recommend some sautéed potatoes with this.

mackerel – 3, filleted
a small onion
tarragon vinegar – ⅔ cup
white vermouth or white wine – ¼ cup
juniper berries – 12, lightly crushed
mustard seeds – ¾ teaspoon
white peppercorns – 6
black peppercorns – 9
superfine sugar – 2 generous tablespoons
bay leaves – 2
sautéed potatoes, to serve

Set the oven at 350°F. Rinse the mackerel fillets and lay them in a shallow oven-safe dish of china, glass or stainless steel (not aluminum). Peel and thinly slice the onion and put it into a non-corrosive saucepan, together with the vinegar and vermouth or wine. Then add the juniper berries, mustard seeds, white and black peppercorns, sugar, bay leaves and a good pinch of salt. Bring to a boil, then pour the mixture over the fish. Add enough water to just cover the fish – no more.

   Cover the dish lightly with aluminum foil and bake for twenty minutes. Serve the fish warm, two fillets each, with sautéed potatoes. Enough for 3

March 1
An English
cheese salad

It is a bit spooky the way the contents of those 'pillow packs' of salad from the supermarket somehow collapse and die within what seems like minutes of opening. Yet the mixed salad leaves you buy at the farmers' market and the ones that come from the organic boxes last several days in the fridge. The bag of leaves I picked up from Marylebone farmers' market – baby leaves of red chard, wild arugula, oak-leaf lettuce, spiky-leaved mizuna and crunchy little Romaine – is still perfect three days after I brought it home. I toss the delicate leaves and their fragile stems with large shavings of young Wensleydale cheese, toasted walnut halves, a bunch of large-leaved watercress and the merest dribble of walnut oil and lemon juice. A gentle, softly flavored salad of unmistakable Englishness.

We follow this with a soup made from fat, old, woody carrots and vegetable bouillon, the root vegetables coarsely grated and then sweated with finely chopped onion in a very little butter. No cream, just the soup put in a blender till smooth, then chopped chives and a knob of butter stirred in at the end.

March 2
Flatbread
and a home-
made dip

Fat flakes of snow are pattering against the panes of the kitchen door, each one sticking on the glass for just a second before dissolving. It is cold enough to have frozen the water in the bucket on the back steps. If ever there was a day to bake bread, this is it. No gung-ho excitement here, just a gentle bit of bread making, the feel of warm, soft dough in the hands, the smell of a fresh loaf coming from the oven and always, always the feeling of 'Why don't I do this more often?'

I use dried yeast rather than fresh, simply because I can buy it in the local health-food shop. The flour is organic white from a small mill. Rather than a loaf, today I make slipper-shaped flatbreads to eat warm with taramasalata and hummus. I have never made hummus better than the stuff you can buy at the Green Valley, just off the Edgware Road. White-coated counter staff serve it by the big spoonful straight into a shallow plastic tray, then drizzle the parchment-colored cream with emerald-green olive oil. But proper tarama is almost impossible to find in England, and shoppers seem to have accepted the bubblegum-pink stuff sold in tubs at the deli as the real thing. It isn't. It's crap. As commercially made food (mayonnaise, tomato soup, pesto) goes, it is the furthest from the real thing. Not even the merest shadow. So I draw a deep breath and pay a small fortune for real smoked cod roe from the fish market, a purple-veined, rusty-pink lobe of roe to beat into olive oil, a clove of garlic and perhaps a little bread to eke it out.

A simple flatbread

white bread flour – 5 cups
sea salt – ¾ teaspoon
dry yeast – 1 envelope
warm water – 1½ cups
olive oil – 2 generous tablespoons

Put the flour into the bowl of a food mixer (you will need the beater attachment), then add the salt. If you are using a coarse salt, crumble it first between your finger and thumb. Empty the yeast into a small glass, pour on enough water to make a thin paste, then stir in the rest of the warm water. (This isn't strictly necessary, you can put the dry yeast straight into the flour, but I prefer to do it this way.) Pour the water on to the flour and turn the mixer on slow. Introduce the olive oil, mixing till you have a stiffish dough. Tip the dough out on to a floured board and knead it with your hands, pushing and folding the dough until it feels springy and elastic to the touch. Set aside in a bowl covered with a clean dish towel and leave to rise for an hour or so. A warm place out of any drafts is ideal.

If you want to make the dough by hand, add the yeast and water to the flour and salt, mixing the two together with your hands or a wooden spoon. Mix in the olive oil – a pleasant, if squelchy, thing to do with your bare hands – then turn the lot on to a lightly floured work surface. Knead for a good nine or ten minutes, folding the far edge of the dough towards you and pushing it back into the dough. It should feel soft, springy and alive. Cover the dough with a clean dish towel as before and leave to rise.

Get the oven hot to 475°F. When your dough is about four times the size it was, break it into six pieces and push each one into a rough slipper shape. Dust them with flour and lie them flat on a baking sheet. Bake for five minutes, then turn the oven down to 425°F and continue baking for a further five minutes or so, until the underside of the bread sounds hollow when you tap it.
Makes 6 small flatbreads

Taramasalata – the real thing

smoked cod roe – a 4oz piece
white bread – 2 thick slices
garlic – a plump clove
olive oil – ¾ to 1¼ cups
the juice of a lemon

Peel the skin from the roe, or scoop the eggs out of the skin with a teaspoon. Soak the bread in water, then wring it out. Mash the bread into the roe with a pestle and mortar or in a food mixer. Add the clove of garlic, finely chopped, then the olive oil, pouring it in gradually as if you are making mayonnaise. When the mixture is a thick cream, stir in the lemon juice. Serve lightly chilled, with the warm flatbreads and some black olives.

Enough for 4

March 3

In my smug haze of good housekeeping from yesterday's baking session, not to mention my arch disdain for factory-produced foods, I fail to notice there is bugger all to eat in the house. At seven thirty I dash to the corner shop, returning with a can of baked beans, a bag of frozen fries and some beers.

March 4
Snow and a
chicken
stew

Snow has fallen as I slept. I fold back the shutters and stare out at the garden without moving for a full ten minutes. Snow brings a hush, a softness, to the city that is all too brief. You have to make time for it. The gravel path, the spindly trees, the little hedges that frame the vegetable and fruit beds are white over. The kitchen itself is icy this morning, its light muffled by the snow that has built up on the skylights. Breakfast is porridge, made with water. No sugar, no molasses, no hot milk. Just rolled oats and water.

Shopping is usually slipped into other jobs and journeys: a dash into the greengrocer's whilst I am on my way to a meeting; a trip to the fish market on my way home. But today's shopping is thought out, with a list and a big bag. There are four of us for supper and it is still snowing. I am not going to get away with a salad and a slice of tart.

One of the advantages of my butcher's free-range birds is that their bones are heavy and strong, as you would expect from something that has had the opportunity to exercise. The availability of these big birds and their fat, sauce-enriching bones makes it seriously worth thinking about chicken stew – a bird cooked slowly, with stock, herbs and aromatics. The results are mild but meaty, which is just what you want when the wind is cold enough to make your eyes water.

Starch is an essential accompaniment to stew – polenta, mashed roots, potatoes slipped into the pot. This time my stew has beans in it. There is quite a lot of juice, which, despite the beans, screams out to be poured over some mashed parsnip or potato, perhaps with some parsley and a dollop of mustard stirred in. Something for the coldest days of the year.

Chicken stew and mashed potatoes

dried cannellini beans – ¾ cup
a large chicken, cut up
olive oil – ¼ cup, plus more for frying
balsamic vinegar – ¼ cup
garlic – 4 plump cloves, peeled
bay leaves – 3 or 4
dried herbes de Provence – 2 teaspoons
the pared zest of a small orange
leeks – 3 medium, thickly sliced
mashed potatoes, to serve

Soak the beans in cold water for three or four hours, though overnight will not hurt (the older your beans, the longer they will need). Bring them to a boil in unsalted water and boil them for forty minutes.

Put the chicken parts in a glass, china or steel dish. Pour over the olive oil and a couple of tablespoons of the balsamic vinegar, then tuck in the peeled garlic cloves and the bay leaves. Scatter over the herbes de Provence, a good grinding of pepper and salt and the strips of pared orange zest. Leave in a cool place, overnight if possible or at least for four or five hours.

Set the oven to 400°F. Heat enough olive oil to cover the bottom of a shallow pan (don't be tempted to fry the chicken in the oil from the marinade; it will spit and pop because of the vinegar). Add the chicken pieces, shaking the marinade from each as you go, and let them fry till they are golden brown on each side. You may find it easier to do this in two batches. Transfer the browned meat to a deep casserole – one for which you have a lid. Drain the boiled beans and add them to the pot.

In the same oil, fry the leeks over a low heat, so that they soften rather than color. Allowing a leek to brown will send it bitter. Now add the garlic from the marinade, then pour in the remaining marinade, the rest of the balsamic vinegar and about 5 cups of water. Don't be tempted to use stock instead; it will make the dish too rich. Bring to a boil, season generously with salt, then pour this mixture over the chicken. Tuck in the bay leaves and orange from the marinade, then cover the casserole and put it in the preheated oven for two hours. Halfway through cooking, check that the chicken is still submerged. Check for seasoning: it may need salt, it will need black pepper and you may feel it needs a little more balsamic vinegar. Serve steaming hot, with mashed potatoes, letting the thick juices from the stew form pools in the potatoes.

March 5   If there is a recurrent theme to my cooking at the moment, it is the clean bite of lime leaves and chili peppers. I appreciate them for the freshness and vitality they bring with them. I have no luck at the greengrocer's with the lime leaves today, nor at the major supermarket that stands, red brick and sprawling, less than thirty minutes' walk from home. I end up catching the bus to the crush of Chinese shops that line Gerrard Street, which have more lime leaves than you could shake a chopstick at. They freeze at a push, and for once I remember to take a second packet home with that in mind.

I have had this problem before, usually when the leaves' inclusion is crucial (Thai fish cakes, perhaps). People say you can use lime zest instead. I agree to an extent, but there is something missing. There is more than just the well-known flavor of lime in those finely shredded leaves. They carry a bite, a spritz, to them that is missing in the skin of the fruit. If lime leaves remain elusive, I would rather add a stalk of lemongrass instead.

While I'm in Chinatown, I pick up a couple of papayas. Unusually, they are perfectly ripe, a deep custard yellow. Tender as a kitten, they get carried home on top of everything else. One of them still gets bruised. After the pork, I slice each fruit and scoop out the black seeds – they look like caviar – then squeeze over a little lime juice. It means there is too much lime in the meal but it has brightened up a wet day.

Pork burgers with lime leaves and cilantro

At first glance, this may seem like a lot of work. It isn't. The whole thing should take about half an hour, plus a little time for the meatballs to chill. I like this with a salad of crisp iceberg lettuce, chopped mint and cilantro, dressed with lime juice and salt. If you need something to fill, then some plain steamed white rice would fit the bill, or some soft buns between which to sandwich the hot pork patties.

scallions – 4
hot red chili peppers and their seeds – 4
garlic 4 medium-sized cloves
the stalks and leaves from a small bunch of cilantro
ginger – a thumb-sized lump
lime leaves – 6
smoked pancetta or fatty bacon – 4oz
ground pork – 1¼lbs
a little vegetable or peanut oil for frying

Chop the scallions, peppers, garlic and cilantro and finely grate the ginger. Roll up and finely shred the lime leaves – they should be as fine as you can get them – then put the lot in a food processor and process till all is finely chopped and well mixed. Scrape the paste out into a large bowl. Cut up the pancetta, then put it into the processor and process it to a coarse mush. Now add it, with the spice paste, to the ground pork.

Mix everything together – I like to do this with my hands – grinding in some salt and black pepper as you go. Set aside in the fridge for about half an hour for the flavors to mingle.

Squash the seasoned pork into about twelve small balls, then flatten them into patties. Pour a little oil into a heavy, shallow pan, just enough to cover the bottom. When it is hot, add half the meatballs and let them cook for several minutes over a high heat, turning them halfway through, till they are cooked in the middle and nicely brown and stickily, sensuously glossy on the outside.
Enough for 4 with rice and salad

I have no idea what I had in mind when I bought the two lamb chops that are now sitting on the kitchen worktop. Actually they are leg steaks and there's enough for two. Whatever it was, the flash of inspiration must have got lost on the way home. In the fridge are mixed salad leaves – arugula, baby spinach and some baby chard – and a bunch of mint. I might also be able to rescue a few leaves from the bunch of basil that has got too close to the back of the fridge and burned on the ice. There is also the usual stuff in the fridge and cupboards.

**March 7
Inspiration
for a lamb
chop**

I put the chops into a bowl with a couple of tablespoons of light soy sauce and a crushed garlic clove and let them sit for twenty minutes. I get the broiler hot and chuck the chops on it, a couple of minutes on each side. Whilst the meat is cooking, I toss the salad leaves into a bowl. Then I knock up a dressing consisting of a couple of small, hot red chili peppers, finely chopped, the juice of half a ripe lime, a tablespoon of dark soy, a handful of shredded mint leaves and a wee bit of sugar. I slice the lamb into pencil-thin strips and, while it is still hot, toss it with the salad and dressing, then divide it between two plates.

The mixture of sizzling meat, mellow, salty soy and sharp lime juice is startling, especially with the green leaves that have softened slightly where they have touched the lamb. The few juices left on our plates are stunning, and we mop them up with crisp white rolls.

Dinner out tonight, so just a quick snack for lunch. The perfect salad sandwich is all about the vitality of the ingredients: the uber-freshness of the watercress, the jelly-soft tomatoes, the crunch of the ice-cold cucumber and the heat of the radishes against the soft, white and impeccably fresh bread. If you are not obsessively fussy about every detail of this sandwich, it won't hit the spot. You might as well not bother. Lunch today is that perfect salad sandwich, with old-fashioned crunchy lettuce, cucumber, radishes, scallions and tomato. There is a slick of mayonnaise, a dusting of fine sea salt and bread so soft, thick and doughy it could double for a duvet. For once, something is as it should be, a sandwich to be proud of.

March 9

March 11
A fiery way
with lamb

The Ginger Pig has a display of lamb chops that is irresistible even to someone who has had them once already this week. Thick, deep red and meaty, they have been cut from the middle of the loin and have a generous bone on which to chew. Rarely have I seen such tempting pieces of meat.

There are two of us tonight so I buy four out of greed rather than necessity. I am set on some sort of meaty supper with Indian spicing, not a curry exactly, but something vibrant. The chops will do fine for this.

At home I raid the spice jars, a teaspoon each of four seeds: mustard, coriander, fennel and cumin, left whole rather than ground. I fry them gently in 2 generous tablespoons of peanut oil, then stir in two peeled and chopped shallots, two hot red chili peppers that I have seeded and chopped, and four crushed cloves of garlic. I let everything soften without coloring, then stir in a grated knob of ginger the size of a walnut in its shell and six chopped tomatoes, their seeds and juice. Once everything has come to the boil, I crumble in some sea salt, turn the heat down and let it simmer, partly covered with a lid, for fifteen minutes.

Off the heat I squeeze in the juice of a lime and add a handful of chopped cilantro leaves and a little more salt. Once the spicy-red slop has cooled, I dunk the lamb chops in it and leave them for an hour or so.

The chops, cooked under an overhead broiler, their marinade still clinging to them, are a fiery, juicy delight. The spices bring heat and savor but in no way overpower the lamb; the fat is crisp and lightly scorched from the broiler, the flesh tender and rich with pink juices. Rarely have I enjoyed a chop quite so much.

March 12
A simple
supper

There have been three restaurant meals this week, including sensationally good plates of hot salt cod fritters at Moro in Exmouth Market and a wonderfully elegant dish of kidneys with lentils and potato purée at Locanda Locatelli in the West End. Add to that a bowl of fried oysters in a clear broth at the 'cheap-as-chips' Japan Centre in Piccadilly Circus and I have barely had to cook at home at all. I don't think the kitchen has ever stayed tidy for that long in its entire life. Eating out remains an absolute treat for me; especially so this year, when for one reason or another I have spent so much time at home. Even if I could eat out every night, I wouldn't. Although I will admit to occasionally getting a bit 'cooked out', I cannot pretend I don't enjoy putting something I have made for someone on the table. To this day, it still sends tingles down my spine.

I have a theory that I love cooking for people after all these years because I rarely attempt too much. Many is the time supper is little more than a bowl of soup and a salad, or perhaps some chicken pieces roasted with butter and served with a handful of green leaves. It is the way I prefer to eat, but it also happens to be a lot less trouble than roast chicken with gravy, spuds and vegetables, followed by dessert and custard. I like to think of it as a love of simplicity, but it could also be a mixture of greed tinged with laziness.

We eat roast chicken, mashed butternut squash and the juices from the roasting tin mixed with a little white vermouth and a shot of lemon juice. Dessert is sliced mangoes and whole rambutans that look like diminutive pan-scrubbers.

It's funny how even on the coldest day people seem to appreciate a salad – if, of course, the ingredients are right. In other words, not tomato, cucumber and lettuce. Hot, spicy leaves such as watercress or arugula go down well, especially when matched with something sharp and bright like orange or grapefruit. With that I would chuck in something meaty, such as bacon, pieces of duck breast (it is almost as cheap as chicken now) or a grilled breast of game bird. Often as not, though, a big salad like this is made to use up cold roast chicken, or perhaps a game bird from the weekend.

**March 13
A refreshing chicken salad**

The oranges right now are as fat and juicy as I have ever known them and I will eat them at every chance. This time, they wake up a salad made from yesterday's roast chicken.

Chicken salad with watercress, almonds and orange
The main-course salads I value the most are those that are refreshing. This, with salty, soy-toasted pumpkin seeds and the clean, fresh taste of oranges, is one of the best. You could serve couscous with it, if you wish, or perhaps a Lebanese tabbouleh.

pumpkin seeds – 3 generous tablespoons
a little dark soy sauce
whole skinned almonds – 2 generous tablespoons
watercress – 1 cup
a large orange
cooked chicken, grilled or left from a roast – 9oz

For the dressing:
olive oil – 3 generous tablespoons
grain mustard – a heaped teaspoon
red wine vinegar – 2 generous teaspoons

Make the dressing: whisk together the olive oil, mustard and vinegar and season with salt and pepper.

Put the pumpkin seeds on a grill pan or in a non-stick frying pan and sprinkle them with soy sauce. Toast them under the broiler or over

a moderate heat for a couple of minutes, until they smell toasty. The soy sauce will have dried.

Toast the almonds under a hot broiler or in a dry, non-stick frying pan. Do not take your eyes off them – they burn in seconds.

Wash the watercress. Peel the orange, scrupulously removing the white pith under the skin with a sharp knife. Cut the orange in half, then cut each half into thin slices, catching as much of the juice as you can and tipping it in with the dressing.

Put the orange slices in the dressing. Tear the chicken into large, juicy pieces, but no bigger than you would want on your fork, then add it to the dressing. Divide the watercress between two plates, lay the chicken and orange on top, then drizzle over the dressing, or as much of it as you need. Scatter over the almonds and pumpkin seeds and serve straight away.
Enough for 2

March 15

Still cold, but there are fat, green buds on the horse chestnut trees opposite the house and the pale jade leaves on the quince tree are opening a little more each day. The roses are sporting new red shoots and the parrot tulips have already sent up furled leaves to announce their intention to flower once again in shades of purple-black, vermilion and orange. I can barely wait. Such signs of life should be uplifting but I can hardly raise an eyebrow. With the exception of a wicker basket of blood oranges at the Spanish grocer's shop in Exmouth market, the shops have never looked less interesting than they are today. I feel we have reached the bottom of the cook's year. I cannot remember a day when I felt so uninspired. For once, getting something on the table (my favorite boiled ham with parsley sauce and mashed potatoes) is truly a chore.

March 18
Sunshine
and smoked
mackerel

I wake an hour earlier than usual, to a sun-filled bedroom. Not the usual clear winter light but a light altogether softer and warmer. As if I have woken in another country. Yesterday was cold enough to see me pile straw round the lemon verbena plant in fear of frost. Today it is like the middle of June, and by mid afternoon the parks are chock full with people lazing on the grass, the cafés bring their pavement tables out of storage, the cats once again sprawl on the hot flagstones outside the kitchen. It is as if we have skipped spring and gone straight from mid-winter to mid-summer. Although I find this sudden change a little disturbing I cannot help but welcome it with open arms. It is as if a silent prayer has been answered.

It may be tempting fate but I get out my short-sleeved shirts and buy some smoked mackerel for a salad. The fish isn't ready and I have to wait, only to be presented twenty minutes later with four golden torpedoes, each whole fish as thick as my arm, their skins shining like

something from Tutankhamun's tomb, their flesh dense and creamy and still faintly warm. The smell of smoke follows me home. A tarry smell that reminds me of oak, boats and old string.

The afternoon cools dramatically and my proposed salad (mackerel, fennel and lemon segments) becomes smoked mackerel on toast. The fish, mixed with a little cream and cheese and piled thickly on rounds of crisp sourdough, suddenly seems one of the most delicious things I have ever put in my mouth. We eat the hot, smoky toasts with a salad of thinly sliced fennel, lemon and parsley leaves.

smoked mackerel – ½lb
heavy cream – 3 generous tablespoons, plus a little more
grated Parmesan – 3 generous tablespoons, plus a little more
chives – 6
slices of sourdough (or whatever you have to hand) for toasting – 4

Remove the skin from the mackerel, put the flesh in a bowl and mash it lightly with a fork. You want it to flake rather than be mashed to a paste. Stir in the 3 generous tablespoons of cream and Parmesan. Chop the chives and stir them in with some roughly crushed black pepper.

Toast the bread on both sides, but lightly. Pile the mixture on to the hot toast, drizzle with a very little cream and add a bit more Parmesan to each one, then broil for three or four minutes, till golden and bubbling.
Enough for 2

**March 19
The first
meal out
of doors**

Looking at last year's diary, the first time we ate in the garden was March 13th. Apparently we ate spatchcocked chicken from the grill with garlic and lemon. I seem to remember it took forever to cook and we ended up tucking in at nearly midnight, in the garden, the candles burning low, and probably by that time more than a little tipsy. This year's first meal is a week later, and I choose one of those neat lamb leg fillets from the butcher. To be honest, I never think they look that interesting, a bit like the sheep's answer to the chicken breast, but as it turns out they roast sweetly and quickly. There is no fat to keep them moist, so a bit of conscientious basting is in order. We sit out of doors, lanterns flickering in the breeze, laughing about how this time last week there was frost on the hedges.

Roast fillet of lamb with anchovy and mint

mint – about 8 sprigs or ½oz
anchovy fillets – 2oz
olive oil – 5 tablespoons
new season's garlic – 4 or 5 cloves, peeled

a large lamb fillet – about ¾lb
new potatoes, to serve

Pull the leaves from the mint and put them in a food processor. Drain the anchovies but don't rinse them; you want all their fishy saltiness. Put them in with the mint, together with the olive oil, the garlic and several serious grinds of black pepper.

Process to a slush – it should be a sort of herby slop – then scrape it into a bowl large enough to take the fillet. Roll the lamb in the paste, cover the bowl with plastic wrap and set aside somewhere cool for a couple of hours, but preferably not quite as cold as the fridge.

Get the oven hot. Ideally it should be at 425°F. Put the lamb in a roasting pan or shallow oven-safe dish, spreading it all over with the marinade paste. Roast for about fifteen to eighteen minutes, which will toast the outside without burning the mint, and leave the meat juicily pink within.

Leave for a few minutes to rest, then slice into thick chunks and serve with just a few new potatoes.
Enough for 4

The potatoes
Rather than just boil the potatoes, I put them in a pan of boiling water till almost tender, then drain them, tip them into an oven-safe dish and press each one hard to split it open. You can do this with the back of a spoon or an oven-gloved hand. A drizzle of olive oil, a seasoning of coarse pepper and chopped rosemary before finishing in the oven with the lamb.

Brown sugar lemon cake with thick yogurt
Cake sounds an eccentric thing to serve after a weekend supper for four. But somehow the lemon note seems right for the day. Almond cakes will keep for several days in perfect condition. I like them with a spoonful of heavy cream, thick Greek yogurt or tart crème fraîche, and with fruit – sliced mangoes, raspberries or poached apricots. That is when they become a dessert rather than something for tea. I think it essential to use unwaxed or organic lemons.

butter – 1¾ cups
brown sugar – 1 cup
all-purpose flour – 1 cup
ground almonds – ⅔ cup
baking powder – ¾ teaspoon
a large lemon
large eggs – 4

For the topping:
a lemon
brown sugar – 2 generous tablespoons
water – 4 tablespoons

For the syrup:
brown sugar – 2 generous tablespoons
the juice of a large lemon

Set the oven at 325°F. Line a loaf pan, about 10 x 4 x 3in deep, with baking parchment (simply cut a piece of paper the exact length of the tin and lay it inside the tin and up the longest sides).

To make the topping, slice the lemon thinly and put it in a small saucepan with the sugar and water. Bring to a boil, then watch closely for five minutes or so, until the water has almost evaporated and the lemon slices are sticky. Set aside.

Beat the butter and sugar together in a food mixer till they are light and fluffy. You can expect it to take a little longer than it would with superfine sugar. Meanwhile, measure the flour and almonds and mix them with the baking powder. Grate the zest of the lemon and add it to the flour mixture.

Break the eggs and beat them lightly with a fork, then add them to the creamed butter and sugar a little at a time. The mixture will probably curdle a bit but don't worry. Remove the mixing bowl from the machine and gently fold in the flour, almonds and baking powder with a large metal spoon (a wooden spoon would knock the air out).

Scoop the cake mixture into the lined pan, then lay the reserved lemon slices on top, overlapping them down the center of the cake. Bake for about forty-five minutes, till risen and golden. Insert a metal skewer to see if it is ready. If it comes out clean, then the cake is done; if it has mixture sticking to it, it needs a few minutes longer. Remove the cake from the oven and set aside.

For the syrup, stir the brown sugar into the lemon juice; it will only partially dissolve. Spike the top of the cake with a metal skewer, then spoon over the lemon and sugar. Leave to cool.
Enough for 8

March 21

One of the reasons I bought this house was because the doors to the small, narrow kitchen opened out on to the garden. And when I found them to be rotten, I rejoiced and replaced them with a much wider pair, hanging them on parliament hinges so each door could be pushed flat against the outside walls, giving the effect of kitchen and garden as one.

I cook with the doors open on even the wettest day. The smell of spring rain as I chop and stir brings with it a gentle freshness and energy. The first home-grown herbs up this spring were chives as fine as babies' hair, and now it's the mint, which has wintered happily in its terracotta pot on the kitchen steps. I grow two varieties: Eastern mint, whose pointed, almost hairless leaves are the best for glasses of sweet, amber Moroccan tea, and a common mint, which is only just starting to wake up from its winter slumber.

Two full days of sunshine and the local gardens are unrecognizable. The playing fields are a mass of chirpy daffodils. At home, leaf buds are suddenly showing on everything from the hazelnuts to the goose-berries. Apart from a couple of sleepy rose bushes (Tuscany Superb, always tardy), every plant, tree and bush seems to have woken up this week.

Shrimp and cilantro rolls

defrosted shrimp – 9oz
garlic – 2 cloves, peeled
scallions – 4, chopped
lemongrass – 2 thick stalks, outer leaves removed, shredded (or 4 lime leaves, rolled and finely shredded)
cilantro – a good fistful
small hot red chili peppers – 2, seeded
flour – a heaped tablespoon
peanut oil for frying
iceberg lettuce leaves – about 8

For the sauce:
sugar – 5 tablespoons
rice vinegar – 7 generous tablespoons
dark soy sauce – a generous tablespoon
red chili peppers – 2 small ones, seeded and very finely chopped
cilantro – a generous tablespoon, very finely chopped
the juice of a lime

Make the sauce: heat the sugar and vinegar in a small saucepan until the sugar has dissolved and the mixture is becoming syrupy. Stir in the soy sauce and leave to cool slightly. Add the chilis, cilantro and lime juice. Leave to cool and thicken.

Put the shrimp, garlic, scallions, shredded lemongrass or lime leaves, cilantro, chilis, flour and a little salt into a food processor and process to a rough paste. Set aside for half an hour in the fridge for the flavors to marry.

Press spoonfuls of the shrimp paste into small patties or flat cakes. You should get about eight from the mixture.

Heat enough peanut oil in a shallow pan to cover the bottom, then

lay the shrimp patties in it, letting them color before gently turning them with a spatula. When they are crisp and golden on the outside yet still moist in the middle, lift the patties out and lay them on the lettuce leaves, spooning some of the sauce over the top.
Enough for 4

March 24
An almost
empty
fridge

I arrive home after a few days in Europe and rummage through the fridge in the hope of inspiration. Celery, scallions, parsley, all still in surprisingly good nick, some chorizo sausage, but not a lot else. The chopped celery and scallions are cooked slowly with olive oil, then the chorizo is stirred in, in fat chunks. Then, as the rust-colored juices leak out into the pan, I stir in a couple of handfuls of rice and some Marigold vegetable bouillon. It simmers, with an occasional stir, till the rice is tender, a matter of ten minutes or so, then I stir in a handful of roughly chopped parsley. The result is a sort of paella-y thing, homely and welcoming. It is exactly what is needed.
Picture on previous page

March 26
Seed day

A fortnight later than I had intended, the day on which I sow the majority of the vegetables for the kitchen garden. Lilac, purple and white sweet peas (Flora Norton, Cupani's Original and Mrs Colville), French pumpkins, rare fava beans from Chelsea Physic Garden and the more pedestrian Red Epicure are all tucked into tall, thin pots full of seed compost and Vermiculite, labeled and watered. This year I do it in the sun, the leaves on the fruit trees slowly unfurling in the spring sunshine. To be honest, it is one of those days you can't quite believe, all blue sky and white damson blossom. Lunch is bread, serrano ham and Manchego cheese at the garden table. Supper is more bread, this time with dishes of olive oil to dunk it in, followed by tomato salad with basil and sea salt. Then we get extraordinarily drunk because I am over-tired and no one has really had enough to eat.

March 27
A new leaf

Baby leeks the thickness of a pencil, still with mud on their white roots; tiny, very early tomatoes from the Isle of Wight; curly kale by the bagful; field mushrooms the size of a side plate; and bags of spear-shaped spinach leaves – these are the stars of today's trip to the farmers' market. The kale is for a side dish to go with a roast chicken stuffed with lemon and tarragon and served with the baked onions with Parmesan and cream on page 336. The stalls are all good spirit-lifting stuff. But nothing quite prepares me for the salad stall. Box after box of greenery in fine fettle: quivering leaves of tender lamb's lettuce, hot, gutsy red mustard, earthy red chard, boisterous celery leaf and pepper-hot arugula all begging to be taken home. Then there are bundles of cilantro, chokingly spiky mizuna and rare and exceptionally tart bundles of sorrel. I buy four bags, keeping the stir-fry leaves separate from the chard, lamb's lettuce and arugula, which will end up in the week's salads. There are also manageably sized heads of frisée, the frilly lettuce that is normally too big for my needs. I only want enough for a couple of frisée and bacon salads, which I still regard as one of the world's best lunches.

I am not an obsessive or even especially passionate foodie but finds like this do excite me. A stall devoted to the art of the salad, where the shopper can pick and nibble and help themselves to whatever they want. Such places make the supermarket pillow pack of 'bistro-mix' salad almost laughable.

A garden day: trimming the yew hedges, clearing the herb garden of sticks from last year's sweet arugula and lemon balm, trying to make space for new tarragon plants, fennel and lemon verbena. I sit on the back steps with green tea and chocolate cake, contemplating Jekka McVicar's herb list. This year I am determined to grow more of the authentic mint for mint tea and find somewhere to plant dill so that it doesn't cross-pollinate with the fennel. Lunch is steamed Chinese broccoli with oyster sauce and ginger. **March 28**

Chinese broccoli with oyster sauce and ginger

Any Chinese greens will do for this, or indeed purple sprouting or European broccoli, or spring greens. What matters is the freshness and vitality of the greens. Time-wise, everything happens at once in this recipe. I get round this by getting the rice ready first, keeping it hot over boiling water, then preparing the garlic and ginger. It is better to let the hot oyster sauce mixture wait off the heat for a second or two than risk over-cooking the greens. They are what it is all about.

steamed rice – enough for 2
cilantro – a small bunch
garlic – 2 large, juicy cloves
ginger – a piece as big as your thumb
peanut oil – a generous tablespoon
Chinese broccoli (*gai lan*), choy sum or other Chinese
greens – 12 stems
oyster sauce – 7 generous tablespoons

When the rice is cooked, keep it warm in a covered colander over a pan of simmering water. Roughly chop the cilantro and fold it into the rice with a few grinds of black pepper. Put a pan of water on to boil for the greens.

Peel the garlic and slice each clove thinly. Pare the ginger, then cut the flesh into matchstick-thick shreds. Warm the oil in a medium-sized saucepan, tip in the sliced garlic and shredded ginger and fry till soft and nut brown.

Cook the greens in plenty of furiously boiling, lightly salted water (the oyster sauce is quite salty, so I tend to go easy on the salt). They will need three to five minutes, depending on the thickness of their stalks. Stir the oyster sauce into the browned ginger and garlic and leave to bubble briefly. Drain the greens and tip them immediately into the oyster sauce. Toss the vegetables around gently in the sauce and aromatics, then serve with the cilantro rice.
Enough for 2

Chocolate almond cake
There are actually very few foods about which I am overly fussy. Coffee, salad, bread and chocolate is pretty much it when it comes to making a list of things I am almost absurdly pernickety about. Where I am normally happy to tuck into pretty much anything if I am hungry enough, these are the things that I will avoid unless they are absolutely as I like them to be. It is not that I am set in my ways, more that I would rather not drink a cup of coffee, say, unless it is perfect, and the same with bread. In matters as simple as these, I just don't see the point of putting up with second best. Of course, some people are like that about everything they eat, which would, frankly, drive me mad. And can you imagine living with someone like that?

Another of my pet obsessions is chocolate cake. Generally speaking, I don't buy into the whole fudgier-the-better school of thought. I actually like my cake to have some 'crumb' to it, rather than be a borderline chocolate mousse. The hazelnut version in *Appetite* is my idea of the perfect chocolate cake, but I admit there are occasions when something more gooey is called for. Today I have a chocolate addict coming round, so I make my darkest, stickiest version for them. It works as both teatime cake and dessert, though if I am using it for the latter I might add some raspberries on the side, and perhaps a scoop of piquant crème fraîche, too.

fine dark chocolate (70% cocoa solids) – ½lb
a small, hot espresso
butter – 1¾ cups
all-purpose flour – ¾ cup
baking powder – 1¼ teaspoons
very good-quality cocoa powder – 2 generous tablespoons
almonds – 1 cup
large eggs – 5
turbinado sugar – ¾ cup

You will need a shallow cake pan, 9in in diameter, about 2in deep, the base lightly buttered and lined with a round of baking parchment.

Set the oven to 350°F. Break or chop the chocolate into small pieces and melt it in a bowl resting over a saucepan of gently simmering water. As soon as it has started to melt, pour the hot espresso over the chocolate. Cut the butter into chunks and drop it into the chocolate and coffee. Resist the temptation to stir. Sift the flour, baking powder and cocoa together. Don't skin the almonds, but pulse them in a food processor until they resemble fine, fresh breadcrumbs.

Separate the eggs, dropping the whites into a large bowl. Whisk the whites till they are thick and stiff, then quickly but gently fold in the sugar with a large metal spoon. Remove the chocolate from the heat and stir to dissolve the last of the butter. Mix the egg yolks together, then stir them quickly into the chocolate, just till the ingredients come together. Fold firmly but gently into the egg white and sugar.

Lightly fold in the flour and cocoa mixture, then the ground almonds. Work slowly and firmly but lightly. Don't over-mix or knock the air out, and stop as soon as the last bit of flour is mixed in. Transfer the mixture to the cake pan and bake for twenty-five minutes. Test the cake for doneness with a skewer. It should come out clean, without any sticky cake mixture attached to it.

Leave to cool a little before turning out and slicing.

Enough for 10

March 29
A stir-fry for
a spring day

Mustard green is just one of the leaves I picked up at the farmers' market last Sunday. Hotter than watercress or arugula, it has a rough edge to it, as if someone has cut round each leaf with pinking shears. The larger the leaf, the more potent it is. It was great with a smoked salmon sandwich, rather like having a thin spreading of wasabi. But there are too many to put in the salad tonight, to which I want to add torn mozzarella and strips of serrano ham. Instead I stir-fry the leaves with mushrooms. The result is a clean and fresh little vegetable dish. No rice, I can't be bothered.

Stir-fried mushrooms, spring leaves and lemongrass

garlic – 3 cloves
small hot red chili peppers – 2
lemongrass – a fat stalk
scallions – 4
portobello mushrooms – 2 cups
peanut oil – 3 generous tablespoons (and maybe more)
tender green leaves (mizuna, spinach, mustard greens etc) – 4 handfuls
sugar and salt – a good pinch of each
light soy sauce – 2 generous tablespoons
toasted sesame oil

Get everything ready before you start to cook. So, peel and finely chop the garlic; halve, seed and finely chop the chilis; discard the outer leaves of the lemongrass and finely shred the inner leaves. Cut the scallions into short lengths and the mushrooms into quarters.

Get the wok hot. By which I mean smoking hot. Pour in the peanut oil, then immediately add the chopped garlic, chilis and lemongrass. Stir and fry for a few seconds, then add the chopped scallions. Once the onions have started to wilt, add the mushrooms and let them color, tossing and stirring until they are golden and soft. Add a little more oil if you need to, but remember that it will bring the temperature down considerably.

Throw in the leaves, then stir and toss until they have wilted but still retain their bright green color. Add a good pinch of salt, another of sugar and the soy. Drizzle over a very little sesame oil (I think a teaspoon is about enough) and eat immediately.

Enough for 2

March 30
A vegetable
curry for six

Six of us tonight for beers and a curry. Nothing mind-blowingly hot, just something that will create a bit of interest with the pumpkin and sweet potatoes that lie idling in the fridge. My problem with any sort of curry is the length of the ingredients list. Once I have divided it into things I already have (chickpeas, onions, garlic, carrots, a forgotten pumpkin and a sweet potato) and raided the spice jars for coriander, turmeric, cardamom and mustard seed, that leaves only curry leaves, chili peppers, mushrooms, yogurt and cilantro to pick up from the shops. So much for the scary ingredients list.

The ingredients here are warm and golden for a day that has been cold and gray since mid-morning. The sauce is fragrant rather than hot and made luxurious by the addition of thick yogurt. The only thing to worry about is overcooking the pumpkin – which will collapse – or boiling the sauce once the yogurt has been added. It needs to be served hot, but kept below a boil once the yogurt is stirred in.

There is a temptation to open a couple of cans of chickpeas instead of cooking them from scratch, mostly because of my incessant habit of letting them boil dry. I resist, and soak and cook them from scratch, though I am not entirely convinced they are any better for it. A bowl of brown rice, put on to cook twenty minutes before the curry is done, ensures that the meal serves six.

Chickpea and sweet potato curry

dried chickpeas – 1 cup, soaked for several hours in mineral water
onions – 2 medium
garlic – 4 cloves
fresh red chili peppers – 3

carrots – 3
coriander seeds – 2½ teaspoons
green cardamom pods – 6
peanut oil – 2 generous tablespoons
curry leaves – 15
black mustard seeds – 1½ teaspoons
ground turmeric – 2½ teaspoons
tomatoes – 1lb
a medium squash or small pumpkin (about ¾lb peeled weight)
a large sweet potato (about ¾lb)
vegetable stock – 3 cups

To finish:
small mushrooms – 5–6oz, halved or quartered
Greek yogurt – 1 cup
a good handful of cilantro

Drain the chickpeas and cook them in boiling water (without salt) until they are reasonably tender (chickpeas are never that tender). This will take about forty-five minutes, depending on the age of your peas.

Peel and chop the onions, garlic, chilis and carrots, keeping them separate. Grind the coriander seeds to a coarse powder. Remove the black seeds from the cardamom pods and grind them to a powder. Pour the oil into a heavy-bottomed casserole dish set over a moderate to low heat and leave the onions and garlic to cook slowly until they are soft, translucent and honeyed. Stir in the curry leaves, which you can leave whole, the mustard seeds and the ground coriander, cardamom, turmeric and chopped chilis. Leave them to sizzle lightly for two or three minutes, then add the chopped carrots and continue cooking over a low heat for four or five minutes.

Roughly chop the tomatoes, pumpkin and sweet potato and add them to the casserole. Stir, then pour in the stock. Turn up the heat and bring to a boil. Scoop off the orange froth that appears at the top of the pot and discard it, then turn the heat down so that the contents simmer gently. Stir the curry from time to time as it cooks, pushing the vegetables down under the liquid and keeping an eye on the softer vegetables. You want them to be tender, but not broken up. Season with salt. It is at this point you can stop the cooking and chill the curry overnight. You will find it will deepen and mellow in flavor if you do.

To serve the curry, drain the chickpeas and stir them into the curry with the quartered mushrooms. Let the curry warm over a low to moderate heat, stirring from time to time. Stir in the yogurt, making sure that the mixture does not boil (it will turn grainy if it does). Stir in the cilantro at the last minute.
Enough for 6 with rice

Orange jelly mold with lemon and cardamom

I get a childish kick out of serving jelly to adults. They always enjoy it, especially after a spicy meal. Use as little plain gelatine as you can get away with, so the jelly shimmers, barely set, on the spoon. I use seven sheets of plain gelatine to 4 cups of liquid, which means the finished dessert is too fragile to turn out so I usually serve it in wine glasses. I add the extra one (leaf gelatine comes in packets of eight) when I am offering it to people who prefer their jelly to have a wobble. The addition of cardamom is a subtle one and, I suppose, gives it a faintly Moorish tone.

large, juicy oranges – 12 (to give just under 5 cups of juice)
an unwaxed pink grapefruit
an unwaxed lemon
green cardamom pods – 6
sheets of plain gelatine – 7–8

Squeeze the oranges. You need about 5 cups of juice, so stop when you have enough, or do a couple more if you stop very short of 5 cups. Much will depend on the size, type and age of your fruit.

Squeeze the grapefruit and the lemon, keeping the juice separate from the orange, then remove three or four strips of zest from each with a short, sharp knife. Pour these juices into a small stainless steel or enameled saucepan with an equal quantity of water and drop in the pared zest. Split open the cardamom pods by pressing gently on them with the flat of a large knife, then add the seeds to the juice and bring it almost to the boil. As soon as the juice is about to start bubbling, cover with a lid and turn off the heat. Leave the juice to cool a little; about fifteen minutes should be long enough.

Now slide the sheets of gelatine – one or two at a time rather than in a big lump – into a bowl of cold water and let them soften for five minutes. Remove the lid from the pan, stopping for a second or two to breathe in the wonderful smell of citrus and cardamom, then pour the juice through a sieve into a large, scrupulously clean bowl. Reserve the cardamom seeds. Lift the softened gelatine sheets from the water – they will be just short of dissolving – and stir them into the warm grapefruit and lemon juice. They will dissolve in seconds.

Pour the orange juice into the grapefruit and lemon juice and stir thoroughly, making certain that every bit of gelatine has melted. Add the reserved cardamom seeds to the juice. They will float around, apparently pointlessly, but will in fact discreetly give some of their flavor to the jelly as it sets. Refrigerate for a good four or five hours.
Enough for 6–8

March 31

I have been doing far too much 'serious' cooking lately and this evening I can't be bothered to do anything more strenuous than chuck something in a wok. It is just as well I seem to be going through one of my wok phases right now. The thin pan, with its stout wooden handle, blackened by constant use, must be a full ten years old. There is a widespread rule that it is wrong to wash a wok. Certainly a new one will rust. An old one, heavy with burnt cooking oil and the legend of meals past, can be washed and quickly dried without danger of rust or of losing its non-stick patina.

This is only my second wok in thirty years of cooking. They are one of those rare things where the cheapest is usually the best. By which I mean the one that becomes a treasured part of your kitchen.

Chicken with mushrooms and lemongrass
Hot, fast and refreshing, this is one of those knee-jerk bowls of food that I make when I have a bit of Thai stuff (lemongrass, limes, ginger and chili peppers) around. As instant suppers go, this is as good as it gets.

garlic – 3 medium-sized cloves
ginger – 4 slices
scallions – 3
lemongrass – 2 stalks
peanut oil
hot red chili peppers – 3
diced chicken – ¾lb
field mushrooms – 3 medium-sized
lime juice – 2 generous tablespoons
nam pla (Thai fish sauce) – 2 generous tablespoons
light brown or palm sugar – a teaspoon
a few leaves of Thai basil or mint

Peel and chop the garlic, shred the ginger, finely chop the scallions and very finely shred the tender inner leaves of the lemongrass.

Heat a couple of glugs of oil in a frying pan or wok. Add the garlic, ginger, scallions and lemongrass and let them sizzle over a moderately high heat till the garlic is golden. Halve the peppers, scrape out the seeds and discard them. Finely chop the flesh and add to the pan. Cook briefly, then tip the whole lot out into a bowl.

Get the pan really hot, pour in a little more oil and then add the chicken. Leave it to color, then stir and fry till the meat is golden brown and sticky on all sides. Cut the mushrooms into small segments and add them to the pan. When they are tender, return the aromatics to the pan. Mix the lime juice, fish sauce and sugar in a cup, then pour this mixture into the hot pan. It will crackle and spit. Toss in the herb leaves and eat immediately.
Enough for 2. Picture on previous page

april

Chicken with mustard seed
and coconut milk

Thai fish cakes

Green curry of shrimp
and Thai eggplant

Mackerel with cumin
and lemon

Thyme and feta lamb

Baked red mullet with
saffron and mint

Bramley apple shortcake

Pork and lemon polpettine

Mustard chops

Orange and lemon cheesecake

A curry of eggplant, tomatoes
and lemongrass

A stunning orange sorbet

Toasted chocolate brioche

Spaghetti with new
season's garlic

Roast chicken wings with
lemon and cracked pepper

Lemon trifle

Chicken with vermouth,
tarragon and cream

Lemon-frosted pistachio cake
and an impromptu sorbet

**April 1
A fragrant
chicken
supper**

A sky as clear and bright as iced water; plum and pear blossom breaking out in the garden; the hot scent of grated ginger coming from the kitchen. If only all days could prick the senses like this one. I fancy a curry, one to stimulate rather than numb our palates, whose point is to be fresh, uplifting and fragrant rather than dark and mysterious.

The basics, coriander seeds and cumin, mustard seeds and turmeric, are there in the cupboard in their black-topped Bakelite jars, a squirrel store of heady scents and warm colors. The little jars have been inspiration for many a meal: for a quick fried rice supper, a slow-cooked curry of lamb or pork, a quick Indian-style sauce for chicken, its edges softened with cream. That is the easy bit. I wish I could say the same for curry leaves, whose addition brings a mild, aromatic warmth. They are certainly the most difficult herb leaves to find in the shops, unless you happen to live near an Asian market. I bought a large bunch of them for the chickpea curry last week from an Indian grocer's shop and now cannot get enough of them. Maybe I'll dry those that I fail to use. (I bet I don't.)

Chicken with mustard seed and coconut milk

If you don't have the curry leaves, this is still a good recipe. They are a sound addition but far from essential.

peanut oil – 3 generous tablespoons
a chicken, cut into 6 pieces
cumin seeds – 1¼ teaspoons
coriander seeds – 2½ teaspoons
black mustard seeds – 2½ teaspoons
small hot red chili peppers – 3
ginger – a walnut-sized knob
onions – 3
garlic – 2 cloves
ground turmeric – 1¼ teaspoons
tomatoes – 1lb, chopped
curry leaves – a handful
coconut milk – 14-oz can
steamed rice, to serve

Warm the oil in a shallow casserole and lightly brown the chicken in it on all sides. Lift it out of the pan on to a plate. Lightly grind the cumin, coriander and mustard seeds, not to a powder, but simply to break open the seeds and release some of their warmth. There is nothing like a mortar and pestle for this, but I have improvised before now with a bowl and the end of a rolling pin. Heat the pan in which you browned the chicken over a low heat, then add the ground spices. Seed and chop the chilis and add them to the pan. Peel the ginger and cut it

into shreds (you can use a coarse grater), then peel the onions and chop them roughly. Stir them into the spices. You can turn the heat up a little, but keep stirring from time to time so that nothing burns.

Peel and chop the garlic and add it to the pan with the ground turmeric, chopped tomatoes, curry leaves and a little salt. Leave to simmer for five minutes. Stir in the coconut milk, lower the chicken back into the pan, then cover partially with a lid and simmer until the chicken is done – a matter of twenty to thirty minutes.
Enough for 3

April 2

There is a little of the curry sauce left from last night's chicken and only myself to feed. To be honest, it is even better after a night in the fridge. I warm it up slowly in a small pan on the burner, then dip pieces of soft flatbread from the Indian shop into it as I watch a DVD.

April 3
A heady
pasta supper

Am I the only person making fewer pasta suppers these days? What was a twice-a-week habit is now more of an occasional treat. Perhaps you can have too much pasta with pesto. What appeal more than ever are those pasta recipes that have a freshness to them, a lightness on the stomach, a spring in their step. The greengrocer has great basil today, fresh-cut leaves whose spicy notes you can detect from a foot away. As basil goes, the large, heavily veined leaves have a more pronounced flavor, one that carries a certain heat with it. The tender leaves of the supermarket packet are fair enough but lack any punch, and make a frail, timid pesto. The leaves I have now, each the size of a bay leaf, if not bigger, bring with them the deeper scents of clove and pepper, and stay green even when they meet a little warmth – basil to be reckoned with.

I boil a pot of linguine, drain it and toss the long, thin strands of pasta with olive oil, grated pecorino, grated lemon zest and masses of basil leaves torn into wide shreds.

April 5

Last weekend the farmers' market had bags of small, tightly budded purple sprouting broccoli. It is still in a fine state of health in the fridge. We eat it for supper, plunged briefly into boiling salted water till its colors sing, then piled on to rounds of hot, thick toast that we have rubbed with garlic and soaked with olive oil. I chop a few anchovy fillets over mine, but others think I am mad.

April 7

Rainbow chard arrives today, the best I have seen, its stems the intense shocking pink and orange of a favorite Howard Hodgkin painting. (*Learning about Russian Music,* 1999, if you are wondering). I plunge it into boiling water, then drain and toss it with green olives, lemon olive oil and roughly chopped flat-leaf parsley. The whole lot gets piled on to rounds of thick-cut sourdough toast. A supper that fills us with joy.

An hour later it is as if we haven't eaten, so I cook bowls of brown basmati rice and stir through them some Geeta's onion chutney I have in the fridge and a handful of chopped cilantro. Sounds weird, tastes great.

**April 9
Another
day, another
curry**

I have the curry bug. Once I make one, a second, third and sometimes a fourth follow within a week or two. Then I won't make another for months. I find cooking is often like that, especially with cakes, bread and, for some reason, risotto. Of the curries I have eaten in the last couple of weeks, one was sharp with yogurt, another rich with coconut and now I want something vibrant and Thai-inspired rather than Indian. The inclusion of lemongrass, which along with chili peppers and ginger is the backbone of such recipes, changes everything in a curry. What was darkly interesting suddenly takes on a vibrancy and energy and moves South-East in character. Perhaps the most exciting of these Asian curries is one I ate near the border of Laos and Cambodia, a curry whose flavor was clean and pronounced and, it must be said, bum-stingingly hot.

I buy lemongrass in a bundle from Chinatown. It lasts for a good couple of weeks in the fridge, losing almost none of its spritz. No matter how young the shoots are, I invariably remove the outer leaves to get at the more tender, pink-tinged growth within. Even then, it is essential not to chop, but to slice it very, very finely, so the slivers are barely thicker than a hair.

Today is my birthday, and it's dinner for four. A trip to the Thai supermarket in Ladbroke Grove for all the ingredients, though I could probably have got pretty much everything in the nearest major supermarket, except that is the last place I want to be on my birthday. What are we eating? Thai fish cakes, a vegetable curry, rambutans and tiny mangoes.

Thai fish cakes

A hot and sticky dip is traditional and essential here. Of course, you can dip anything you like into a chili dipping sauce but to my mind little fish cakes, the sort flavored with lime leaves or lemongrass, are just about perfect. The hot, jammy sauce flatters the cakes' citrus and fish flavors like nothing else. I use chopsticks for this, even though the Thais wouldn't. It just feels right. I don't make the cakes too big here; they seem to work best when about the size of a gingersnap.

small red chili peppers – 4
scallions – 6
garlic – 4 cloves
lime leaves – 12 medium-sized
cilantro – 2 large handfuls
nam pla (Thai fish sauce) – 2 generous tablespoons
white fish (haddock, hake, cod, whatever) – 2lbs, skinned
a little flour
oil for frying

Discard the stems and seeds from the chili peppers and roughly chop the scallions. Drop them into a food processor. Peel the garlic and drop it into the processor along with the lime leaves, cilantro and fish sauce. Process to a smooth paste, then tip into a stainless steel or glass bowl. Cut the fish into chunks and pulse in the food processor to a rough paste.

Mix the fish and the spice paste together. Add a little salt and black pepper, then set aside in the fridge for half an hour, covered with plastic wrap.

Flour your hands and shape the mixture into 12 small, flat patties. Leave them to settle for a while in the fridge – they will be quite fragile. Then fry them in shallow oil till golden on both sides. Drain on paper towels and serve with the dipping sauce below.
Enough for 4

A deep, sweet dipping sauce

large hot red chili peppers – 2
nam pla (Thai fish sauce) – 3 generous tablespoons
water – 7 generous tablespoons
rice vinegar – 3 generous tablespoons
superfine sugar – 7 generous tablespoons
a thumb-sized knob of ginger
the juice of 2 limes
light soy sauce – 1¼ teaspoons

Remove the stems from the chilis, halve the flesh and chop it finely. Don't discard the seeds; you need their heat for this. Put the fish sauce, water, rice vinegar and sugar in a small saucepan and bring to a boil. Peel the ginger and chop it finely with a heavy knife, then crush it to a pulp with the flat of the knife blade. Add the ginger to the pan and let the mixture boil till it has started to thicken slightly.

Let the sauce cool, then add the lime juice, chopped chilis and soy sauce.

Green curry of shrimp and Thai eggplant

shallots – 2 (about 5oz)
peanut oil – 3 generous tablespoons
small purple Thai eggplant – 5 (about 5oz)
Thai green pea eggplant – 20 (available from Chinese and Thai grocers)
fresh green peppercorns – 2 generous tablespoons
cherry tomatoes – 12
coconut milk – 1 cup
nam pla (Thai fish sauce) – a generous tablespoon
large cooked shrimp – ⅔lb

For the green spice paste:
green bird's eye chilis – 4
lemongrass, chopped – 2 heaped tablespoons (2 large stalks)
lime leaves – 6
the roots of 4 cilantro sprigs
garlic – 3 large cloves
ginger – a 2oz lump
cilantro – 7 heaped tablespoons

To finish:
fresh mint leaves and Thai basil – ¼ cup in total
cilantro – a handful
large lime leaves – 2
steamed white rice, to serve

Make the spice paste: discard the stems from the chilis, then chop the flesh and tip it into either a blender or a food processor. Add the chopped lemongrass. Roll the lime leaves tightly and slice them into fine shreds. Chop the cilantro roots, peel and chop the garlic, then peel the ginger and cut it into shreds. Tip everything into the blender. Add the cilantro and pulse to a paste with enough water to make the mixture go round – two or three tablespoons. Continue to mix until you have a coarse paste.

Peel and finely slice the shallots. Warm two tablespoons of the oil in a shallow pan, then add the shallots and cook them over a moderate to high heat until they are golden and soft. Once they have softened, slice the Thai eggplant into quarters lengthways and add them to the shallots with the pea eggplant and green peppercorns, letting them soften and color. Expect them to take about five to seven minutes. Scoop the shallots and eggplant out into a dish, then add the remaining tablespoon of oil to the pan.

When the oil is warm, add the green spice paste. Let it fry briefly – the water will evaporate – and then halve the cherry tomatoes and add them to the pan. Continue cooking for a few minutes, then return the shallots and eggplant to the pan and pour in the coconut milk. Season with the *nam pla*, adding more if you wish. Slip the shrimp into the sauce and leave to cook for a minute or two – no longer.

Roughly chop the mint, basil and cilantro. Roll and finely shred the lime leaves, then spoon the curry on to the rice on serving plates and divide the herbs amongst them.

Enough for 4. Picture on previous page

Pools of water have collected on the sagging seats of the garden chairs. At seven in the morning they have turned to ice thick enough to crack with a hammer. By lunchtime, it is warm and sunny enough to eat outdoors. (Pity the garden seats are wet.) We lay out a picnic on the table and pick at it standing up – toasted sourdough bread; hummus spiked with lemon juice, hidden under a pool of vivid green olive oil; baba gannouj with its smoky eggplant flavors; a bunch of scrubbed radishes and a bowl of mint leaves and tight lettuce leaves.

The tomato plants arrive this morning, each no bigger than a little finger. I plant them out into deep rooting pots and label them meticulously: Marmande, Costoluto Fiorentino, Gardener's Delight and a new variety that guarantee flesh the hue of a ripe apricot. They promise much, but if there is one thing I can grow it is this fruit. They survive black fly and scorching sun, my forgetfulness and occasional absence. In my house they grow all the better for their cocktail of rough treatment and neglect.

The downside of my inability to eat eggs is that it rules out a hundred quick suppers. My loss. However, I can manage a frittata or a Spanish omelette. My version is lighter and crisper than the traditional one that uses thick slices of potato. I coarsely grate my potatoes instead, using about 2lbs of them to three large beaten eggs and just a single tablespoon of flour. I season the mixture with six chopped scallions and a handful of mixed parsley, mint and tarragon leaves. I push the mixture down into an oiled 10-in non-stick frying pan and let it cook for fifteen minutes or so before coloring the top under a hot broiler and cutting it into wedges.

April 11
A new way
with eggs

Cold roast chicken, sautéed potatoes, spinach. Pretty much perfect.

April 12

A great day at the garden center in Petersham that I have been trying to visit for ages, where they prepare lunches with vegetables and fruit grown on the premises. The nursery is quite the most romantic I have seen around London but stupidly I fail to check that their restaurant is open today. Not only is it closed, but they are grinding and roasting spices in the kitchen and leave the menu lying about just to tease me. I'm intrigued all the more now and can't wait to go back. I go home

April 13
A way to
perk up a
cheap fish

with big pots of thyme and new garden seats, then finish the day with a grilled mackerel made interesting by rubbing it with spices and following it with ripe Indian mangoes.

Mackerel with cumin and lemon

mackerel – 2, glistening with freshness
ground cumin – 2½ teaspoons
olive oil – 3 generous tablespoons
lemon juice – 2 generous tablespoons
garlic – 2 cloves, crushed to a paste
cayenne pepper – ¾ teaspoon

Lay the fish on a broiler pan and make half a dozen slashes across each one. Mix the cumin with a little black pepper and some salt. Spread it over the fish, smoothing it down into the slashes. Set the fish under a moderately hot broiler, not too close to the heat, so that it cooks right through to the bone. Mix the remaining ingredients together and baste the fish with them every few minutes, turning once. Watch carefully that it does not burn. Cook until the fish are an appetizing gold and black – about six to seven minutes on each side. Serve with the juices that have collected in the pan and plenty of crusty bread to mop them up.

April 16
Real fast
food

Busy day in town and I have barely ten minutes to shop before they close. I dash into a vast Middle Eastern store in the Edgware Road and join the queue at the long counter. There are lamb's testicles, sweetbreads and paper-thin escalopes of veal; there are sweet pink kidneys and thirty or forty quail all cozied up to one another in a box. There are hot chickens and a turning spit of seasoned lamb, which they slice to order and tuck into warm, honey-colored dough before your eyes. There is no time to cook tonight, to watch something simmer and putter its way to tenderness, just time for a quick 'flash in a pan' before I have to go out again.

I spot a vast pyramid of tiny lamb cutlets, each no bigger than a baby's hand, a good hundred cutlets placed in row after soldierly row on white waxed paper. I grab twelve for the three of us, then a tub of brilliant white tsatziki with shreds of cucumber and a whiff of garlic and mint. Once the lamb is grilled, the fat gilt and black, I scatter feta cheese, mint and thyme leaves over it and we eat the stingingly hot chops with the cold cucumber dip at their side. For dessert, three syrup-soaked pastries, stickily seductive squares of filo and chopped pistachios, brought home in a white paper box.

Thyme and feta lamb

small lamb loin chops – 12
lemon juice – 2 generous tablespoons
olive oil – 2 generous tablespoons
garlic – 2 cloves, crushed
fresh young thyme leaves – 2 generous tablespoons
feta cheese – ¼lb
mint leaves, chopped – a small handful
extra virgin olive oil, to finish

Put the lamb chops in a small dish. Squeeze the lemon juice into a small bowl, add the olive oil, some salt and coarsely ground black pepper and the garlic. Chop the thyme leaves and stir half of them into the oil and lemon. Pour this marinade over the lamb and set aside for a good hour.

Crumble the feta cheese into a small bowl and add the mint and the remaining thyme leaves.

Grill the lamb, either on a charcoal grill or in a ridged cast-iron griddle pan. When the outside of the lamb is golden, its fat toasted to an appetizing amber, transfer to warm plates. Sprinkle the feta cheese and herbs over the lamb, then add a single glug of olive oil to each plate. Eat immediately, whilst all is hot, herbal and piquant.
Enough for 3–4. Picture on previous page

April 17
Sorrel and a plump spring pigeon

Could there ever be the perfect day? Maybe not, but today is as close as it gets. Bright sunshine and cool breeze, the scent of wallflowers and narcissus on the air; a farmers' market with sorrel, young pigeons and good rhubarb, and an afternoon so hot and sunny you could fry eggs on the pavement. I gave in and bought my first tomatoes too, a vine or two of the early Campari. Small, round and bright as a button, they smelled and tasted as they should, a treat. A larger fruit called Tiger Soul disappointed in the way that only flabby and flat tomatoes can.

I roasted the pigeons, four of them, plump and young, for lunch and served them with a purée of the sorrel. Over a pound of soft green leaves and yet they made only a spoonful of sauce per person. Even tossed gently in hot butter, they still dissolve to nothing. Heaven knows what would happen if the leaves met boiling water.

April 19
Pink fish and a deep apple pie

Like salmon, red mullet catches your eye on the fish market slab. Unlike salmon, these rose-pink and silver fish are interesting to eat, carrying an earthy flavor that sings out for the robust seasonings of the Med: thyme, olives, lemon and garlic. I would go so far as to say that their juicy flesh also benefits from the inclusion of the earthy notes of saffron and the freshness of mint.

Baked red mullet with saffron and mint

Beautiful colors here, with the pink fish and green-speckled cooking juices. Part of the pleasure is squishing the new potatoes into the minty, saffron-freckled juice as you eat. A good, light dish for a spring day.

red mullet – 4 medium-sized
olive oil – 5 tablespoons
white wine or white vermouth – 3 generous tablespoons
mint leaves – a handful
a good pinch of saffron stamens
small waxy potatoes such as La Ratte, to serve

Put a pan of water on to boil. Set the oven to 425°F.

Rinse the fish and pat them dry, then lay them snugly in an oven-proof dish. Pour the olive oil into a small bowl, add the white wine and a little salt and ground black pepper. Roughly shred the mint leaves and stir them into the wine and oil with the saffron stamens. Pour the marinade over the fish and leave it for anything up to an hour (though you don't have to leave it at all if time isn't on your side).

Salt the water, and put the potatoes on to boil. Put the fish in the oven to bake, basting it once during cooking with the juices that surround it. It will take about twelve to fourteen minutes, but check it after ten. The exact timing will depend on the size of your fish.

Serve the fish out on to warm plates or shallow bowls, spooning over the mint and saffron juices as you go.
Enough for 2

After a light main course, a dessert of substance. The local apples for sale in the market are still crisp and sweet, despite having been picked months ago. The Cox's make an interesting bowl of stewed apple for breakfast but I prefer a big, tart apple in a pie, such as a fluffy, fat Bramley. They weigh a ton, so I buy them as near to home as possible, then cover them not with pie crust but something altogether more tender – a butter-rich shortcake crust. It needs a careful hand to transfer the pastry from work surface to pie dish but the result is an exceptionally crumbly crust, a perfect match for the soft, juicy apples.

Bramley apple shortcake

butter – 1¼ cups
turbinado sugar – ¾ cup
large egg – 1
all-purpose flour – 2½ cups
baking powder – 1¼ teaspoons
a little milk and superfine sugar to finish

For the filling:
Bramley apples* – 2½lbs
lemon juice
butter – 4 tablespoons
superfine sugar – a heaped tablespoon

Lightly butter a 10-in (7-in across the base) shallow metal pie plate. Cream the butter and sugar in a food mixer till light and fluffy. Mix in the egg, then gently add the flour and baking powder. Remove and roll into a ball on a heavily floured work surface. Knead the dough for a minute or two, until it is smooth and soft.

Cut the pastry in half, roll out one half and use it to line the pie tin. Wrap the remaining pastry in wax paper and refrigerate it with the lined pie plate for twenty minutes.

Set the oven to 350°F. Peel the apples, remove their cores and slice them thickly, as you would for apple pie. Drop them in cold water to which you have added a squeeze of lemon juice to stop them discoloring.

Melt the butter in a non-stick frying pan and, when it sizzles, add the apples. You want them to color here and there and soften somewhat, but without breaking up. Scatter the sugar over them and continue cooking until they are very lightly caramelized. As soon as they show signs of frothing, turn off the heat.

Place a baking sheet in the oven to heat up. Brush the edge of the lined pastry shell with juice from the apples. Fill the plate with the cooked apples, then roll out the second half of the pastry and carefully lay it over the fruit. Press the pastry edges together and patch where necessary. Brush the pastry crust tenderly with milk and sprinkle with sugar. Bake for forty minutes or until the pastry is golden and crumbly. Leave to cool briefly, then sugar again before cutting.
Enough for 8

April 20
A meatball
to beat
them all

I never make my own chopped meat. Maybe it is because I trust my butcher. Who has room for a mincer attachment in their kitchen anyway? I like the look of pale, naked ground pork with its little flecks of white fat that will enrich the meat as it cooks, knowing that by stirring in a couple of cupboard staples I have mouth-popping little meatballs to tuck into.

Today I want something Italian, a supper with notes of thyme, lemon and Parmesan. There is also some bread to use up. It is not until you start mashing together the ingredients that you remember just how quick and effortless this sort of cooking is. Chop, roll, fry, eat. I love it.

Pork and lemon polpettine
Delectably moreish little balls, these. You probably wouldn't mind a

---

Granny Smiths could be substituted.

few wide and slithery Italian noodles on the side, or perhaps some rice. Or maybe just a plate of greens such as sprout tops or purple sprouting broccoli.

fresh white breadcrumbs – 1¼ cups
ground pork – 1lb
a lemon
parsley leaves – a large handful
thyme – about 6 bushy sprigs
grated Parmesan – 2 heaped tablespoons
anchovy fillets – 10, chopped
a little flour

To cook:
olive oil – 2 heaped tablespoons
butter – 3 tablespoons
chicken stock – ¾ cup

Put the breadcrumbs and pork into a mixing bowl. Grate the lemon zest in with the pork, then halve and squeeze the lemon. Add the lemon juice to the pork with the roughly chopped parsley leaves and the thyme leaves stripped from their stems. Tip in the grated Parmesan, then the chopped anchovy fillets. Season the mixture with a little salt, then more generously with black pepper. Mix thoroughly.

Make about eighteen small balls of the mixture, using a heaped tablespoon of pork for each one. I find it easiest to shape them into a rough ball, then flatten them slightly. Put each one on to a floured baking sheet.

Warm the olive oil and butter in a heavy-based pan that doesn't stick. Roll the patties lightly in the flour on the baking sheet, then fry them in the oil, about eight at a time, for four or five minutes, until they are crisply golden on each side. Lower the heat and leave to cook through to the middle – a matter of six to eight minutes more. I tend to turn them no more than once or twice during cooking, so they develop a crisp, slightly sticky exterior.

Tip the fat, or at least most of it, from the pan, then pour in the chicken stock. Leave to bubble for a good two or three minutes, scraping up and stirring in any pan stickings. Let the stock bubble down a bit, then divide the patties between four plates and spoon over the juices from the pan.
Enough for 4

I make no secret of the fact that Nigella Lawson's *How to Eat* (Wiley) is **April 21** my favorite cookbook. She has a recipe in there for a miso dressing that I use all the time. Tonight I make it as usual, beating a couple of tablespoons of hot water and a teaspoon of rice vinegar into a table-spoon of thick yellow miso paste. As she suggests, I stir in just the merest drop of sesame oil too. Nigella uses this dressing with beans, and it is good that way, but tonight I use it to dress cold soba noodles, which I scatter with sesame seeds and handfuls of cilantro, then eat with chopsticks in front of 'the box'.

April 22
A spicy
chop and
a citrus
cheesecake

Today as so often, I stand at the butcher's counter and hear the weary sigh, 'Oh, I'll just have a couple of chops.' This time it is me who is saying it. The chop is the knee-jerk supper for when you haven't got the imagination or energy to come up with anything more exciting. A bit of a no-brainer really, but a delicious one nevertheless.

I love a lamb chop, seared over a hot grill, with its rose-pink meat and its frame of crisp fat. I love to pick up the bone and tug at the last tiny fibers of juicy flesh. A lamb chump chop, and especially a demure little cutlet, needs a generous hand with the seasoning if it is to be of any interest. It is simplicity itself to unwrap your meat when you get it home, put it on a plate and rub fat and flesh with olive oil, black pepper and chopped thyme leaves. I use oregano too, or sometimes rosemary, with its warm hints of the Mediterranean.

As a rule I go for the darker meat, with its promise of an older animal and therefore more flavor. Pale pink spring lamb is not something I can get excited about. I said in *Appetite* that this meat responds to robust seasoning and I stand by that. This is why it is especially suited to being cooked over a grill, where the fierce cooking and sharp seasoning add the notes of charcoal, robust herbs and lemon.

As lamb ages, its color darkens, bringing with it promises of deeper flavor but perhaps slightly firmer flesh. I hold flavor in higher esteem than I do tenderness, so in my kitchen lamb is more a meat for summer and autumn than for the spring.

The bone is a toothsome bonus (though lamb steaks grill well enough), whether it is the round bone that lies in the middle of a leg chop or the neat little 'handle' on a chop cut from the loin. The thickness of the cut will depend on what treatment I am going to give them. A thin loin chop is delightful when dipped in flour, beaten egg and grated Parmesan, then fried in butter till crisp as a twig. Thicker chops are more suitable for grilling, where there is room for the inside to stay a deep rose pink whilst a suitably tantalizing crust forms outside it.

Mustard with lamb. Some people find it controversial. I insist the flavor works superbly with properly hung meat of almost any sort. There's a bunch of decent spinach in today's organic bag, not too many holes, and clean as a whistle. It will work well with both the chops and the mustard.

Mustard chops

garlic – 2 plump cloves
grain mustard – a generous tablespoon
lemons – 2
olive oil – 2 generous tablespoons
lamb chops – 4, about 5oz each

Peel the garlic and mash it to a pulp with a couple of good pinches of sea salt with a mortar and pestle. Stir in the mustard, the juice of one of the lemons, then the olive oil. Mix to a slush, grinding in some black pepper as you go, then scrape it into a dish. Roll the chops in the marinade and set aside for as long as you have. Ideally an hour or so.

Cook the chops under a broiler, spooning over any remaining marinade as you turn them. They will probably need three to four minutes on each side, depending on the heat of your grill. They are especially good if the fat has singed a little. You'll need the other lemon, a half on each plate.
Enough for 2 with spinach

Orange and lemon cheesecake
And today I made a cheesecake that turned out to be one of those perfect recipes that you have been after all your life, a really fudgy, creamy filling and crisp base.

butter – 7 tablespoons
graham crackers – 9oz
mascarpone cheese – 1¾ cups
cream cheese – 1 cup
superfine sugar – ½ cup plus 2 tablespoons
large eggs – 3
an egg yolk
an orange
a lemon
heavy cream – 1 cup
vanilla extract – ¾ teaspoon

Melt the butter in a saucepan. Crush the graham crackers to a fine powder. You can do it the traditional way with a plastic bag and rolling pin or, as I do it, in a food processor. Tip the crackers into the butter and stir to mix. Set the oven at 275°F.

Press two-thirds of the buttered crumbs into the base of a deep 9-in loose-bottomed cake pan. The sort you might make a fruit cake in. Set aside in a cold place to harden. The freezer is ideal.

Put the kettle on to boil. Put the mascarpone, cream cheese, sugar,

eggs and the extra yolk in the bowl of a food mixer (you will need the beater attachment). Finely grate the orange and lemon zest into the cheese and sugar, then beat until thoroughly mixed. Fold the cream, juice of the lemon (not the orange) and vanilla extract into the cheesecake mix.

Wrap the tin in aluminum foil, covering the bottom and sides with a single piece. I do this twice to ensure the water doesn't seep in. Pour the cheesecake mixture on top of the hardened crumbs. Pour the water from the kettle into a roasting pan. It needs to be enough to come halfway up the cake pan. Lower the cake pan into the roasting pan and carefully, very carefully, slide them into the oven. Bake for fifty minutes, then switch off the oven and leave the cake to cool in it.

When the cake is cold, remove it from the pan and press the reserved crumbs around the edge.

April 23
A meal in
perfect
harmony

There is something perfect and harmonious about a meal that has a stinging-hot principal dish followed by a sharp citrus dessert. A meal that works on all levels, exciting and soothing the palate. Tonight's vegetable curry is followed by a startling orange sorbet, made with Italian fruit of a deep orange flecked with scarlet.

A curry of eggplant, tomatoes and lemongrass
As always with curries, lots of ingredients but very little hands-on cooking time. For which I say, thank God.

peanut oil – 3 generous tablespoons
mushrooms – 14oz
vegetable stock – 1⅓ cups
baby (egg) eggplant – 8
large tomatoes (not beefsteak) – 6
coconut milk – ¾ cup
cilantro – a small handful
steamed basmati rice, to serve

For the spice paste:
small hot red chili peppers – 4
lemongrass – 2 plump stalks (or 3 smaller ones)
ginger – a walnut-sized lump
small red shallots – 2
garlic – 4 cloves
shrimp paste – ¾ teaspoon

Make the spice paste: halve the red chilis, scrape out the seeds with the point of a knife, then chop the flesh finely. Remove and discard the tough outer leaves from the lemongrass and roughly chop the tender

inner ones. Peel and shred the ginger, peel and roughly chop the shallots and garlic, then put them, together with the chilis and lemongrass, into a food processor. Add the shrimp paste and a tablespoon of water, then process to a rough paste.

Warm the peanut oil in a shallow pan. Fry the spice paste in the oil, moving it round the pan so it does not burn. Slice the mushrooms in half and add them to the pan, letting them cook, with a little more oil if things are looking dry, till soft and sweet. Pour the stock into the pan (you can use water in a pinch) and bring to a boil. Slice the eggplant into quarters, roughly chop the tomatoes and add them to the pan. Leave to simmer, partially covered with a lid for ten to fifteen minutes, then pour in the coconut milk and simmer for a further five to ten minutes. Scatter over the cilantro so that their fragrance rises with the warmth of the warm milk. Serve with basmati rice.
Enough for 2–3

A stunning orange sorbet

superfine sugar – 1 cup
mineral water – 1 cup
the grated zest of 2 oranges
orange juice – 3 cups (about 6–8 oranges)
the juice of a lemon

Put the sugar and water in a pan over a moderate heat until the sugar has melted. Tip in the grated orange zest, then leave to cool (I invariably cannot wait, so I pour the syrup into a heatproof bowl and put it in a sink of cold water to cool it quickly).

Once the syrup is cool, strain it to remove the orange zest. Pour the orange juice into the syrup and stir in the lemon juice. Pour the mixture into an ice-cream machine and churn till almost frozen. Remove from the bowl and freeze for twenty minutes or so before serving.
To serve 6

April 24
A rummage
through the
fridge

I snack. Dried figs, apricots, pistachio nuts, cashews, brazils, and in summer fresh cherries, the odd cookie and occasionally, in desperation, those polystyrene ceiling tiles known as rice cakes. Such nibbles, they are really no more than that, are not always enough, so I can often be found rummaging through the fridge to fill the endless gap between lunch and supper. A bowl of yesterday's trifle, a cold sausage, an unwanted roast potato have all found a welcome home with me. (A word of advice to those who find themselves in similar straits – almost anything is edible with a dab of French mustard on it.) But sometimes the cupboard is well and truly bare, and I have to put something together quickly.

The usual route to instant pleasure involves a piece of toast spread with mustard, then topped with slices of old cheese (even grated Parmesan works) that will toast nicely under the broiler. Failing that, I have been known to spread cream cheese on warm bagels, no matter how stale they are, reheat bits of pizza from last night's takeaway (though nowadays I draw the line at actually fishing the box out of the trash), and eat beans directly from the can without going to the bother of heating them up. Anything that can be toasted is. Rarely do I go as far as making a sandwich, which would seem too much like a proper meal, instead eating the ingredients that could have been a sandwich, the bread, a tomato, some scraps of cheese, as I come across them. It seems less like greed that way. Right now there is a brioche left from a notion I had of using it in a trifle (horrid, don't ever try it) and some cooking chocolate. Together they make the most sophisticated and indulgent of snacks, worth buying a loaf of brioche for.

Toasted chocolate brioche

Brioche is both rich and feather-light. Toasted, it is a tender mid-morning pick-me-up with a cappuccino, but it is wonderfully decadent when stuffed with shavings of chocolate and toasted till the filling melts. Brioche loaves are not as easy to track down here as they are in France but most major supermarkets have them.

Per sandwich:
brioche – 2 thin slices
dark, smooth chocolate – 2oz

Heat a ridged griddle pan (or a toasted sandwich-maker). Lay the brioche slices flat on a work surface. Grate or shave the chocolate so that the pieces are small and thin enough to melt quickly. Spread them over one slice of the bread, almost to the edge. Cover with the second slice.

Toast the brioche on the hot griddle till the underside is done, then carefully turn it so that the filling doesn't escape and toast the other side. It is ready when the chocolate has melted and is starting to ooze out.

Two cloves of the mild, new season's garlic seem hardly enough in **April 25** pasta for two, but you need it only as an underlying whiff behind the real star ingredient – the Parmesan. This recipe demands the freshest, green-tinged spring garlic, the sort that offers no more than a gentle, garlicky breeze.

spaghetti – ½lb
new season's garlic – 2 cloves
butter – 4 tablespoons
freshly grated Parmesan – ½ cup, plus extra to serve

Get a big pan of water on to boil. Salt it generously. Boil the spaghetti in it till it is tender but still has a bit of bite to it – about ten minutes. Peel and finely chop the garlic.

Drain the spaghetti, leaving a good couple of tablespoons of the cooking water behind. Put the pan back on the heat and add the butter, chopped garlic and grated cheese. Toss the pasta in the butter and cheese, grinding in plenty of black pepper as you go, and serve immediately with a bowl of extra cheese.
Enough for 2

April 26 The big-name potato-based snacks, especially the very highly flavored potato and corn chips designed for munching while you watch TV, all make me feel a bit queasy. I think it must be the oil they use in them. So when I am in a couch-potato mood I tend to make something cheap and fast but 'real'. Chicken wings are number-one couch fodder for me, chucked in the oven and left till deep gold and crisp. I can get through a good dozen of them if they aren't too big, absentmindedly gnawing at the bones whilst watching re-runs of *Sex and the City*.

Roast chicken wings with lemon and cracked pepper
This is finger food at its very best. So simple you could do them with a blindfold on, these roast chicken wings can easily be doubled up for larger numbers. The trick is to roast them till they are almost stuck to the roasting tin. Don't even think of using a knife and fork here.

chicken wings – 12 large (about 2lbs)
a large, juicy lemon
bay leaves – 5
black peppercorns – 1 heaped tablespoon
olive oil – 2 generous tablespoons
sea salt flakes – 2½ teaspoons

Set the oven to 400°F. Check the chicken wings for stray feathers – they seem to be more prevalent on the wings than on any other part of the bird. Put the wings into a roasting dish, halve the lemon and squeeze it over them, then cut up the lemon shells and tuck them, together with the bay leaves, between the chicken pieces.

Put the peppercorns in a mortar and bash them so they crack into small pieces. They should still be knobbly, like small pieces of grit, rather than finely ground.

Mix the peppercorns with the olive oil, then toss with the chicken and lemon. Scatter the salt flakes, without crushing them, over the chicken. Roast for forty to forty-five minutes, turning once. The chicken should be golden and sticky, the edges blackened here and there.

Enough for 2

April 27
A new trifle

I have a fancy for those custard-cup desserts that graced Edwardian dinner tables. This trifle – for want of a better name – in all its cream-laden and liqueur-sodden glory, is the nearest I have come to it. No fruit here, just deep, billowing layers of cream and ladyfingers and fine, artisan-made lemon or orange curd. I regard the sugary crunch of crystallized violets on top as essential. The trifle is all the better for a night in the fridge.

Lemon trifle

ladyfingers – 4oz
orange or lemon curd – $\frac{1}{3}$ cup
Limoncello liqueur – 3 generous tablespoons
heavy cream – 2 cups
superfine sugar – $\frac{1}{2}$ cup
lemon juice – $\frac{1}{3}$ cup

To finish:
heavy cream – 1 cup
a small orange
crystallized violets

Break the ladyfingers in half and spread them thickly with the orange or lemon curd. Put them in a glass or china dish and sprinkle the Limoncello liqueur over them.

Pour the 2 cups of cream into a saucepan and add the sugar. Bring to a boil over a moderate heat, then turn down the heat and leave to simmer for a good two or three minutes. Remove from the heat, stir in the lemon juice, then pour this mixture over the ladyfingers. They may bob about a bit in the lemon custard but just push them down and leave to cool. When the mixture has cooled, refrigerate for a couple of hours, or even overnight, until set.

To finish, whip the 1 cup of cream until thick, but stop before it will stand in peaks. It should still be able to slide slowly from a spoon. Smooth the cream loosely over the trifle, then finely grate the orange zest over the top and add a few crystallized violets. Return briefly to the fridge until needed.

Enough for 6

April 28   A still, quiet morning, as humid as a Turkish bath. I sit barefoot in the garden, sipping green tea and listening to the sound of church bells. The Mirabelle plum tree at the bottom is a mass of infant fruit the size of a peppercorn. Now in its fourth year, this will be the tree's first real crop. The damson, for so long a spindly and struggling bush, has got a spurt on this year, and is dotted with young fruit. I worry, though, that it will never produce enough for a pie or a pot of jam.

This is the time of year I want to sit in the garden and breathe. To drink in its luminous greens, to sit under its white blossom – hawthorn, pear, quince and plum – to watch the bees going from apple blossom to greengage, each petal washed with faint brushstrokes of marshmallow pink.

As the soil has warmed up over the last couple of weeks, so indeed have the markets. Today, a change of market: the first asparagus – short stems, tight points – in bundles for the early comer; tiny leaves of baby rainbow chard the color of a box of children's candies; pale, shallow-cupped field mushrooms; fat curls of local butter, pots of cream and the first true crisp-heart lettuce, whose stems snap like ice and exude their milky white and gently soporific sap. There are pots of tarragon and sweet cicely to flavor an omelette and crates of lemon-sharp sorrel and earthy parsley. No strawberries or gooseberries yet, but there are plants to take home for the garden and bunches of late hyacinths to sit on the kitchen table.

Away from the market, there are tiny Indian mangoes the size of hen's eggs, their flesh the deepest saffron; miniature lamb chops and bunches of fresh mint; young potatoes with soil sticking to their moist skin. You need no recipes with such inspiration in your hand. But there is a dilemma. The butcher by the farmers' market tells me about some baby monkfish he has seen at the fish shop. Curiosity gets the better of me. There on the ice is a shoal of young monkfish. Each pearl-white fish is plump, sparkling with freshness, and barely longer than a man's middle finger. Yet I cannot imagine there are many fish quite so environmentally unsound. They would be a joy on the grill, their flesh tinged with the scent of lemon, rosemary and charcoal. But they would have been even better in the sea, where each can grow and feed four apiece, or maybe left where they are so we can eat a species less threatened by over-fishing.

Did I buy them, dear reader? Yes, I did. Eight of them to feed four of us – grilled in the open air after an hour in a marinade of olive oil, chopped leaves of young green rosemary and the merest whiff of a garlic clove. When they were done, the outside a lattice of brilliant white and crusted black, we dressed them with lemon-scented olive oil and a dish of fava beans the size of a thumb nail, so young we didn't think to skin them. Once the plates were empty (we started with new asparagus), I brought out a simple salad of crisp lettuce with a timeless dressing of oil and vinegar, though thicker than is usual. We followed with rhubarb fool – deepest pink fruit from the garden stewed with sugar and a few sweet cicely seeds, then chilled and folded into cream whipped till it lay in soft, dreamy folds. Sometimes appetite gets the better of conscience.

Chicken with vermouth, tarragon and cream

Thumbing through my diary, I note how few creamy main courses I have eaten this year. Yet the cream available at the farmers' market is glorious – thick, yellow and sweet. It seems a crime not to use it in some way or another, and to my mind there are few better ways to use good-quality cream than with the aniseed notes of fresh tarragon. If I can steer myself away from the grill at this time of year, then it will be to make a simple chicken sauté such as this. The amount of tarragon you use is up to you, but you should start with a bunch of about ten sprigs, adding a few more near the end of cooking. Some green beans and some rice would be good here, too.

chicken pieces on the bone, preferably thighs – 8
butter – 6 tablespoons
a wine glass of dry vermouth
tarragon vinegar – 2 generous tablespoons
the leaves from a small bunch of tarragon
heavy cream – $1\frac{1}{4}$ cups
a squeeze of lemon juice

Season the chicken pieces with a little salt and some ground black pepper, then melt the butter in a large, shallow pan over a moderate heat. Lightly brown the chicken in the butter, taking care that the butter does not burn. If it does, you need to wipe out the pan and start again with some fresh butter. Remove the chicken, tip off and discard most of the butter and put the pan back on the heat. Pour the vermouth and vinegar into the pan and, as the steam rises, scrape away at the sticky deposits in the pan with a wooden spoon, letting them dissolve into the wine.

Once the vermouth has reduced for a minute or so, bubbling away by about a third, add the tarragon leaves and cream and stir them into the wine. Return the chicken and its escaped juices to the pan, partially cover with a lid and set the heat quite low, so that the sauce bubbles gently around the chicken. Let it simmer like this for fifteen to twenty minutes, stirring from time to time and checking that the cream does not thicken too much or stick to the bottom of the pan. If it looks in danger of becoming too thick – you want it to have the texture of a light cream sauce – then add a little more vermouth.

Check that the chicken is cooked: its juices should run clear, not

pink, when the flesh is pierced with a skewer at its deepest point. Season with salt, a little black pepper, a squeeze or two of lemon juice to sharpen and lift, or a dash more of tarragon vinegar.
Enough for 4

**April 30
Mint tea and
a pistachio
cake**

Friends for tea and it's the most magical of days, a cool summer afternoon in the garden, all full-blown roses and cucumber sandwiches. We drink mint tea by the potful. I have now finally accepted the fact that I can bake a pretty fine cake, be it a rich chocolate brownie or an old-fashioned plain sponge, and am happy to do so whenever the occasion calls for it. Today's cake is not a light-as-a-feather sponge but a moist affair, heavy with pistachios and ground almonds. I flavor it gently with rosewater but this is not essential. For once, I buy my pistachios ready shelled. To crack enough to give ⅔ cup would be more than most people's fingers could cope with.

Lemon-frosted pistachio cake

butter – ½lb plus 2 tablespoons
superfine sugar – 1 cup plus 2 tablespoons
large eggs – 3
shelled pistachio nuts – ⅔ cup
ground almonds – ⅔ cup
an orange
rosewater – 1¼ teaspoons
all-purpose flour – ½ cup plus 1 tablespoon
crystallized rose petals and shelled pistachio nuts, to decorate (optional)

For the icing:
confectioners' sugar – ¾ cup
lemon juice – 2 generous tablespoons

Preheat the oven to 325°F. Line the bottom of a non-stick 9-in cake pan with baking parchment.

Cream the butter and sugar in a food mixer until very light and fluffy. Add the eggs one at a time, beating between each addition. Process the pistachios to fine crumbs in a food processor, then add them, with the ground almonds, to the butter and sugar. Finely grate the zest and squeeze the orange, then stir it in with the rosewater. Lastly fold in the flour with a large metal spoon.

Scoop the mixture into the lined baking pan and bake for fifty minutes, covering the top lightly with foil for the last ten minutes. Check the cake by inserting a metal skewer into the center. It should come out fairly clean, without any wet mixture stuck to it. Leave to cool in the pan before running a knife around the edge and turning it out. Make the icing by mixing the sugar and lemon juice together till smooth, then pouring it over the cake. Decorate, if you wish, with crystallized rose petals and shelled pistachio nuts. Leave for half an hour for the icing to set.

Enough for 12. Picture on previous page

An impromptu sorbet

After everyone has gone, it crosses my mind that some thick yogurt would be good with the remaining slices of cake. Pistachio . . . rose-water . . . yogurt – it's a short jump. What starts out as a simple idea of yogurt on the side slowly becomes one for yogurt sorbet. It occurs to me that if I stir sugar directly into the yogurt it will save me making a sugar syrup. I pour a tub of yogurt (16oz) into a bowl, whisk in 5 tablespoons of confectioners' sugar and leave it to churn in the ice-cream machine. The result is one of the most startling sorbets I have ever made.

may

Lemon and basil linguine

Chickpeas with harissa,
basil and ham

Lamb chops with lemon and
mint and potatoes crushed into
the pan juices

Orange and ricotta pancakes

White bean and tarragon soup

Salmon and dill fish cakes

Lemon amaretti cream pots

A hot, sour bean sprout salad

A really fast cake with
blueberries and pears

Goat cheese puddings and a
salad of young lettuce hearts

A deli sandwich

Five-spice quail

Roast pork with lemon
and potatoes

Lemon ice cream

Asparagus and lemon risotto

May 1 **Roses, and an** **extraordinary** **salad**	The short-lived, single flowers of the *Rosa chinensis mutabilis* have opened. At first light they are pale amber flecked with crimson. By dusk they will lie flat over the bush like so many exhausted butterflies. In the larder is a jar of French rose petal jelly. On a clear, bright Saturday morning such as this, I should unscrew the cap and eat the quivering pink conserve with spoonfuls of thick sheep yogurt. It could be a magical moment. Instead I put one of the croissants I bought yesterday under the broiler, letting it blacken across the top, then eat it whilst thumbing through the papers with buttery fingers and drinking coffee.

Saturday mornings in summer are sacrosanct. Coffee, croissant, the papers, which are so much more readable than those in the week, then a trip to the shops for salad, fish, a cheese, slices of prosciutto, some fruit. Then I potter about in the garden. Lunch is early, a lazy kitchen picnic – a rambling meal of shop-bought stuff eaten straight from its wrapping. This is as much of a ritual as opening a bottle of champagne on a Friday evening, or making soup when I clean out the fridge. My Saturday mornings are one of the few predictable things about this kitchen and I love them for that.

I found pea shoots today. A white felt mat covered with soft green leaves and curling tendrils, from which the purchaser is allowed to cut off as much or as little as they want. Farm shops and farmers' markets are the usual hunting grounds for these short-season treats. I spot mine in the herb section of a smart food shop, nestling between the ubiquitous bags of arugula and sweet little trays of mustard and cress. I could fry them for a few seconds in hot oil and sprinkle them with flakes of sea salt. Instead I get the full hit of clean, pea-greenness by tossing the shoots in a salad with tiny spinach leaves and hot, skinny arugula. Eaten raw, they are the very essence of freshly podded peas and possess a mouthfeel quite unlike anything else. Dressed only with lemon juice and a very light and fruity olive oil, they make a late-spring salad with textures that amaze and delight.

I save some of the pea shoots to go with three vast slices of halibut I am cooking tonight, which will be respectfully seasoned with salt and oil, then grilled and served to friends with nothing more fancy than lemon halves and black pepper.

The shoots were supposed to surprise and amuse everyone. Truth told, no one even notices them.

May 2 **Lemon** **and basil** **linguine**	Few sights lift the spirits like a crate of lemons with their glossy leaves intact. They keep well, so I buy them by the dozen. I snap their stems and sniff the cut ends as I pile them into a bowl. They carry with them the faintest ghost of their white blossom. Lemons are as much a part of this kitchen as pepper and salt, but right now their spring-like freshness is more welcome than ever. Sometimes, I start my day with a slice or

two in a glass of hot water, actually a little Moroccan tumbler, its snowy etching and gold rim almost worn off with age.

In our house, a lemon will find itself accompanying a grilled pork chop or even a steak, or sometimes I'll toss one in with a roasting chicken or a pan of sliced potatoes as they crisp in the oven. Lemons are squeezed into a rasping green-oil mayonnaise, instantly lightening its color and flavor, and even find their way into the velvety gloop of a risotto. I have only recently started to use lemons with pasta (even though lime is a given with Asian noodles). Squeezed or grated into a cream sauce and matched to fat, peppery basil leaves, they introduce a vitality all too often missing in Italian pasta 'comfort' suppers.

Today I don't bother with the cream. This 'sauce' is all about the sharpness of the lemon tempered by the Parmesan, and the warmth of the pasta gently bringing out the fragrance of the basil. I'm not sure if it's about chemistry or art. All I know is that it is sumptuous and incredibly simple.

Grating ¾ cup of Parmesan takes longer than you might think, but no longer than it takes the pasta to cook. This turns out to be another ten-minute supper.

linguine – ½lb
the juice of a large lemon
olive oil – ⅓ cup
grated Parmesan – ¾ cup
basil leaves – a large handful

Put a huge pot of water on to boil. When it is bubbling furiously, salt it generously, then add the linguine. Let it cook at an excited boil for about eight minutes.

Put the lemon juice, olive oil and grated Parmesan in a warm bowl (warmed under a running tap, then dried) and beat briefly with a small whisk till thick and grainy. Tear up the basil and stir in with a grinding of black pepper.

Drain the pasta and quickly toss in the lemon and Parmesan 'sauce'.
Enough for 2

May 4
Chickpeas
with harissa,
basil and
ham

There is the constant patter of rain on the kitchen roof and the gentle rattle and putter of a pan of simmering chickpeas. I don't always cook these hazelnut-sized legumes from scratch, and often as not open a can instead. I guess I just wanted to smell them cooking today – a mealy, nutty smell that must have filled Middle Eastern kitchens since time immemorial. That said, they do survive the canning process more successfully than any other ingredient.

The chickpea thing has been set in motion by my finding a jar of organic harissa in the health food shop. I usually buy this brick-red spice paste in beautiful little cans with yellow and blue writing and scenes of Fez. I use a tablespoon or two to add depth to a stew or bite to a baked eggplant, then leave the opened can in the fridge. I find it a few weeks later when I am having a clear out, sporting a layer of blue fur. I must have thrown away scores of them over the years. Harissa in a screw-top jar could change my life.

There always seems to be an eggplant and a few tomatoes around. They come, with a slight monotony, in the weekly organic sack. If they are still there by Wednesday, I roast them with olive oil and maybe oregano, cumin or garlic, then eat them as a warm salad with sesame bread and fresh basil leaves. To add substance, I may stir in some cooked navy beans or chickpeas. If you do this whilst the beans are hot, they soak up all the sweetly tart juices from the roasted vegetables. A good supper, but I tend to use it just as much as a salad to sit on the table when we eat outdoors, a knubbly, luscious side dish to accompany grilled lamb.

tomatoes – 6 large ones or a mixture of sizes
a medium-sized eggplant
olive oil – ½ cup
red wine vinegar – ¼ cup
cumin seeds – 1¼ teaspoons
chickpeas – two 14-oz cans
large basil leaves – 12
Spanish ham or prosciutto – 9 thin slices

For the dressing:
harissa paste – 1¼ teaspoons
olive oil – ¼ cup

Set the oven to 400°F. Twist the tomatoes from their stalks. Cut each one into six pieces, then put them into a roasting tin. Discard the stalk from the eggplant, slice the flesh in four lengthways, and then into short chunks. Put them in the roasting pan together with the oil, vinegar, cumin seeds and a generous grinding of black pepper and sea salt. Roast for about an hour, until the eggplant is soft and golden brown, the tomatoes are caught slightly at the edges and the whole lot is fragrant, sizzling and juicy.

Lift the tomatoes and eggplant from the tin with a slotted spoon, putting them in a mixing bowl but leaving any roasting juices behind in the pan. Mix the drained chickpeas with the tomatoes and eggplant.

Make the dressing by stirring the harissa and olive oil into the roasting juices, then tip it in with the vegetables. Leave a film of dressing in the pan. Leave the basil leaves whole, even if they are very large, and fold them into the salad. They will wilt and soften in the slight heat from the vegetables.

Set the roasting pan over a moderate heat, lay the slices of ham in the film of dressing and cook till they start to crisp lightly. A matter of a minute or so. Transfer the salad to a small serving platter. Lift the ham out and lay the slices on top of the salad.
Enough for 4

And the best mangoes ever

From now until the end of June, the Alphonso mangoes are around. Smooth-skinned, custard yellow and heavily fragrant, they are about as sweet and juicy a fruit as you could ask for. You can pick them up by the box for a bargain price at Indian or Middle Eastern grocers. I sometimes think they are the finest fruit on earth.

They come, six or eight to a box, each highly prized fruit bedecked with a single strand of tinsel and swaddled in yellow or magenta tissue paper. Opening a box of Alphonso mangoes is like peeping in on a carnival. Their deep orange flesh is at its most welcome after a meal spicy enough to make your lips smart.

May 7
Lamb chops with lemon and mint and potatoes crushed into the pan juices

Some new potatoes barely bigger than fava beans have come my way. They will take not much longer than ten minutes in boiling water, so I want something to eat with them that takes about the same length of time. Though grilled food always sounds the right note for me, I sometimes long for the more gentle flavors of an old-fashioned sauté. Lamb steaks, or indeed any chops, work well when cooked in a little oil in a shallow pan, remaining juicy in the extreme. If you add the torn leaves of an herb and maybe some lemon juice to the toasty sediment at the bottom of the pan, you end up with extraordinarily delicious, fresh-tasting pan juices. Just the thing to crush the new potatoes into.

new potatoes – 20 or so
lamb leg steaks or chops – 4
a lemon
mint leaves – 15–20
olive oil – 5 tablespoons

Put the potatoes on to boil in deep, salted water. Season the chops on both sides with black pepper and sea salt. Finely grate the lemon zest and roughly chop or tear the mint leaves. Mix the olive oil with the grated zest of the lemon, the mint and a little pepper and salt.

When the potatoes are almost tender, warm the oil and lemon mixture over a moderate heat in a shallow, heavy-based pan. As it starts to sizzle, lay the seasoned lamb in the pan and let it color for a couple of minutes. Turn the meat over and cook the other side for a minute or two, making sure that the lemon and mint aren't burning. The meat should remain juicy, its surface caught golden brown here and there, rose-pink within. Lift the meat on to warm plates.

Squeeze the juice of the lemon into the hot pan and let it bubble for a few seconds, scraping at the gooey sediment left behind by the chops and stirring it in. Pour it over the chops and vegetables, crushing the potatoes into the cooking juices as you eat.
Enough for 4

There are already recurring themes in my shopping this month. Fava beans and ham, fava beans and goat cheeses, fava beans and olive oil. The latter with the finger-length beans simmered whole with the oil, lemon and chopped dill, then eaten with sesame bread and thick yogurt. The asparagus has been a good price this year, pretty much the same as last. So far I have eaten it as plain as paper, with softening, not quite melted butter, and last week grilled and tossed with olive oil and grated pecorino. Other shopping-bag regulars have been lemons, sheep yogurt, spinach, blueberries (Polish, Spanish, whatever), a little wild salmon and some hugely disappointing apricots.

May 8
Pancakes at
the stove

A friend turns up at two forty-five in the afternoon. Too late for lunch, too early for tea.

They sit on a stool at the side of the cooker whilst I make pan after pan of thick, soft pancakes. Normally they would get a cookie and a mug of tea, but I am testing a recipe for the column and there is something faintly relaxing about exchanging gossip whilst tossing pancakes. If I had some blueberries, I'd bubble them up in a small pan with a spoonful of sugar till their skins burst and then pour them and their purple syrup over the little cakes. I haven't, so we make do with confectioners' sugar and a puddle of melted apricot jam. At this time of year, this is probably as near as I get to a hot dessert.

Orange and ricotta pancakes

ricotta cheese – 1 cup
superfine sugar – 5 tablespoons
large eggs – 3, separated
the finely grated zest of a large orange
all-purpose flour – $\frac{1}{2}$ cup
melted butter – 2 generous tablespoons

In a large mixing bowl, combine the ricotta, sugar and egg yolks. Grate the orange zest into the bowl and stir it in gently with the flour. Beat the egg whites with a balloon whisk till they are stiff, then fold them

lightly into the ricotta mixture. I do this surely but gently, so as not to knock the air out.

Warm a non-stick frying pan over a moderate heat, add the butter, then, as it starts to sizzle lightly, place a heaped tablespoon of mixture into the pan. You will probably get three in at once, but leave room for them to spread. Let them cook for a minute or two till they have risen somewhat and the underside has colored appetizingly, then, using a spatula, flip them over to cook the other side. Let them color, then serve immediately, with a little melted jam and a slight shake of confectioners' sugar.
Makes 8

May 9 and 10
A bean soup
to celebrate
a spring
clean

Cleaning out the kitchen cupboards invariably inspires a bean soup. It is only then, with the Kilner jars and scrunched cellophane packets laid out on the table, that I realize just how many borlotti, cannellini, lentils and fava I actually have. I have no basil for a summer pesto soup, and anyway I am not sure the days are yet warm enough for that. Along with French pissaladière, salade niçoise and slices of watermelon, the sun must be very high in the sky for a *soupe au pistou* to feel right.

There is tarragon in the garden though, and a hot bean soup, creamy rather than tomato-flecked, would warm a chilly late-spring evening without sending us into a sweat. After the soup there is a plate of Tuscan prosciutto and some wide wedges of a smooth-skinned yellow melon that turned up in my organic bag and is now, three days later, dripping with juice.

White bean and tarragon soup

dried navy, cannellini, or borlotti beans – 1¼ cups
2 or 3 bay leaves
a thick slice of butter or a tablespoon of olive oil
scallions – 5
a medium-sized carrot
a clove of garlic
chicken or vegetable stock – 4 cups
tarragon – a good ¼ cup

Soak the beans overnight. The next day, drain them and cover with deep, cold water. Bring the water to a boil, add a bay leaf and a tiny slick of olive oil, then turn down to a simmer and leave for about an hour, until the beans are completely soft. They should have little or no bite in them. Drain them and discard the water.

Warm the butter or oil in a heavy-based pan. Roughly chop the scallions and stew them for a few minutes in the fat. Once they have

softened, peel and finely dice the carrot and garlic and stir them into the onions, letting them soften for five minutes over a low heat.

Tip the beans into the onion and carrot, pour in the stock and bring to a boil. Turn the heat down after a few minutes of enthusiastic boiling, then leave to simmer with salt, black pepper, the leaves of half the tarragon and the remaining bay leaves. Leave for a good half hour, until the beans are starting to collapse. Add the remaining tarragon and process in a blender till smooth and thick, adjusting the seasoning as you wish. Enough for 6

To the Lebanese shops that line London's Edgware Road. Here are bunches of dill the size of horses' tails and tubs of thick, tart yogurt. I cannot resist either. The aniseed smell of the dill reminds me of a restaurant I once worked in, where a nightly job was to walk through the walled garden picking great handfuls of the herb to go in a sauce for the local salmon.

Dill and salmon is a made-in-heaven marriage that works in so many forms: as gravlax, as a retro mousse, or as a piece of gently poached fish with an accompanying green sauce. A long-time fan of this particular culinary partnership, I have a go at making fish cakes with chopped dill but without potato. Tiny cakes that crisp up in the pan and weigh less heavily on the stomach than the traditional variety. I put them on the table with a tub of yogurt into which I have stirred chopped dill, a spoonful of grain mustard and a smidgin of black pepper.

They are rich but light and, despite a side dish of green beans with parsley, they leave us in need of dessert.

Salmon and dill fish cakes

salmon – 2¼lbs
a large egg white
dill – a small bunch
flour – a generous tablespoon
grain mustard – 1¼ teaspoons
the juice of half a lemon
olive or peanut oil

To serve:
lemon wedges
thick yogurt with dill and grain mustard

Remove the skin from the salmon, then chop the flesh finely. Put it in a bowl with the egg white, a couple of tablespoons of finely chopped dill fronds, the flour, mustard and lemon juice, then mush together with a generous grinding of salt and black pepper. Squash spoonfuls of the mixture together lightly with your hands to make ten small balls. Flatten each one slightly and set aside for a few minutes.

Get a little oil hot in a shallow pan. Place the patties in the hot oil (I do this in two batches) and leave them for two or three minutes, until they have colored on the underside. Turn them over with a spatula and color the other side. Cut one in half to check for doneness. The fish should be lightly cooked within and golden and crisp on the outside.

Eat with wedges of lemon and the mustard sauce.
Enough for 3

Lemon amaretti cream pots

I am all for spooning out a dessert from a vast dish in the center of the table but there is a certain elegance, a charm if you like, about a dessert served in individual dishes – like those classic French chocolate mousse pots. This is one for serving in small portions and it needs something crisp to accompany it, such as waffle wafers or those chocolate-dipped wafer curls. A delicate little recipe this, best served well chilled.

heavy cream – 1 cup
thick, natural yogurt – 1 cup
good-quality lemon curd, preferably home-made – ¾ cup
ratafia biscuits or crisp amaretti – 4oz

Pour the cream into a cold china bowl and whisk gently till it starts to thicken. Take care not to over-whip; you are after soft, billowing folds rather than pointy peaks. Now fold in the yogurt and the lemon curd with a large metal spoon.

Put the ratafia or amaretti in a plastic bag and bash them carefully with a heavy object – a rolling pin will do. I use a wine bottle for such tasks. You need large crumbs and small lumps – the size of gravel – rather than fine breadcrumbs. Fold them into the cream.

Scrape the mixture into 6 of those small, classic French chocolate mousse pots or espresso cups (or small ramekins will do) and cover tightly with plastic wrap. Refrigerate for at least 2 hours. This will give time for the biscuits to soften a little and the flavors to marry. Serve with a tiny biscuit on the side or a *langue de chat*.
Enough for 6

Ten-minute tortellini and a few light 'sauces'

My pasta consumption dwindles with the increasing sunshine. Ready-made tortellini, bought from Rocco, my local pasta maker, still features strongly, though at this time of year I ask for it stuffed with ricotta and spinach rather than mushrooms or meat. It's enough, I think, to drizzle over some peppery olive oil and a shaking spoon of grated Parmesan, but at other times I ring the changes.

Green olive paste, bought in jars from the gourmet shop, is an impromptu and fragrant 'sauce' in which to toss freshly drained tortellini, as are sliced, bottled artichokes with olive oil and a handful of chopped flat-leaf parsley. Both offer a light alternative to cream, cheese or tomato-based sauces. I also think this is the perfect time of year in which to toss your pasta with nothing more complex than glossy, grassy olive oil. The very best you can get your hands on.

I can't get enough of those Vietnamese-style salads that manage to be hot, sour, crisp and refreshing all at once. In summer they do as lunch, perhaps with a couple of spring rolls (ready-made – I'm no kitchen slave), but I also use them as a stirring first course or side dish for a larger meal. Their crunchy texture and mouth-popping vibrancy make them a perfect match for grilled fish. I take my time over washing the bean sprouts and spinach and picking the leaves from the stems of the herbs. There is much pleasure to be had from making a salad.

May 15
A hot, sour
bean sprout
salad

scallions – 6–8
lime juice – 2 generous tablespoons
nam pla (Thai fish sauce) – 2 generous tablespoons
sugar – a generous tablespoon
bean sprouts – 2½ cups
half a cucumber
small hot red chili peppers – 1 or 2
spinach – 1 cup (2 large handfuls)
cilantro – a good handful
mint – the leaves from 4 or 5 sprigs

Trim the scallions and grill them till they are a soft brown on all sides. Meanwhile, make the dressing by briefly whisking the lime juice with the fish sauce and sugar. Wash the bean sprouts and leave them to soak for a few minutes in cold water. Cut the cucumber into matchsticks and add it to the dressing. Chop the chilis finely, discarding the seeds, and mix them with the cucumber.

Rinse the spinach, drain the bean sprouts and add them to the dressing, along with the scallions as and when they are ready. Rinse the herb leaves and toss them with the rest of the salad.
Enough for 2

And a really fast cake with blueberries and pears
I have never really been good at the 'perfect hostess' thing. That slightly annoying person who can produce a cake in the time it takes

unexpected guests to walk up the drive. One of the reasons I live near a row of decent shops is that it allows you to produce a piece of shop-bought pâtisserie when the situation calls for it.

Today an emergency cake is called for. On this occasion it has to be home-made. I use the classic 'equal butter to sugar to flour' base, then top it with whatever fruit is to hand. This time it's a couple of slightly manky pears and a box of organic blueberries I was saving for breakfast tomorrow. The result is served warm, with a jug of heavy cream. Though it could just as easily have been fromage frais or vanilla ice-cream. The cake is a dream. It has the perfect open crumb and a beautiful purple-smudged top. It is difficult to imagine a cake that is simpler to make.

butter – ½ cup plus 2 tablespoons
superfine sugar – ½ cup plus 1 tablespoon
ripe pears – 2
large eggs – 2
all-purpose flour – 1⅓ cups
baking powder – 1¼ teaspoons
blueberries – 2½ cups
a little extra sugar

Set the oven 350°F. Line the base of a square 9-in cake pan with a piece of baking parchment.

Beat the butter and sugar until pale and fluffy. A food mixer will do this far more efficiently than you ever could by hand. Whilst this is happening, peel and core the pears and cut them into small chunks. Break the eggs, beat them with a fork, then gradually add them to the butter and sugar. Sift the flour and baking powder together and fold them gently into the mixture. Scrape into the lined cake pan. Rinse the blueberries, then tip them, together with the pears, on top of the cake mixture. Scatter a couple of tablespoons of sugar over the top. Bake for fifty-five minutes, then test for doneness with a skewer. If it comes out clean, remove the cake from the oven, then leave to cool for ten minutes before turning out.
Enough for 8

May 18
A cheese pudding and a salad of young lettuce hearts

At this time of year it is all too easy to swoosh past the Roquefort, the Gorgonzola and the Brie and head for the raffia-lined shelf of goat cheeses. The sharp, chalk-white cheeses seem right for late spring. They have a light spritz to them. But there is no reason why it has to be goat cheese. This week the young Lancashire is as mild and milky as I have ever tasted it. Like fresh, still-green hazelnuts. With rough chunks torn from a soft, white farmhouse loaf, it is all too easy to eat.

My eyes lit up when I first came across Sally Clarke's method of making shallow soufflés without flour. Now I make them no other way. I swap goat cheeses according to what looks good when I go shopping. This week the Ticklemore is particularly young and moist. It is one of those gently goaty, chalk-white British cheeses of rare beauty that I wouldn't normally dream of cooking with, but in this case I am glad I did. It lent a freshness of flavor I wasn't expecting. No doubt due to its young age. I also fancied the idea of Ticklemore with thyme. In truth, any relatively moist goat cheese will work.

Goat cheese puddings

a little butter
freshly grated Parmesan – $1\frac{1}{3}$ cups
large eggs – 4
soft English goat cheese – 12oz
heavy cream – $\frac{1}{2}$ cup
fresh chopped thyme leaves – 1 tablespoon (about 5 stems)

Set the oven to 400°F. Lightly butter three shallow oven-safe pasta bowls or soup plates. Dust them with a little of the grated Parmesan.

Separate the eggs, putting the whites in a bowl big enough to whisk them in. Mash the goat cheese into the egg yolks, then stir in the cream, chopped thyme and a seasoning of black pepper and a very little salt.

Whisk the egg whites till they are almost stiff, then fold them firmly but tenderly into the cheese mixture, using a large metal spoon. Lastly fold in all but a couple of spoonfuls of the grated Parmesan.

Divide the mixture between the three buttered bowls. Scatter over the remaining Parmesan, put the dishes on a baking sheet and bake for ten to fourteen minutes, by which time the center should be lightly risen and creamy inside. I usually test one after nine minutes by opening the middle of it carefully with the edge of a spoon. If there is any sign of liquid at the bottom, I close the oven for a couple of minutes.

Serve immediately, with the salad below, while they are still puffed and golden.
Enough for 3

A young lettuce salad
The heart of a young lettuce is more yellow than green, and has a soft and subtle crunch. This is spring salad at its simplest, and I do no more than toss the unwashed heart leaves with the tiniest drop of walnut oil and a handful of toasted walnut halves. A mild salad to wipe up the last cheesy stickings from the soufflé dishes.

A deli sandwich

If the bread is perfect, by which I mean it has a crust that crackles and shatters when you split it, if the ham is thinly sliced from the bone and the mustard is fresh and hot, then I am not sure you can improve on a *baguette au jambon*. But sometimes you need just that little bit more. It is then that the bottled artichokes come out. If you slice them and toss them in olive oil and chopped parsley, they work superbly with the ham. Or, of course, you can add some thinly sliced cheese, a mild, nutty Gruyère perhaps. Whatever, it must have mustard too. The really hot stuff that packs a punch.

Too often, all my corner shop has left is soft, open-textured ciabatta. At one time it was the small brown loaves and pita bread that were left hanging around at the end of the day. Now it's ciabatta. The soft, flour-topped bread makes a good enough ham sandwich if the ham is paper-thin and Italian, otherwise it just doesn't feel right. Adding mustard becomes precarious here, the large holes in the bread holding enough to make your eyes water.

What I end up with today more than makes up for the lack of a baguette. I slice the short, slipper-sized ciabatta in half lengthways, then drizzle it with my best olive oil. I cover one half with thinnish slices of fat-marbled coppa, some leaves of arugula, eight pitted black olives and a shower of neat little curls of Parmesan taken off the block with a vegetable peeler. For once I throw in some oil-bottled sun-dried tomatoes. Another drizzle of oil, then I press down the top and squeeze. You have to squeeze hard so that the oil soaks into the bread a bit. A bottle of cold San Pellegrino and an exceptionally sparkling Nasturo beer, and that is supper.

May 20 Five-spice quail with loquats to follow

I am not sure I could ever tire of quail. Its skin, saltily blistered over a hot grill, is possibly the most savory mouthful of all. The flesh is rich, clean, and toothsome, the bones a joyous and sensual feast.

What to eat with it, apart from a wedge of lemon, is always a puzzle. I just happen to have a plastic bag of spinach in the fridge, which I cook without really thinking. Its silky leaves are curiously soothing after the rough, charred edges of the bird and its spindly bones, and the mild Chinese spicing works just as well with the green vegetable as it does with the moist, lightly pink meat.

This is the most diminutive bird we can roast and it demands to be picked up at the table, its bones nibbled and sucked clean. Wincing at such table manners and going at it with a knife and fork would be to miss a treat beyond measure.

Five-spice quail

a large clove of garlic
hot chili powder – 1¼ teaspoons
Chinese five-spice powder – 2 slightly heaped teaspoons
the juice of a lemon
peanut oil – 2 generous tablespoons
oven-ready quail – 4

Peel and mash the garlic, put it in a glass, steel or china bowl, then stir in the chili, five-spice powder, lemon juice and oil. Season generously with sea salt – a good ¾ teaspoon. Dip the quail into this seasoned slush and toss them gently round. You can leave them like this for several hours if it suits you, though just one will do.

Set the oven to 425°F. Put the birds and any marinating juices into a small roasting pan. They should be close, but not touching. Roast them for twenty to twenty-five minutes, depending on their size, turning once. The little birds will look quite dark after the full cooking time, but this is fine. Serve them piping hot, with orange or lemon wedges to squeeze and some crusty bread.
Enough for 2

One of the Turkish greengrocers up the road has a wooden crate of pockmarked apricot-colored loquats outside his shop. They glow richly in the late-afternoon sun. Fruit that holds so much promise in a gray, filthy street.

They are not perfect, but good enough to eat on their own. Originally from China, they are at their best when their skin is spotted with small, caramel-colored blotches. The marks rarely go through to the flesh. That is when they are sweetest.

May 23
A citrus roast

There are four of us for Sunday lunch and the day is unusually cool and windy. We are hearty meat eaters all, and exceptionally fond of potatoes. I make the most of this situation by cooking the meat with sliced waxy salad potatoes, which sponge up the juices from the roasting meat. I usually roast my pork on the bone, a sure way to get succulence on to everyone's plate. But today I want something neater and easier to carve. Yesterday I queued for a boned loin, string-tied and scored across the fat by the butcher. If you roast it this way, on a bed of sliced lemons and potatoes, you end up with a gorgeously sticky, citrus-scented little roast.

As always, I like my vegetables or salad after the meat and potatoes rather than piled on the same plate. Today we will mop up the meat juices and the last of the potatoes with a watercress salad, dressed very lightly with walnut oil, red wine vinegar and a smidgen of

grain mustard. It mingles delectably with the lemony meat juices on our plates.

Roast pork with lemon and potatoes

new potatoes – 16
lemons – 2
fennel seeds – 1¼ teaspoons
olive oil – 3 generous tablespoons
boned, rolled pork loin – approximately 3lbs, scored and tied

Set the oven to 425°F. Wipe the new potatoes, cut them in half length-ways, then drop them into a mixing bowl. Cut the lemons into thick wedges, eight or ten to each fruit, then add them to the potatoes, together with the fennel seeds, a tablespoon of the olive oil and a generous grinding of sea salt and black pepper.

Rub the pork generously with salt. Warm the remaining olive oil in a roasting pan and place it over a high heat. As soon as it starts to shimmer, lay the pork in the pan and let it color, then roll it over and continue until all sides are seared. This will help the fat to crackle.

Tip the potatoes and lemons into the roasting pan with the pork. Roast for twenty minutes, then reduce the oven temperature to 400°F and continue roasting for twenty-five minutes per pound or until the juices run clear when the meat is pierced deep with a metal skewer.

You won't need to baste the meat as it cooks but it is a good idea to toss the potatoes around halfway through cooking, so that they turn golden and sticky on both sides. Carve the meat and serve on nicely warmed plates with the roast potatoes.
Enough for 4 with second helpings. Picture overleaf

I dearly want to end this meal with a dish of stewed gooseberries, the jade-green tartness cutting through the preceding richness. But there is not a gooseberry to be seen. Cheese of any sort would be too much, as would chocolate. I decide, perhaps rashly, to continue the lemon theme into the dessert. What could have been citrus overkill turns out to be a huge success, a meal in honor of the fruit.

Lemon ice cream
A few months ago I phoned Jane Pelly, one of my oldest friends. Her voice was as calm and gentle as ever. 'I'm just making some lemon ice cream for the kids to have in the freezer while I'm away in the hospital. I'll phone you as soon as I get back.' Jane never left the hospital. This recipe is for her, with love.

whipping or heavy cream – 2 cups
plain yogurt – ¾ cup
artisan-made lemon curd – 1 cup
zest and juice of 2 lemons
small meringues, home-made or bought – 4oz (about 4)

Whip the cream until it is thick. Not so thick it will stand in peaks, but just so that it lies in slovenly folds. Stir in the yogurt, lemon curd and the zest and juice. Crush the meringues roughly – you don't want them to be smashed to crumbs – then fold them in.

Tip everything into a shallow plastic freezer box and freeze for three or four hours, stirring occasionally. Remove from the freezer thirty minutes before serving.

Enough for 4–6

May 24
Fava beans
and bacon

The fava beans in the garden are still holding on to their flowers. It is as if a hundred black and white butterflies are climbing up the stems. Until next month I have to rely on the greengrocer's for my beans. For lunch today I boiled a whole load of them, then tossed them with bits of fried, smoked bacon and its hot fat and a good handful of chopped parsley.

May 25
Asparagus
and bread
and butter

We stop at the first sign we see. A gray wooden barn with a set of scales on a makeshift counter and a shallow wooden tray of spears. To our right is a pea field, the shoots barely a finger high. To the left a deeply furrowed asparagus field where the pickers are still at their backbreaking work. We buy four bundles, each as thick as a farmer's arm. There are trays of fresh eggs too, as if to remind us to make a foaming hollandaise sauce. But with spears as fresh as this, it will be just softened butter for me. Butter not melted but soft enough to sink a finger in. Sweet, white butter from an organic farm.

At home I eat my spears the way I was taught by an asparagus farmer in Evesham. You boil them in deep, salted water till they will bend and are a dull, muted green – 'that way, they have more of a flavor to 'em'. You eat them with nothing but a china plate of brown bread cut as thin as you dare, buttered as if you were plastering a wall.

May 26
A risotto
for spring

I don't mess around with asparagus, though come the end of the season I might make a tart with crumbling pastry and a quivering filling. But I bought too much yesterday, as you might expect of a townie let loose in a farm shop, so this evening I make risotto with the remaining bunch, grating in a palmful of lemon zest to stave off its tendency to cloy. You could use vegetable stock instead of chicken. The flavor will be much the same, but your risotto will lack the soul, not to mention

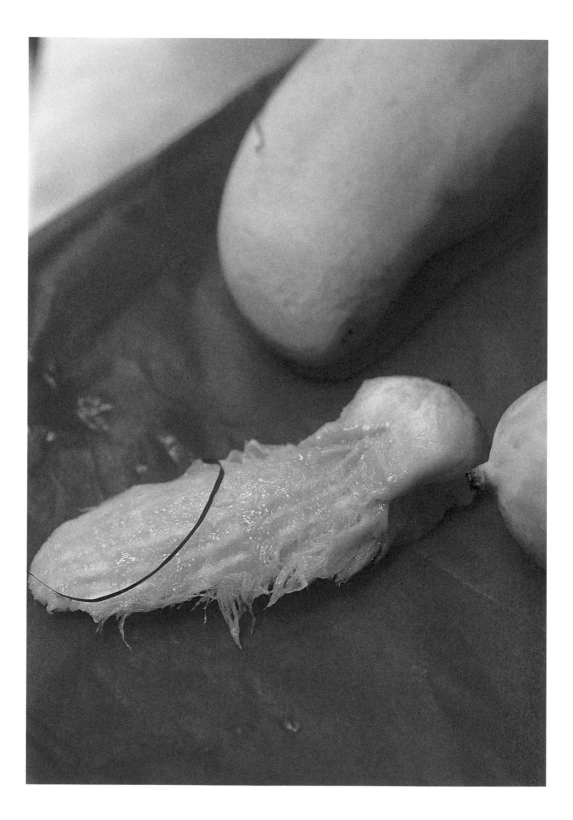

the silky texture, that can only be achieved with a fine, gelatinous chicken stock.

Asparagus and lemon risotto

butter – a thick slice, about 4 tablespoons
a small onion
arborio rice – 1 cup
a glass of white wine or Noilly Prat
asparagus – 1lb
hot chicken stock – 4½ cups
lemons – 2
grated Parmesan – 3 generous tablespoons

Melt the butter in a wide, high-sided pot over a very low heat. Peel the onion and chop it finely. If your onion is larger than a golf ball, you will only need half of it. Let it soften in the butter, stirring from time to time so that it does not color but instead becomes translucent and silky.

Stir in the rice, folding the grains over briefly in the butter with a wooden spoon. Pour in the wine or vermouth and let it bubble down until the liquid has pretty much disappeared, chopping the asparagus into short lengths as it does so.

Add a hefty ladleful of hot stock, turn the heat up a bit, then let the liquid almost disappear before adding the pieces of asparagus and a second ladle of stock. Continue adding the stock as it boils down to almost nothing. Stir the rice often, grating and squeezing the lemons as you go.

Season with salt, pepper, the lemon zest and juice and continue cooking till the rice is creamy but has a little bite left in it. Stir in the cheese and eat immediately.
Enough for 2

**May 30
A bunch of beets, a cheese and a loaf**

There were beets at the farmers' market today. I buy six, each the size of a plum and the color of damson jam. The stalks are young and translucent, a vivid magenta-purple, yet the beets have the coarse, curly whiskers of an old man. They need no washing, just a rub with a wet thumb and a while in a very hot oven. I cut off the stalks, leaving a short tuft behind, then put the beets in a roasting tin with a splash of water and cover the tin with foil. An hour in the oven and they are done. Their skin slides off effortlessly to reveal sweet, ruby flesh.

Beets need no oil. Just a splash of vinegar – red, white or tarragon – and a crumbling of salt. I always do this as soon as they are cut into segments, while their earthy flesh is still warm. The vinegar sets the color and the warm beets take up the flavor.

I rinse the leaves and drop them, stems and all, into a shallow pot with a glass of water. Brought to a boil for two minutes, they are drained and tossed in with the beets in seconds.

Two of us ate the beets and their greens with slices of crumbly goat cheese, hacking off bits of cheese and pushing them on to the still-warm beets with ruby-stained fingers. After the fudgy, chalk-white cheese and sweet, claret roots, we filled up on slices of thickly buttered soft white bread cut from a cottage loaf. Oh, and I bought pinks too, a fat bunch of them, and sat them in a creamware jug on the kitchen table.

june

Steamed sea bass with
ginger and cucumber

A chicken roasted with
new garlic and a fresh
pea pilaf to go with it

Strawberries with
fromage blanc

Chicken and rice salad

Gooseberries with
mascarpone cream

Fava beans in their pods
with dill and yogurt

Vietnamese beef salad

Orecchiette with ricotta,
fava beans and mint

A radish, mint and feta salad

Orecchiette with roast tomato
and basil sauce

Fava bean and dill 'hummus'

Roast lamb with cumin
and fresh mint

Grilled chicken with harissa
and mint

A cooling crab salad

Strawberry mascarpone tart

A warm summer fruit compote

Clams with ham and sherry

June 1
A simple
lunch

Today, a lunch of the softest goat cheese (Dorstone from Neal's Yard Dairy, though it could have been any young, softly crumbling *chèvre*), eaten with crisp, chewy sourdough bread and perfectly ripe peaches. A gentle, snow-white cheese, so young and fresh it has only had time to develop the thinnest of crusts. Perfect food for a summer's day, the slight sourness of the cheese and the glorious sweetness of the peaches is as good a marriage as you will get. Two long loaves, eight peaches and four cheeses between four of us, and we could have eaten more.

June 2
A basket of
lychees and a
steamed fish

I take a shopping list to Chinatown: scallions, ginger, cilantro, Thai mangoes and lemongrass. There is a crowd of Chinese shoppers hanging around the back of a van from which small wicker crates the size of wastepaper baskets are being unloaded. There seems to be a mild sense of excitement. The crates turn out to be holding lychees. Not the fat, deepest-carmine Emperor lychees that are such a treat but bargain-basement fruits, pale in color and quite small. I am unsure how sweet they will be, but everyone seems to be buying them. The crates are sealed and no one offers me any to taste. I join in the scrum and part with my cash, then curse myself all the way home, thinking I have been done, knowing full well that lychees that color are always sour.

Steamed sea bass with ginger and cucumber

It is raining, and not especially warm. Neither am I feeling at my best. Time for a solitary, soothing supper. Something mild and gently flavored. Perhaps even a little bit extravagant. Who says food cannot heal?

The fish market has whole wild sea bass at about a fiver apiece. So fresh as to be bent with their tails pointing to the sky, they look as if they have been caught mid leap. Their firm flesh will steam beautifully. As it's not so warm today, I use a small amount of Chinese spicing, just enough to lend a subtle aromatic note, a warm herbal depth, to the broth in the dish.

My kitchen doesn't have a large enough steamer for this. I get by with a Chinese wicker basket suspended over a heavy casserole of boiling water. It will take a shallow dish long and wide enough to hold a small whole fish, albeit rather snugly.

a small sea bass
ginger – a piece about 2in long
scallions – 2 large
limes – 2
light soy sauce – 2 generous tablespoons
nam pla (Thai fish sauce) – 1 generous tablespoon
stock (chicken or vegetable) – ¾ cup

sugar – a pinch
lemongrass – 2 plump stalks
cucumber – a piece about 2½in long
cilantro – a small bunch

Rinse the sea bass, checking that all the scales have been removed. Off with its head, then score the fish deeply two or three times across its width. This will help the seasonings permeate the flesh and encourage it to cook gently right through to the bone. Lay the prepared fish in a shallow, heatproof dish that will sit comfortably in your steamer. Ideally there should be enough space for the steam to come up around the sides of the dish.

Peel the ginger and cut it into fine shreds, then scrape it into a bowl. Trim the scallions, then cut them similarly and add to the ginger. Squeeze over the juice from one of the limes, add the soy and fish sauce, the stock and the sugar and mix together. Spoon this over the fish. Smash the lemongrass stalks with the back of a heavy knife and tuck them into the broth around the fish.

Lower the dish into the steamer basket and steam for ten to fifteen minutes, until the fish will part easily from the bone in fat, pearl-white chunks. While the fish is cooking, peel the cucumber and slice it thinly lengthwise, then cut each slice into long shreds about the width of a chopstick. Add these to the fish halfway through the cooking time. You want them to retain a bit of crunch.

Roughly chop the cilantro. Lift the dish from the steamer, scatter with the cilantro and squeeze over the juice of the second lime.
Enough for 1

A pleasant surprise
After eating the fish I remember the basket of lychees. It occurs to me that if they are really bad I can always use the wicker basket for something. Despite their pallid color and diminutive size, they turn out to be some of the sweetest and juiciest I have ever eaten. What was going to be a quick taste ends up with my sitting there for a good half hour, shelling and eating fruit after fruit without stopping. Honeyed fruits as sweet and fragrant as a summer rose.

I get a bit overexcited this morning when I see six giant bunches of new purple garlic at La Fromagerie. Bunches so large it would be easier to carry them on your shoulder. Yet for all its size, there is only the faintest aroma of garlic in the house, for which I am grateful. The skins, ivory streaked with rose and mauve, hold the plumpest cloves, yet there is a subtlety to their scent, as if someone has wafted through the room carrying a plate of garlic bread on their way to somewhere else. The smell you get in the market in Nice. Yes, it was

**June 3
A lunch of lettuce and new garlic; supper of roast chicken and more new garlic**

more than a fiver, but anyone would be tempted. As irresistible as a bunch of violets.

I don't normally get quite so carried away, but I make salad within half an hour of coming home. I cut one clove in half and rub it round the inside of the salad bowl. I mean to put in mustard, too, but end up with just salt, black pepper, the merest dash of red wine vinegar and a drizzle of olive oil. It doesn't thicken, of course, but it doesn't matter. Then I pile in the leaves of two Little Gem lettuces, organic and with leaves so tight I can barely separate them without tearing, and toss them gently around till every leaf is lightly coated with oil. Two thick slices of bread, and that is lunch. There is a little coffee afterwards, but that's about it.

A chicken roasted with new garlic and a fresh pea pilaf to go with it

a large chicken – about 3½lbs
olive oil
young summer garlic – 2 whole heads
white vermouth – 2 wine glasses

Set the oven to 400°F. Rub the chicken all over with olive oil, massaging in a generous amount of sea salt and black pepper as you go. Put the seasoned chicken breast-side down in a roasting pan in which it will not have too much space around it. Put it into the hot oven and leave it to roast for just over an hour.

Break open the heads of garlic and separate the cloves but don't peel them. Drop them into a small pan of boiling water and let them simmer for five minutes. Drain them and add to the chicken pan. Turn the chicken over for the last twenty minutes. Continue roasting until the chicken is golden and puffed and its juices run clear. To test, push a skewer into the thickest part of the leg; if the juices that come out are clear rather than pink, it is done. It should take an hour to an hour and a quarter.

Lift the chicken from the tin and leave it somewhere warm to rest. Crush the garlic cloves with the back of a spoon so that the soft centers squish out of the crusty brown skins into the pan. Pour in the vermouth and bring to a boil. Stir, scraping at any crusty bits in the pan, and leave to simmer enthusiastically for a couple of minutes. Season generously, then pour the juices through a small sieve into a warm pitcher or small bowl. Keep this warm whilst you carve the chicken. Stir the gravy a bit before you pour it over.

For the pilaf:
You should make the pilaf once the chicken has been roasting for almost an hour. It should be ready for when the chicken has rested.

Put a couple of handfuls of fresh peas into a small pot of boiling water, let them simmer for five minutes and then drain.

Fry a finely chopped small onion in a little olive oil. When the onion is pale gold, add a cinnamon stick and a couple of cloves, then pour in a large cupful of rice, say two or three handfuls. Stir, letting the spices cook briefly – you just want to warm their oils – then pour in the same volume of water as rice and bring to a boil. Add salt generously, turn down the heat to a simmer and cover the pan with a lid. After ten minutes, switch off the heat. Avoid the temptation to lift the lid for ten minutes, then stir in the cooked peas and fluff the rice up with a fork. Cover with a lid if you are not quite ready for it. Part of the joy here is the garlic gravy spooned over the rice.
Enough for 4

Strawberries with fromage blanc
The squirrels have wolfed most of the strawberries in the garden but the ones at the farmers' market are as good as they come: small, sweet, deeply flavored and red right through. None of that ice-white core that so many of them have. I pile them in a dish so full that they are falling off the edge, then bring out a bowl of the fromage blanc below to go with them.

heavy cream – ⅔ cup
thick plain yogurt – ½ cup
a large egg white
confectioners' sugar – 1 tablespoon

Put a large mixing bowl in the fridge to chill. When it is cold, pour in the cream and beat until it will stand in soft folds. Gently fold in the yogurt. Beat the egg white until it will stand in stiff peaks, then fold it tenderly into the cream and yogurt. Taste and add sugar as you wish. Chill, then use within an hour or so.
Enough for 4

**June 5
Sometimes
lunch just
happens**

The remains of the chicken are sitting peacefully in the larder wearing a dish towel. If there was enough white meat left on the bones I would cut it away in long, thin slices and have it with nothing but a bowl of thick, glossy mayonnaise and enough salt to make the golden skin feel gritty on the tongue. Maybe there would be a few leaves of plain English lettuce, too. But there isn't. Any decent slices went yesterday. Instead I wheedle out every bit of brown and white meat left on the carcass, first with a short-bladed knife and then, finally, with my fingers. Fifteen minutes later the bones are almost clean and I have a bowl of thick, juicy nuggets of meat, enough for a salad.

I don't normally do rice salad. The words stir no passion in me. But there is rice pilaf left from yesterday, too, and the marriage seems inevitable. The healthfood shop has bags of sprouts, which I often buy but for some reason rarely finish. Green and white mung, lentils and the odd chickpea make for a bag of fresh, green pea flavors and sharpen the dull texture of cold rice.

I won't assume you have both chicken and leftover rice, so in the recipe that follows I cook the rice from scratch. A nice garden lunch, this one.

Chicken and rice salad

basmati rice – 1 cup
sprouts (mung, lentils etc) – 1¾ cups
small hot red chili peppers – 2
mint – 6 bushy sprigs
nam pla (Thai fish sauce) – 2 generous tablespoons
lime juice – 2 generous tablespoons
olive oil – 3 generous tablespoons, or include a little walnut oil, too
several handfuls of leftover chicken

Wash the rice, put it into a small pot and cover with about the same volume of water. Add a little salt and bring to a boil. Turn down to a jolly simmer and cover with a tight lid. When the water has evaporated (and deep holes have appeared in the surface), test the rice for tenderness. Turn the heat off and leave the rice, covered with its lid, for ten minutes. Fluff up the rice with a fork and leave to cool.

Rinse the sprouts in cold running water and drain. Make the dressing by chopping and seeding the chilis, chopping the mint leaves (and discarding the stems) and mixing them together in a serving dish with the fish sauce, lime juice and olive or walnut oil.

Cut the chicken into thin strips. Toss them with the dressing, then add the cooled rice. Mix gently and check the seasoning. You may need a little salt. Leave for twenty minutes or so for the flavors to marry. Enough for 3

Gooseberries with mascarpone cream

Gooseberries are a rare treat, the season lasting no more than three or four weeks. Some years my own bushes fruit, other years they stand barren. I tend to get gooseberry fever, first poaching the fruit with sugar and bringing it to the table with a jug of yellow organic cream, then I usually bake it under a crumble topping, the butter, flour and sugar sometimes flecked with shredded almonds. Then, towards the end of the season, I stir the raw fruit into a cake, beads of warm green tartness to flatter the sweet crumbs. When I am serving the berries

185

poached, the simplicity of a jug of pure cream on the side is positively soothing, but I often make this custard-flavored cream instead.

gooseberries – 1lb
sugar

For the mascarpone cream:
large eggs – 2
superfine sugar – 2 generous tablespoons
mascarpone cheese – 1 cup
vanilla extract – a couple of drops

Top and tail the gooseberries. Not such a bad job if you do it in the garden and, unlike podding peas, you won't be tempted to eat half of them raw. Drop the fruit into a stainless steel pot (aluminum will taint the fruit), shake over a little sugar – a tablespoon or so should do – then add a tablespoon of water. Simmer over a low heat for ten minutes, until the sugar has dissolved and the fruit has almost burst.

To make the mascarpone cream, separate the eggs, put the yolks in a bowl with the sugar and beat for a few seconds until thoroughly mixed. Beat in the mascarpone till you have a creamy, custard-colored cream. Stir in the vanilla, but don't be tempted to add more.

With a clean whisk, beat the egg whites till they stand stiff, then fold them into the creamed mascarpone. Cover with plastic wrap and chill for a good thirty minutes.

Put the gooseberries and their juice into a serving bowl and the cream into another.
Enough for 2–3

June 6
An avocado and bacon salad

Tiny, knobbly avocados arrive in the organic bag this week, so small and nutty you could eat them like sweets. But there's three of us for lunch, so I make (a bit of) an effort. I peel away the hard shells, cut the green flesh into thick slices and drizzle it with bits of fried smoked bacon, hot and crisp from the frying pan. I then throw a splash of sherry vinegar into the pan, scrape up the pan-stickings with a wooden spatula and tip it over the avocados. We eat the salad with thin slices of dark rye bread I found at the back of the cupboard and everyone thinks I am a genius.

June 7
Fava beans from the garden

The largest fava beans in the garden are no bigger than an index finger. Caught at this early stage, while the beans inside are the size of a child's fingernail, they can be eaten pods and all. I need olive oil for this, and settle on Greek rather than Italian, which feels more appropriate to a dish whose origins are embedded in that part of the world. A lunch like this needs bread, the sort encrusted with sesame seeds, and yogurt, too – preferably the true Greek sort, a yogurt so sharp and thick you can stand a spoon up in it.

Fava beans in their pods with dill and yogurt

young fava beans in their pods – 9oz
scallions – 6
olive oil – 6 tablespoons
water – 1 cup
dill – 6 bushy stems
thick, sharp yogurt

Wash the bean pods and cut off their stalks, pulling away any strings from the sides of the pods as you go. There shouldn't really be any if the beans are young enough, but you may find one or two. Cut each pod into four.

Put the beans, still in their pods, into a medium-sized pot for which you have a lid. Cut the scallions into short lengths, discarding the very dark green tips, then add them to the beans together with the olive oil, water and a good grinding of both black pepper and sea salt.

Bring to a boil, turn down the heat so the beans simmer gently and cover with a lid. Leave, bar the occasional stir, for about fifteen minutes, then check for tenderness. Chop the dill and stir it into the beans. Turn off the heat and leave for ten minutes.

Serve with crusty bread and dollops of thick yogurt, drizzling the meager olive-oily pan juices over the yogurt.
Enough for 2 as a light lunch with bread

June 9

The urge for fish sticks and peas gets the better of me. As I am waiting to pay in the corner shop, a total stranger turns to me and says, 'Well, well, Nigel Slater with a bag of frozen peas!' As I scuttle out of the door I glance guiltily over the road at the greengrocer packing up for the day, no doubt wondering what to do with his unsold crate of fresh English peas.

June 10

I tend to recoil from most recipes with more than half a dozen or so ingredients. Unless we are talking curry or Christmas cake, the result is almost certain to be confused, the main ingredient losing its integrity in a muddle of flavors.

Vietnamese beef salad

Then there is the Vietnamese salad. Only the right balance of sweet, sour, hot and cold will give you the sensation you desire, the mix of flavors that always manages to wake the senses. If this means a shopping list as long as my arm, then so be it. The results are spectacular.

2 small sirloin steaks (4oz each)
a little oil
a bird's eye chili
a lime
a good pinch of sugar
Vietnamese or Thai fish sauce – 2 generous tablespoons
sweet chili sauce – a generous tablespoon
lime leaves – 4 large or 6 smaller ones
cilantro – a large handful
mint leaves – a large handful
cucumber – a piece 2in long
a medium carrot
a bunch of watercress
tomatoes – 2 large or 8 cherry tomatoes

Season the steaks with black pepper and a little oil and set them aside while you heat a broiler or griddle pan.

Halve the bird's eye chili, then scrape out and discard the seeds. Shred the flesh finely and put it into a mixing bowl with the juice of the lime, the sugar, fish sauce and sweet chili sauce. Mix thoroughly.

Remove the stem and central vein from the lime leaves, then roll up the leaves and shred them very, very finely. Put them in a serving dish. Roughly chop the cilantro and mint leaves (if they are small, you can leave them as they are). Cut the cucumber and carrot into matchstick-sized pieces, peeling them first if you wish, then add them to the lime leaves with the chopped herbs.

Wash the watercress and remove the toughest of the stems. Slice the tomatoes into thin segments or, in the case of cherry tomatoes, in half, then add them to the rest of the salad with the watercress.

Grill the steaks briefly, salting them as they cook. They should be nicely singed on the outside and a deep, rosy pink within. Remove them from the heat and let them rest for a good five minutes. Slice them in finger-thick strips, then toss them with the salad and the dressing. Serve straight away, whilst the steak is still hot.

Dessert is mangoes with lime juice. Fruit so ripe and messy to peel that I need a shower afterwards.
Enough for 2 as a main dish

As a rule, I take my meals in the garden at this time of year, even on the rare occasions I am eating alone. The fava beans are ripening as you look at them and from now until the end of the month they will turn up on the table in some form or another every few days. After a succession of highly spiced meals my mouth needs something peaceful and calming, a gentle, mildly flavored pasta dish for a summer meal in the garden. **June 11**

Orecchiette with ricotta, fava beans and mint

fava beans in their pods – 2lbs
pasta, such as orecchiette – 2 cups
young garlic cloves – 2
olive oil – a generous tablespoon
mint – a small, bushy bunch
ricotta cheese – 1¼ cups

To serve:
extra virgin olive oil – at least 2–3 tablespoons
grated pecorino cheese – a good ⅔ cup

Pop the beans from their pods (you should end up with about 2 cups) and cook them in deep boiling salted water until tender. Seven to ten minutes should do it. Drain the beans, rinse under cold running water and remove the skin from any beans bigger than your thumbnail. Tiny beans will have a thin skin that is perfectly edible.

Bring a large, deep pot of water to a boil and add the pasta. It should be ready after about nine minutes, depending on the type. Peel and finely slice the garlic, put it in a shallow pot with the olive oil and let it soften over a moderate heat without coloring. Remove the mint leaves from their stems and chop them roughly, then stir them into the softening garlic. Tip in the beans and then the ricotta, in dollops. Add the drained pasta and fold the mixture together lightly with a fork.

Divide between two warmed pasta bowls and drizzle generously with extra virgin olive oil and grated pecorino.
Enough for 2

**June 12
Another
ten-minute
pasta dish**

If you open a jar of green olive paste and let it down with a few glugs of olive oil, you have an instant sauce for pasta. Add a handful of grated Parmesan at the table and a bottle of very cold Pinot Grigio and you have a very fine lazy-boy's supper for two.

**June 14
A crisp,
salty salad**

You can grow radishes in a window box, set in between spring bulbs, or, as I do, in the garden. They fit neatly into the gaps between the zucchini, the melons and the sweet peas. They are usually something I pick as I walk round the garden, wiping off the soil with my thumb before crunching into them. They rarely make it as far as the kitchen.

The reputation of most salads is made by their dressing. Today I make a salad that is by contrast almost naked – just a splash of fruity oil for lubrication and some sharp red wine vinegar for punch. The result is a dish that possesses a refreshing crunch and salty bite. An early-summer lunch of singular freshness and vitality.

A radish, mint and feta salad

cucumber – a medium to large one
radishes – a large bunch
scallions – 6
feta cheese – ¾lb
mint – a small bunch
flat-leaf parsley – a small bunch
olive oil
red wine vinegar (not too smooth)

Peel the cucumber lightly, removing the coarse skin but leaving behind as much of the bright green that lies directly under the skin as possible. Otherwise the salad will appear insipid. Cut the cucumber in half lengthways, then scrape out the seeds with a teaspoon and discard them. Slice each long half lengthways again, then cut each piece into short, fat chunks and tip into a large mixing bowl.

Wash the radishes and top and tail them. Cut them in half or quarters, according to their size, then add them to the cucumber. Trim the scallions and chop them into thick rings.

Crumble the cheese into small chunks. Tear the mint leaves into large pieces – you can leave the small leaves whole – and toss them with the whole parsley leaves, cheese, cucumber, onions and radishes. Drizzle over a little olive oil and vinegar (you don't need a formal dressing here, just a splash of both), then grind over a little black pepper, but no salt.
Enough for 4

June 15
A shrimp
omelette

You can make a very nice little omelette by folding in a carton of cooked shrimps, minus the butter topping, as it cooks. It is surprisingly filling and somehow, with a glass of white wine, rather decadent.

June 16
Bulgur
wheat and
mangoes

This is what it says in my notebook: 'Soaked fine bulgur wheat for five to ten minutes in cold water. Squeezed it dry and fluffed the grains up with a fork. Stirred it through with roughly chopped ripe mangoes, masses of chopped fresh mint and parsley, several shots of olive oil and a lot of coarse black pepper. Wonderful with slices of cold ham.'

June 17
Summer
pasta for
four

Just outside the kitchen door is a long, north-facing wall that is bathed in summer sun. I stand giant terracotta tubs against it – two of Costoluto Fiorentino tomatoes and Roma zucchini and a smaller one of basil, the plants grateful for the wall's shelter and excessive warmth. The first fruits appear in mid June, and continue producing until October. This year they are late. I spotted the first tomato today, a good fortnight later than last year. But the tomatoes that have been

turning up in the organic box have been fine this summer: sharp and rich, with that deep, herbal smell that comes when the fruit is allowed to bake in the sunshine.

There is a glut of the fruit in the house this week. The usual delivery came, but then I got tempted by those at the market – smaller tomatoes with orange and green freckled shoulders. Now there's enough for a sauce. So sauce it is, a thick one to serve with orecchiette, to sit in the pasta's little hollows, making each mouthful sweet-sharp and luscious. I didn't mean to put the cream in, but the charred bitterness of the roast tomato skins and the bite of the tomatoes demanded it. What we got was a sauce that was robust and yet somehow luxurious.

Orecchiette with roast tomato and basil sauce

cherry or small tomatoes – 3lbs
garlic – 4 fat cloves
olive oil
dried orecchiette – 1lb
large basil leaves – 30
heavy cream – 5 tablespoons
grated Parmesan or pecorino cheese, to serve

Remove the stalks from the tomatoes and put the fruit into a small roasting pan. Peel the garlic and slice the cloves thinly, drop them in with the tomatoes and drizzle over a little olive oil. Put the tomatoes under the broiler and leave them until their skins are golden brown and black here and there and their insides are juicy and starting to burst. Don't pussyfoot around here; broil the tomatoes till their skins are truly blackened in some places. Meanwhile, cook the pasta in a deep saucepan of boiling, generously salted water.

Remove the tomatoes from the heat and crush them, skins and all, with a fork. Drop in the basil leaves and stir them in. They will wilt and soften with the heat of the fruit. Stir in the cream, correct the seasoning with salt and coarsely ground black pepper, then eat straight away, with a spoon or two of grated Parmesan or pecorino.
Enough for 4 as a main dish

Eating in the garden
The roses are better, stronger, more floriferous than they have been before. The soft, white flowers and long, yellow stamens of the climbing white Direktor Benschop are on their second flush. When there is a breeze, the flowers dance on their fragile stems. The long, white stems of the sweet arugula are entangled with the deep magenta-purple of the Tuscany Superb. The sweet peas – lavender, cream and white – are just bursting into flower. In the evening, the smell of the roses, light, fruity,

romantic, wafts over to the garden table. Even with a chilly evening breeze it is almost impossible to resist the temptation to eat amongst all this billowing, fragrant chaos whenever you get the chance.

To the Lebanese shops on the Bayswater Road. I eat lunch walking down the street – a piece of hot flatbread from their in-store oven with a thin, nutty spice paste on top. Not an easy thing to do whilst struggling with a bag containing fresh mint, dill, Lebanese yogurt, cumin seeds, arugula, a bottle of orange blossom water and a bag of apricots. Afterwards I eat a square of their pistachio baklava. I end up with sticky, oily fingers and no way of washing them.

June 18 Dinner for six in the garden

There is an ancient flavor to hummus, a pleasing mustiness. A flavor as old as God. I have always fancied making a brighter, fresh-tasting recipe for summer using fresh beans or peas, whipping the cooked legumes with olive oil and maybe a few herbs. Today I do just that, beating freshly boiled fava beans with olive oil and dill to achieve a sort of summer hummus. A dish for people to dip into as they talk.

Fava bean and dill 'hummus'

fava beans in their pods – 3½lbs
olive oil – 5 tablespoons
the juice of a small lemon
fresh dill – a large handful (about ½oz)

Put a pot of water on to boil. Pod the beans, then drop them into the boiling water and cook for seven to nine minutes, until tender. Drain them and blitz to a coarse purée in a food processor. Pour in the olive oil, add the lemon juice and dill and a grinding of salt and pepper. Continue to process until the mixture is bright green and almost smooth.
    Scrape into a dish, then pour over a little olive oil. Eat with hot pita or crusty bread.

Roast lamb with cumin and fresh mint
I have used a shoulder here, but in fact any cut of lamb would work.

shoulder of lamb –3½–4lbs
garlic – 4 cloves
cumin seeds – 3 large pinches
mint leaves – a large handful, plus more for the gravy
the juice of 2 lemons
enough olive oil to make a slush
a glass or two of white wine or stock for the gravy

Make three or four deep cuts into the lamb from one side to the other, going right through the fat to the meat. You will need a very sharp knife for this. Then put the shoulder in a roasting pan. Peel the garlic and put it into a food processor with the cumin seeds, a fat handful of mint leaves and the lemon juice. Add a grinding of salt and some black pepper. Process to a coarse paste, adding enough olive oil to make it into a spreadable slush. You want it thin enough to be easy to spread but thick enough to cling to the lamb.

Massage the joint of meat well with the spice paste, spreading it over the skin and into the cut sides of the flesh. Now set aside in a cool place, preferably not the fridge, for an hour, basting occasionally with any of the paste that has run off.

Preheat the oven to 400°F. Roast the meat for forty-five minutes to an hour, depending on how you like your lamb (forty-five minutes should give you a roast that is still pink and juicy inside). Remove from the oven and rest the meat for a good ten minutes before carving.

To make a gravy, remove the meat from the roasting pan, put the pan over a moderate heat and pour in a couple of glasses of wine or stock. Bring it to a boil and stir with a wooden spoon, scraping away at the pan to dissolve any stickings into the gravy. Let the liquid bubble a little, then add a last handful of fresh mint leaves and check it for seasoning – it may need salt and pepper. Keep the 'gravy' warm whilst you carve the lamb.

An arugula salad with which to wipe our plates
To go with the lamb: a pile of arugula leaves on each plate, so that they wilt slightly under the slices of warm lamb and serve as a green mop to sponge the juice from our plates.

Warm apricots with orange blossom and pistachios
Apricots disappoint. Sure, you can tease out their flavor with warmth. They will improve somewhat if you leave them in a brown paper bag on a warm windowsill for a day or two, but even then their eating quality depends more on luck than good judgement. When they fail to come up trumps, I bake the saffron-colored fruit and eat them at room temperature. Warmed gently with orange blossom water and sugar, or sometimes honey, this shy fruit will often come to life.

Cut the apricots in half, remove the stones and lay the fruit snugly in a baking dish. Shake a little sugar over them, or a drizzle of honey, and a splash or two of orange blossom water. Cover them with foil and bake at 400°F for about thirty-five to forty-five minutes. Serve warm or at room temperature as they are or, if you wish, with thick sheep milk yogurt and a few chopped pistachios.

This evening I cooked three of the big garlic cloves, peeled and sliced very thinly, in butter. I let them soften without coloring for five minutes or so, then tipped in three double handfuls of freshly podded peas. I covered them with a little water, added salt, and simmered them for about twelve minutes. I tipped them on to a thick slice of hot toast and let the sweet, garlicky, buttery juices soak through. A sort of summer beans on toast.

I adore the food of warm climates. The home cooking of India, Thailand and the Middle East always interests me more than anything nearer home. There is a quiet excitement about eating that goes hand in hand with hot countries and seems missing in cooler climates. Beirut versus Calais, Mumbai versus Birmingham. No contest.

Much has to do with fragrance. It is what makes me buy an ingredient, it is what brings me to the table. Mint, garlic, rosewater, lemons (both pickled and freshly cut), cilantro, cumin, orange blossom water. These are scents that make me want to cook, that make me want to eat. I bought a can of harissa the other day, the gentlest of all chili pastes and, to my taste, one that has more depth and less vibrancy than the Asian varieties. Even then, there are times when I temper its cayenne heat with yogurt – usually the thick plain yogurt that you can buy by the big white tubful in Middle Eastern groceries.

I cannot remember a day when I didn't eat yogurt. It is as much a part of my life as mineral water, salad or coffee. Sometimes I buy the Lebanese variety, so white and dense you could spread it with a knife. Other times it has to be the delicate French sheep yogurt that comes in glass pots the size of an egg cup. Mostly it is British goat yogurt from the healthfood shop. It is not the thickness that matters so much to me but the sharpness, the clean taste that accompanies the best artisan-made varieties. The only yogurt I will not eat is the mild, bland, sweet stuff the supermarkets excel at. Yogurt disguised as a dessert.

**June 21
An homage
to yogurt:
a succulent
and spicy
grilled
chicken and
a delicate
dessert**

Grilled chicken with harissa and mint

Unless you are a dab hand with the boning knife, you will have to ask the butcher to bone the chicken legs for you. Ask him on a quiet day though, or better still a day in advance. I tend to eat nothing but a spinach salad with this, dressed with lemon and olive oil and maybe scattered with a few toasted pine nuts.

harissa paste – 2½ teaspoons
yogurt – 2 generous tablespoons
olive oil – 3 generous tablespoons
chicken legs – 4
mint leaves – a handful

Stir the harissa paste into the yogurt, then beat in the olive oil, a little salt and some black pepper with a small whisk or a fork. You will end up with a somewhat curdled, pale brick-red paste. Don't worry, it'll be fine. Roll the boned chicken legs in this.

Heat a broiler. Place the chicken, still coated in the paste, on the broiler pan and leave to cook until it is tender inside, without any trace of blood, and the meat is browned in appetizing patches. Scatter with mint leaves and eat whilst it is still hot and sizzling from the grill.
Enough for 2

Rosewater and yogurt panna cotta
My recipe, and one that will leave purists screaming. I make no apologies. The yogurt lends a welcome freshness, while the rosewater offers the faintest whiff of mid summer. It is utter bliss. I have served the passion fruit purée below with this, but some white currants or loganberries would be good, too.

heavy cream – ½ pint
whole milk – ½ cup
vanilla pods – 2
gelatine sheets – 1½
confectioners' sugar – 4–5 tablespoons
rosewater – 2½ teaspoons
thick, creamy yogurt – ⅔ cup

Put the heavy cream and milk into a small saucepan. Split the vanilla pods down their length and scrape out the seeds with the point of a knife. Stir the seeds into the cream, then set the pan over a moderate heat and simmer for five or six minutes. During this time the mixture will reduce a little. Soak the gelatine leaves in a bowl of cold water. Within a few minutes they will have softened to a slippery, rubbery shape.

Remove the cream from the heat and stir in the confectioners' sugar. Once it has dissolved, add the drained gelatine and the rosewater. Fold in the yogurt. Pour the mixture through a sieve balanced over a jug, then pour into six demitasse cups and leave to cool.

Once the panna cotta is cool, cover with plastic wrap and refrigerate till set. Turn out and serve with berries or fruit purée.
Makes 6, but will keep in the fridge for a day or two

A passion fruit purée for panna cotta
Cut eight ripe (wrinkled) passion fruit in half and squeeze the seeds and pulp into a sieve balanced over a jug. Push as much of the pulp as you can through the sieve, ending up with a dry mass of seeds. Spoon the purée over the turned-out panna cotta.

June 23
Loaves and
fishes

Five people turn up for a meeting that ends up dragging on later than anyone expected. They keep looking longingly at the oven, hoping I will suddenly produce a meal out of nothing. In truth, I'm tired and I cannot wait for them to go, and so offer them the only thing I have around – sardines on toast. We end up eating round after round with bottles of beer, till every crumb of bread is finished and my larder is looking distinctly depleted.

June 24
A cooling
crab salad
and a simple
strawberry
tart

I keep meaning to buy an umbrella for the garden table, so that on days as hot and bright as this one you can eat lunch outside without squinting at your salad. Mr Hatt had crab today, already dressed, their sweet flesh piled up in their shells in a neat row on the ice. Crab salad in the garden is one of those summer meals to be cherished. Perhaps I would feel less fortunate if I lived by the sea, where a decent crab salad is just a short walk away across the pebbles. In the city, you always feel grateful when you find spanking-fresh seafood.

Rather than take the usual route with a crab salad, I fancy something with a brighter, more refreshing edge to it. With melon, watercress and limes to hand, what I end up with is an exhilarating jumble of tastes and sensations: cool, pepper-hot, salty and sour all come into play. The real point here is the salad's cooling quality. I would normally suggest a mixture of both brown and white crab meat but with the melon it is best to stick to white meat. The brown will be used in a sandwich later, or maybe tomorrow.

2 small, ripe green- or orange-fleshed melons, well chilled
cucumber – half a small one
watercress – ¼lb
fresh crab meat – ¾lb

For the dressing:
a lump of ginger the size of a walnut
freshly squeezed lime juice – ⅓ cup (about 2 ripe limes)
palm sugar (or superfine sugar) – 1¼ teaspoons
mild olive oil – a generous tablespoon
mint leaves – 15

Make the dressing. Peel the ginger and grate it over a bowl. You should get about a heaped teaspoon of ginger purée. Stir in the lime juice (I use a tiny whisk for this), sugar and olive oil. Season with a little salt and a generous amount of black pepper – coarsely ground pepper always complements chilled melon, as does salt. Roughly chop the mint leaves and stir them in.

Peel the melons, cut the flesh in half and scrape out the seeds with a teaspoon. Cut the flesh into fat chunks. Peel the cucumber, remove the seeds and cut the flesh into chunks, but smaller than those of the melon. Toss the melon and cucumber gently with the dressing. Wash the watercress, trimming off only the toughest stalks, then add it to the melon.

Divide the melon and watercress between two large plates or salad bowls, leaving any extra dressing behind in the bowl.

Season the crab meat with a little salt and black pepper, then pile it on top of the melon and watercress. Add the remaining mint leaves and eat straight away, whilst all is well chilled and before the salad becomes wet.

Enough for 2 as a main dish

Strawberry mascarpone tart

Pastry hates a hot kitchen. I decide not to make a pie crust base for a strawberry tart but to make one from cookie crumbs, like the base of a cheesecake. Except that I want it to be more crumbly than the average cheesecake bottom, which can vary from the rock hard to the downright impenetrable. This is to be a crust that collapses at the merest pressure from your fork, then sticks to the cream filling in fat, pebbly crumbs. Graham crackers will work, but something softer and with a more open texture will give the consistency I am hankering after, especially if you put in less butter than usual. Posh cookies, the sort that come in boxes rather than bags, are probably the best. If they are almond or orange, then all to the good. It is hard to think of a more easily made tart than this.

egg – 1 large
superfine sugar – a generous tablespoon
mascarpone cheese – $1\frac{1}{4}$ cups
vanilla extract – 2 drops
strawberries – $\frac{1}{2}$lb

For the crumb base:
butter – 6 tablespoons
almond, orange or sweet oat cookies – 9oz

You will need a rectangular tart pan with a removable bottom. I used a long, thin one, 14 x 5in, but you can make it in something shorter and wider if that is what you have.

For the crumb base, melt the butter in a small saucepan. Crush the cookies to a coarse powder. A food processor will do this in seconds or you can put the cookies in a plastic bag and bash them with a rolling pin. Do it gently or the bag will split. Thoroughly mix the crumbs with the butter. Spoon the crumbs into the tart pan and smooth them into

the corners and up the sides. Press firmly, but not so hard that they become compacted. The cookie base is better when short and crumbly. Refrigerate till the base has set.

Make the filling. Separate the egg, put the yolk in a bowl with the sugar and beat for a few seconds until thoroughly mixed. Beat in the mascarpone till you have a custard-colored cream. Stir in a little vanilla extract; a couple of drops should be enough. With a clean whisk, beat the egg white till it stands stiff, then fold it into the creamed mascarpone.

Spoon the mascarpone into the cookie crust, spreading it smoothly right out to the edges. Hull the strawberries, slice them thinly, then arrange them on top of the mascarpone. Keep cool, removing the tart from the refrigerator a good twenty minutes before serving.
Enough for 6–8

June 25
A bag of cherries

The cherries are as juicy and plump as I can ever remember them. Must be all that rain. So far I have resisted every call to make cherry pie, cherry cobbler or cherry tart, instead eating the shirt-staining fruit straight from the bag. The nearest I have got to cooking them is to pit a few of the deepest-claret-colored fruits and scatter them over a salad of Little Gem lettuce and folds of thinly cut English ham. It was all right, but not as good as the cherries eaten straight from the paper bag.

June 28
Rice with spinach, and a shining compote of summer berries

A simple supper of freshly cooked white rice into which I fold a pile of lightly cooked spinach (wash, then pile still-wet spinach into a deep pot, cover and put it over the heat for a minute or two to cook in its own steam, then drain and lightly chop) scattered with toasted pine nuts and the smallest amount of grated nutmeg. Pure and green and perfectly nice enough if you cook the spinach only till it is bright green, and are generous with the toasted nuts, salt and pepper.

A warm summer fruit compote

Few summer desserts are as beautiful as this shimmering red compote. The berries soften and a few of the currants burst; their juices glow ruby red and give a rich, deeply flavored syrup.

loganberries – 3 cups
red or white currants – 2 cups
superfine sugar – 2–3 tablespoons
crème de Cassis – 3 generous tablespoons

Hull the loganberries, pull the currants from their stalks and rinse gently. Put the fruit into a stainless steel saucepan, add the sugar and the crème de Cassis, then bring slowly to a boil. Turn the heat down to

a slow simmer, cover with a lid and leave to cook gently for seven to ten minutes. Taste the syrup; it should be only slightly sweet. Serve the fruit warm, without cream, in all its glistening beauty.
Enough for 4

Off to the Spanish deli in Exmouth Market for ham, olives and some fat dried *judión* beans for a salad for next week. I come back not just with carefully packed layers of thinly sliced serrano ham (and sardines, three sorts of olives and smoked paprika in a red can) but also with a single slice of ham the thickness of a shoe sole. I dice it and cook it with some clams from the fish shop. It turns out to be an absurdly fast supper of deep smoky-fishy flavors, light though not insubstantial. A sound supper for a cool, rainy summer evening.

June 27 Clams and Spanish ham

Clams with ham and sherry
Clams always look good served in small, deep bowls, like teacups. Put a plate in the center of the table for everyone to dump their shells on. You might want a bit of bread to mop up the juice.

small clams – 2¼lbs
olive oil
garlic – 2 cloves
diced serrano ham or pancetta – 5 tablespoons
dry sherry – a wine glass full
flat-leaf parsley – a small bunch

Wash the clams thoroughly, discarding any that have broken shells or fail to close when you tap them against the sink. Heat a thin film of oil in a deep saucepan with a lid, add the peeled and chopped garlic, then, before it has time to color, add the diced ham. Move the ham and garlic around the pan from time to time, letting it color, then, once all is golden and sizzling, throw in the clams and the sherry. Cover with a lid and leave to cook for two or three minutes, till the clams have opened. Chop the parsley roughly and toss it in. Check the seasoning – it may need black pepper but not salt – then divide between six small, warm bowls.
Enough for 6

july

Red mullet with lemon
and rosemary

Strawberry water ice

Roast lamb rolls with
oregano and garlic

A soup of roasted
summer vegetables

A lunch of baked tomatoes

A supper of grilled mackerel
and more tomatoes

Zucchini cakes with
dill and feta

Peach and blueberry
sour cream cobbler

A refreshing salad
for a hot day

Melon sorbet

Baked salmon

Nigel's delightful trifle

Roast tomatoes with anchovy
and basil

Saint-Marcellin with tomatoes
and basil

Lamb-filled flatbread

July 1
A new farmers' market and a basket of loganberries

I avoid my local street market with its stalls of cut-price CDs and big pants. The sort of market that sells imported cherries at the height of the Kent cherry season and boxes of wizened satsumas in July. The only stall worthy of more than a cursory glance is the banana table, a small stand of fruit at every level of ripeness from acid green to black and seeping. There is usually the perfect fruit to suit your taste. Which in my case means long, thick fruit without blemish, fruit that banana aficionados would no doubt consider unripe. I know ripe bananas taste richer but I find truly ripe bananas too sweet, almost verging on sickly.

Yesterday, the Arsenal T-shirts and pre-packed meat stalls were joined by a small contingent of farmers' trestles – five or six of them set out with local produce picked that morning. There were lettuces with their cut stalks still beaded with milky sap; tomatoes whose warm, herbal scent you could detect from a foot away; bags of freshly picked spinach, black-leaf kale, and ruby chard so fresh it still had the dew on. There were baskets of gooseberries and redcurrants; beets with a tuft of blood-veined leaves (to be steamed like spinach); and summer cabbage so crisp and fresh it squeaked when you touched it.

Best of all was a stall with rare pink currants sitting like jewels in a tiny casket, and another of loganberries, the fruit's rich juices already staining the bottom of the carton in claret-colored blotches. Had this been the Sunday market further down the road I could have bought a carton of unpasteurized Jersey cream to go with them. As it was, I picked up a tub of organic cream from the deli.

Tart red fruit, silky yellow cream, a summer treat beyond measure.

July 2
A baked red mullet and a vivid scarlet water ice

To Notting Hill and the fish market at Kensington Place. The fish you see on the ice here, with its eyes sparkling and scales glistening like mother of pearl, is as good as it gets. Sometimes, once you have chosen your wing of skate or wild sea bass, the assistant goes into the vast fridge behind the counter, rummages around and brings out other beautiful specimens for you to inspect. They then wash, gut and fillet, if you wish, and pack your purchases in heat-sealed foil bags so that none of the fishy juices escape in your car. At Kensington Place you walk out of the shop with a smart bag complete with fishy logo. Like leaving my local fish market, you walk out thanking God such a shop exists.

I bought red mullet today. Pink, actually. It is the large, juicy flakes of fish that appeal so much here. I always find you need one large fish per person, or two smaller ones. This sounds a lot, I know, but trust me when I say they have quite big bones. I asked the fishmonger to gut but not head the little fishes, so that I can serve them whole, their pink skin crisped and salty from the grill.

Red mullet with lemon and rosemary

large red mullet, cleaned but with the heads left on – 4
garlic cloves – 2
rosemary – a couple of bushy sprigs, chopped
olive oil
a lemon, halved

Heat the broiler. I find the one in the oven is actually easier for this particular fish. Rinse the mullet, pat them dry with kitchen towels and lay them snugly in a stainless steel pan. Peel the garlic, then mash it in a mortar and pestle with half a teaspoon of salt, the rosemary leaves and enough olive oil to make a thin paste. Rub this over the fish and leave for fifteen minutes or so. Longer will not hurt. Broil the fish till the skin has crisped in places and the flesh will come easily from the bone when pulled. Plate the fish whole, with the lemon squeezed over at the table.
Enough for 4

A simple tomato salad
Nothing sits better with red mullet than a tomato salad. This time I slice two large tomatoes per person quite thickly and add just the merest smidgen of olive oil and black pepper.

Strawberry water ice
The deeper flavor and vivid red juice of the small, late-ripening strawberries make them a good candidate for a water ice. I pick up two baskets of tiny, meltingly ripe berries today, one to eat with yogurt in the morning, the other for a sorbet to follow the salty, herbal mullet. A scarlet sorbet of the purest flavor.

superfine sugar – ½ cup
water – ½ cup
ripe strawberries – ½lb
the juice of half a lemon

Put the sugar in a saucepan with the water and bring to a boil. You can remove it from the heat as soon as the sugar has dissolved. Set aside to cool.

Rinse and hull the strawberries, then process them in a blender or food processor till smooth. Add the lemon juice, then stir the strawberry purée into the cold sugar syrup. Now either pour the mixture into an ice-cream machine and churn till frozen or pour into a freezer box and place in the freezer. Leave for a good couple of hours, then remove and beat the freezing edges into the middle with a whisk. Refreeze for a

further two hours, then beat once more, again bringing the ice crystals from the outside into the middle. Return to the freezer till firm.
Enough for 4–6

The butcher had a few small legs of South Downs lamb yesterday. I bought one for today's roast. One of a neat size that will do for four of us, but with a little left over for the day after.

**July 4
Oregano
and a lunch
of roast lamb
sandwiches**

The oregano in the garden is in its third year and just about to come into flower. Even with this summer's rain, the scent from the leaves is as strong as I have ever known it. Rub a leaf between your fingers and close your eyes. Suddenly you are in Greece, on a mountain slope white with rocks, and underfoot are wiry clumps of wild marjoram.

Made into a rub with olive oil and garlic, the leaves give a soft, aromatic note to the meat and in particular to its fat. Mixed salad leaves are what we are having on the side, just a few leaves to melt in the heat of the meat and its juices.

One of the bakers at this morning's farmers' market had some soft white rolls, their pale crust freckled with sesame seeds. Few breads would be nicer with the roast lamb, the spongy dough soaking up the lamb's herb-enriched juices. So what was going to be a semi-formal Sunday roast for four suddenly becomes an informal lunch, eaten outdoors, with me carving somewhat badly and everyone piling wafer-thin slices of rose-pink meat into flat, fluffy rolls.

Roast lamb rolls with oregano and garlic

a small leg of lamb

For the rub:
garlic – 4 cloves, peeled
anchovy fillets – 6, rinsed
a small palmful of oregano leaves
olive oil – 7 generous tablespoons

To make the rub, crush the garlic with a little salt under the flat of a knife blade, then scrape the resulting slush into a small bowl. Chop the anchovies very finely, then stir them into the garlic, along with the oregano and a grinding of black pepper. Beat in the olive oil with a fork or small whisk.

Lay the lamb in a roasting pan and massage with the herbal rub, making sure to get into the exposed flesh as much as you can. Set aside for at least half an hour, or longer if possible.

Set the oven at 400°F. Roast the lamb for fifteen minutes per pound plus an extra twenty minutes. This will give you meat that is pink inside. Before carving, let it rest for fifteen minutes in the switched-off oven with the door open (unless there are kids around, in which case I leave it on top of the stove, a piece of foil placed lightly over it).

When the meat has rested, carve it thinly, then pile up the slices in the soft white rolls, adding a few salad leaves and a dribble of the pan juices. Tuck in.
Enough for 4, plus leftovers

Dark red cherries and a goat cheese

Chalk-white cheeses with a mild tang are flattering to sweet cherries. We finish our meal with a pure white log of goat's cheese, a *buchette de Banon*, a single sprig of dried savory embedded in its thin crust. And with this faintly piquant *chèvre*, a vast bowl of late-season English cherries, their juices staining the white cheese as we eat and finish the cheap pink wine we have poured with the lamb.

**July 7
A melon
from France**

There are foods you only really appreciate on hot, bright days, such as Charentais, those jade-green, orange-fleshed melons from France. My greengrocer has a box, for once in perfect condition. So often you see them past their best, dented and bruised at the greengrocer's or rock hard and unyielding in the supermarket. You should treat a Charentais with the same tenderness you would a tiny baby, and with the same awe and wonder, too. I bring the fruit home.

An air-cured French ham such as Bayonne is a delight with a melon like this. Salty ham and drippingly sweet fruit – a lunch of quiet perfection. One of those meals to make only when you have found a melon that is fragrantly, blissfully ripe. I have, so that is lunch today, a plate of dark maroon-colored ham and fruit that is a gift from the gods.

a ripe Charentais melon
thinly sliced Bayonne ham – 8–10 slices

Cut the melon in half and remove the seeds and pulp, but try to lose as little juice as possible. Cut the flesh into four pieces, then cut the flesh away from the rind. Sometimes I am so worried about losing any more of the precious juice than necessary that I let everyone remove their own rind as they eat. Divide the pieces of melon between two plates and lay the strips of ham alongside.
Enough for 2

**July 10
A soup of
roasted
summer
vegetables**

A dish of roast vegetables – onion, tomato, eggplant, zucchini and anything else that roasts sweetly – turns up time and time again in my kitchen. It is useful to have around as a salad or a pasta sauce but if neither sauce nor salad fits the bill, then I use the melange of roast vegetables for a summer soup. This is something that needs only olive oil and Parmesan to finish. From time to time I add pasta, too.

Today I have to get rid of a whole heap of vegetables that arrived with the organic bag and need using. There are also a couple of zucchini that I want to pick from the garden before they turn into big squashes.

tomatoes – ½lb
a medium onion
small summer carrots – 2 or 3
a small bulb of fennel
garlic – 2 large cloves
olive oil – 3 generous tablespoons
a medium zucchini, thickly sliced
hot vegetable stock (vegetable bouillon powder is fine) – 5½ cups
bay leaves – 2
small dried pasta – 1 cup
the tight heart of a summer (pointed) cabbage
Parmesan cheese – about 1oz
a small bunch of basil – about ¼ cup
extra virgin olive oil, to serve

Set the oven to 425°F. Remove the stalks from the tomatoes and discard them, then put the tomatoes in a roasting pan. Peel and roughly chop the onion, then slice the carrots into short lengths, halve and slice the fennel and add all to the tomatoes. Peel the garlic and slice it thinly, then toss it with the vegetables and the olive oil. Roast for forty to forty-five minutes, till the vegetables are soft and pale gold.

Tip the vegetables into a deep saucepan, add the thickly sliced zucchini and pour over the stock. Season with salt, pepper and the bay leaves. Bring to a boil, then turn down to a simmer and leave to cook for twenty minutes.

Bring a large pot of water to a boil, salt it and add the pasta, letting it cook until it is tender but still has some bite – probably about nine minutes or so.

Shred the cabbage, grate the Parmesan, tear the basil into pieces. Check the seasoning of the soup, then stir in the cooked and drained pasta, the cabbage and half the basil. Continue to simmer for five minutes or so.

Ladle into warm bowls, spoon over a little extra virgin olive oil, then scatter over the remaining basil and the grated Parmesan.
Enough for 4–6

**July 12
A lunch
of baked
tomatoes**

I wake to find that the tomato plants outside the back door have flopped over in the early-morning rain. When I lift them up, I discover a bunch of shiny green fruit hidden under the leaves. Further attempts to tie the wayward plants to their sticks reveal a whole series of bunches, green, healthy and in good condition. There are bundles of tiny Gardener's Delight, like emerald-green cherries, knobbly Marmande and lightly ridged Costoluto Fiorentino, a good dozen of them, all peeping out through the hairy, matte-green branches.

By the time I have finished securing the plants and snipping off any leaves smothering the fruit, my hands reek of their sap – warmly aromatic and peppery. A smell five times that of the most fragrant shop-bought tomato. I go on sniffing my hand right through breakfast, which today is a croissant with neither jam nor butter and, as usual, two espressos.

At the shops I get carried away buying sacks of tomatoes, some tiny and green shouldered, others striped red and orange, and a few perfect oval fruits, which I admit are nothing till they are cooked. On my return I leave some in their paper bags to ripen a little more whilst I bake the largest with rosemary from the garden and grated Spenwood from Neal's Yard Dairy, a sort of English Parmesan.

medium tomatoes – 6
garlic – 2 cloves
a bushy branch of rosemary
olive oil
freshly grated Spenwood or Parmesan cheese – 3 generous tablespoons

Set the oven to 400°F. Slice the tomatoes in half horizontally and lay them snugly in a shallow baking dish. Peel and crush the garlic, finely chop the rosemary leaves, then scatter them both over the tomatoes, together with a good grinding of salt and pepper. Pour over a little olive oil – each tomato should glisten with oil – and bake for twenty-five minutes.

Remove the tomatoes from the oven, dust thickly with the finely grated cheese and bake for a further fifteen minutes, till the cheese is golden and has formed a thin, crisp layer on top of the tomatoes.
Enough for 2–3 as a side dish

A supper of grilled mackerel and more tomatoes

Strong, bright flavors here. I don't think there is any point in eating mackerel unless you are prepared to make the most of its strident notes and broil or roast it till the skin starts to singe. The smack of lemon juice with the crisp skin is stunning.

whole mackerel, cleaned and filleted – 2
olive oil
ripe tomatoes – 4

For the dressing:
fresh thyme leaves – a generous tablespoon
a small garlic clove, peeled
olive oil – 5 tablespoons
the juice of a large lemon

Salt and pepper the fillets, oil them lightly and lay them skin-side up on a broiler pan. You can save a great deal of washing up by lining the tray with a piece of aluminum foil first. Put the mackerel under a hot broiler and let its skin color and catch a little. The smoky results will add to the robust flavors of the mackerel and thyme.

Put the thyme leaves in a mortar and pestle and pound them with the garlic clove and a good fat pinch of sea salt. Mix in the olive oil and lemon juice.

Slice the tomatoes thinly and season with black pepper and a small amount of salt.

Check the fish for doneness, then lift it on to warm plates. Pour the dressing over the hot fish and serve with the tomato salad.
Enough for 2

July 13
Roast garlic,
a raw milk
Wensleydale,
a Kentish
loaf, Italian
nectarines

Roasted in its skin with a little olive oil, the garlic has taken on an unusual spiciness (I use the recipe in *Real Food*). I put the dish on the table and we pop each caramel-colored clove out of its skin with our fingers and thumbs, then we squish the warm garlic on to hunks of sourdough baguette with a crumb or two of soft, young Wensleydale. With a dish of watercress, undressed out of laziness, the effect is peppery, tempered only by the mild, nutty cheese. The nectarines are from the supermarket and eaten chilled from the fridge. Juicy and refreshing after the garlic, but I'd rather have had a peach, with its young, soft fuzz, like a teenager.

July 15
Zucchini
from the
garden

Two zucchini plants stand either side of the kitchen doors in terracotta pots. Each morning for the last three weeks they have greeted me with open yellow flowers the size of a hand, like huge golden birds squawking to be fed. Today there are four fat zucchini too. It's not often you get the chance to use a zed. Anyway 'zucchini cakes' sounds too naff to describe the crisply tender little patties I had for supper, with their salty green flavor and moreish quality. Two of us ate three apiece and I wouldn't have minded a fourth.

Zucchini cakes with dill and feta

zucchini – 3 large ones (about 1lb)
salad onions – 4 (or a medium onion)
olive oil
garlic – 1 clove
all-purpose flour – 3 generous tablespoons
large egg – 1
feta cheese – ¼lb
dill – a small bunch, chopped
a coarse, fine-quality chutney, to serve

Coarsely grate the zucchini into a colander, sprinkle lightly with salt and leave in the sink for half an hour or so.

Chop the onions finely and warm them gently with a little oil in a shallow pan. They should soften but not color. Pat the zucchini dry with paper towels or wring them out lightly in your hands. Peel and chop the garlic and stir into the onions with the zucchini. When all is soft and starting to turn pale gold, stir in the flour and continue cooking for a couple of minutes or so, with the occasional stir, to cook the flour. Beat the egg lightly and stir it into the onion mixture, then crumble in the cheese and the chopped dill. Season with black pepper and a little salt.

Heat four tablespoons of olive oil in a shallow pan, drop heaped tablespoons of the mixture into the hot oil and let them cook until they are golden on the underside. Turn carefully – they will be fragile – and cook the other side. Lift the cakes out with a spatula and drain briefly on paper towels. Serve with the chutney.
Makes about 6. Picture on previous page

A hot dessert for summer

You dare not ask my greengrocer if something is ripe. To do so is to risk having to watch his testing technique. A wincingly painful scene that involves pressing his thumb so hard into a peach, an apricot or a melon that it leaves a lasting dent in even the hardest of fruits. You are better off taking pot-luck. Today he is offering four peaches for a pound. Okay, they are not the biggest you have ever seen but they are meltingly ripe, their skin a short fuzz of darkest crimson. There are the first of the dusky Dorset blueberries, too.

July desserts are, as a rule, eaten cold: gooseberry fool, Eton Mess, strawberry fool, summer pudding. I could go on. Many of the richest summer fruits lend themselves to being served warm, when their deep, honeyed sweetness or tart edge becomes even more pronounced.

The American cobbler, so beloved of Shaker bakers, is one summer dessert I usually file under 'overrated', the dessert's scone-like

topping seeming somehow too heavy and bland for the warm fruits below. Today I have mastered it, tweaking the traditional recipe to give a topping that is much lighter than the norm. I have upped the rising agent, lowered the sugar and swapped the heavy cream for the sharper notes of sour cream. The result is soft, golden fruit streaked with deepest purple and topped with light cobbles of sweet dough. You might want some crème fraîche or vanilla ice-cream to serve with it.

Peach and blueberry sour cream cobbler

ripe peaches – 3
blueberries – 3½ cups
the juice of a lemon
superfine sugar – a generous tablespoon
all-purpose flour – a generous tablespoon

For the cobbler crust:
all-purpose flour – 1½ cups
a pinch of salt
baking powder – 2½ teaspoons
superfine sugar – 1 gently heaped tablespoon, plus extra for sprinkling
butter – 6 tablespoons
sour cream – a small container (4oz)

Set the oven to 400°F. For the cobbler crust, put the flour, salt, baking powder, sugar and butter in a food processor and process for a few seconds, until the mixture resembles soft, fresh breadcrumbs. Tip into a bowl.

Slice the peaches, pulling the stones out as you go and dropping the fruit into an oven-safe dish. Toss the sliced peaches with the blueberries, lemon juice, sugar and flour. At this point it will look less than inviting, but don't worry.

Mix the sour cream into the crumb mixture. You will have a soft dough. Break off walnut-sized pieces and flatten them lightly. Lay them on top of the fruit. Dust the rounds of dough with sugar, then bake in the preheated oven for twenty-five minutes, till the cobbler is golden and the fruit is bubbling.
Enough for 4

**July 16
Shopping
for melons**

Shopping in a foreign market, the rue de Seine in Paris, say, or the sprawling markets of Nice or Florence, you will catch the occasional waft of ripe melons. Sweet as Sauternes and thick as honey, it is a smell to walk through, rather than one by which to linger and inhale. It hangs still and heavy on the air. A smell of high summer.

Here, few people sell their melons truly ripe, and when they do it is usually small greengrocers rather than major supermarkets, who must find such tender, potentially troublesome cargo a worry to have on their shelves. British shoppers are left to bring their melons to perfection themselves.

Today at Borough Market, there are boxes of jade-green Charentais and craggy cantaloupe. I pick up three Charentais, heavy for their size, two cantaloupe the size of small soccer balls, some raspberries and a bunch of scarlet runners – the first of the year.

At home, the melons go straight into the larder to sit on the marble shelf, where they will be subjected to a daily ritual of turning and sniffing. Listen, some people make a big fuss over choosing their wines, I get a buzz out of bringing fruit to its point of perfection. I do it with mangoes, papaya and pears, too. Okay. So I am a ripeness geek, there are worse things to be.

One of the melons I bought at Borough Market on Friday is ripe, the criss-cross of rough 'netting' on its green skin heavily pronounced, feeling like unglazed pottery as you turn the fruit over in your hand. This fruit is announcing its perfection from six feet away, its honey-and-cream scent filling the little larder.

**July 19
A refreshing
salad for a
hot day**

The heat means we can get away with a salad of melon, ham and milky mozzarella this evening – but only because there are fat hunks of thick apricot tart from a posh new takeaway food shop that opened in the High Street this week. Robust Mediterranean cooking in a cool white room.

lemon juice – 2 tablespoons
olive oil – 5 tablespoons
cantaloupe melon – 1 medium
Parma ham – 6 slices
buffalo mozzarella – 6 baby or 1 large ball
flat-leaf parsley – a few bushy sprigs
arugula – $1/2$–$3/4$ cup

Mix the lemon juice and olive oil together and season lightly with salt and pepper. Cut the melon into thick slices, then remove and discard the seeds, retaining as much of the juice as possible. Cut the flesh into large chunks – they should be a bit bigger than bite-sized if the salad isn't to look muddled – and drop them into a bowl. Tear or cut the ham into wide strips. Break the mozzarella in half or, if you are using a large ball, cut it into thick slices. Add all to the melon. Chop the parsley, toss gently with half the oil and lemon dressing, then toss the melon mixture in it.

Wash and shake dry the arugula leaves, then dress them with the remaining half of the oil and lemon. Divide them between two

large plates. Tuck the melon salad amongst the arugula leaves and serve immediately.
Enough for 2

I want the last of the melons out of the larder. On a passing breeze in the South of France, its rich perfume would be heavenly; locked inside my little pantry it is cloying and not altogether pleasant. Crushed, its flesh beaten with sugar syrup, it makes one of the most sublime sorbets of all, subtle, elegant, enchanting.

July 20
Melon sorbet

superfine sugar – ½ cup
water – ½ cup
melon – a large cantaloupe or 2 Charentais
the juice of a lemon

Put the sugar and water in a small saucepan and bring to a boil. Avoid any temptation to stir it. Remove the syrup from the heat as soon as the sugar has dissolved, even if the water is nowhere near boiling. Let it cool, then refrigerate.

Cut the melon in half and, losing as little of the juice as possible, scoop out and discard the seeds. Put the flesh and juice into a blender and process to a smooth purée. Stir in the sugar syrup.

If you have an electric ice-cream machine, pour the melon mixture into it and let it churn as normal. If you prefer to do it by hand – in which case you won't get such a smooth finish – then scoop the mixture into a plastic container, cover with a lid and put it in the freezer. Check after an hour or so that the mixture is freezing around the edges. Bring the frozen edges into the middle with a whisk, return it to the freezer for a further hour, then do the same again. Continue like this until the sorbet is almost frozen. How long it takes will depend on your freezer but it should be at least four hours. Serve in chilled bowls.
Enough for 4–6

Picked up some Cornish new potatoes, skins and soil intact, organic certification on the bag. Served the nutty, buttery, earthy little spuds as a main dish with a bowl of crème fraîche from Neal's Yard and lumpfish roe from a jar. Yum.

July 21

Arms red and tingling from the sun and sea air. We have huge, kite-sized pieces of flounder in batter, with lemon and thick fried potatoes, eaten on the beach. Worth the wait, the drive there and the drive back home in the dark with the windows open and the music on too loud.

July 23
A quick trip to the seaside

**July 24
Dinner for
six. Baked
salmon and
a black-
currant
trifle**

Six for dinner. I sometimes feel like a cooking machine. We start with a salad of tiny French beans boiled briefly, then plunged into iced water, their color glowing emerald in the colander. Drained and tossed with Tuscan olive oil and slices cut from a large log of soft, crumbly goat cheese. Green and white and simple on cool, white plates.

For our main course there is cold wild salmon. A vast piece rubbed with butter, salt and pepper, a handful of fennel stalks and three bay leaves tucked in its belly, tightly wrapped in foil and baked. On the bone, I usually allow fifteen minutes per pound for a fish cooked at 425°F. We eat it in fat chunks with home-made mayonnaise stirred through with finely chopped fennel fronds and the merest drip of Pernod. There are boiled new potatoes served warm (I add mint – a mistake, I think, with the fennel) and a salad of warm green peas tossed with tiny Gem lettuce leaves and, as a last-minute silliness, nasturtium flowers from the garden. A picture. To follow, a trifle so divine that I wish I had made two, the last one to eat alone, in my bathrobe, at breakfast.

Nigel's delightful trifle

plain sponge cake – 12oz
a large egg, separated
superfine sugar – 2 generous tablespoons
mascarpone cheese – 1 cup plus 2 tablespoons
vanilla extract – a couple of drops
whipping or heavy cream – 1 cup
a few sprigs of blackcurrants and some crystallized violets, to decorate

For the blackcurrant layer:
blackcurrants – 5 cups
water – 5 tablespoons
superfine sugar – 2 generous tablespoons

Pull the blackcurrants from their stalks and put them in a stainless steel pot with the water and sugar. Put them over a low to moderate heat and leave to simmer for seven to ten minutes, until they are starting to burst. Once there is plenty of purple juice, remove the currants from the heat.

Break the sponge into small pieces and push it into the bottom of a large serving bowl. Spoon the hot blackcurrants and their juice over the sponge and leave to cool. During this time the sponge will soak up much of the blackcurrant juice.

Put the egg yolk and sugar in a bowl and mix well, then stir in the mascarpone and vanilla. Whip the cream until it is thick enough to lie in soft folds (rather than stand in stiff peaks), then fold it lightly into

the mascarpone mixture. In a separate bowl, beat the egg white until it is almost stiff, then fold it into the mixture.

Spoon the mascarpone cream over the cool blackcurrants and sponge. You can smooth it flat or leave it as I do, in deep, billowing folds. Refrigerate for a good hour or so before serving, so that the whole thing has time to come together. Decorate with fresh blackcurrants and, if you like, crystallized violets.
Enough for 6

July 25
Tomatoes
in the oven

There is something of a surfeit of tomatoes in the house. Several large, round ones on the vine; a plastic carton of yellow Sungold without their stems (why is it that yellow tomatoes are so often sold without their stems?); and a bag of oval San Marzano, which I bought with the idea of bashing out some tomato sauce, then failed to get round to it. And at the back of the fridge are a couple of slightly wrinkled fruits that should really be chucked out.

This isn't a one-off occurrence. Things often multiply in my fridge while my back is turned. It is usually kiwi fruits and turnips, but right now I have to find a use for more tomatoes than most people would get through in a month. A more organized cook would make sauce and bottle or freeze it. Though if they are so organized, how come they have a glut in the first place? I will roast them. An entire roasting pan of oddball fruits cooked till blistered and softly squishy, dressed with a high-summer vinaigrette, heady with basil, and served with floury, airy ciabatta to sponge up the juices.

Roast tomatoes with anchovy and basil

tomatoes – 2lbs
garlic – 6 cloves
a little olive oil

For the dressing:
small anchovy fillets, rinsed – 6
olive oil – 6 tablespoons
white wine vinegar – 2 generous tablespoons
a good handful of basil leaves

Set the oven to 400°F. Put the tomatoes, still on the vine if you wish, into a roasting pan. Crush the garlic cloves in their skins, so they are flattened but still in one piece. Drop these in with the tomatoes, then trickle over a little olive oil and a very light grinding of salt (the anchovy dressing may mean you need no more than a very little).

Roast for about twenty to twenty-five minutes, until the tomatoes are starting to color and are ready to burst. Meanwhile, mash the anchovies until they are a lumpy paste, then stir in the olive oil, vinegar and basil leaves – torn if they are very large – and a good seasoning of pepper but no salt.

When the tomatoes come out of the oven, toss them immediately in the dressing. Leave to cool to room temperature, then serve with bread or bruschetta to mop up the juices.

**July 26
Saint-
Marcellin
with
tomatoes
and basil**

I couldn't quite roast all the tomatoes yesterday. Without anyone coming over to eat, I would have been eating the same salad for days. I refuse to waste them. Lunch today is a garden affair of sweet-sharp roasted tomatoes, melting cheese and hunks of crusty sourdough bread, a meal for a blazing summer's day. The Saint-Marcellin, a small, softly crusted cheese from the Dauphiné region of France, is pretty much spot-on right now, but any small, creamy cheese will work here.

tomatoes – 4 medium
olive oil
a couple of bushy sprigs of basil
2 small, creamy, easy-melting cheeses, such as Saint-Marcellin

Set the oven to 400°F. Cut the tomatoes in half horizontally and lay them cut-side up in a dish – an earthenware baking dish would be fine. Sprinkle olive oil over them. It should not completely cover the bottom of the dish, just lie in puddles on and around the tomatoes. Crumble over a little sea salt and grind some black pepper over.

Bake for about thirty to forty minutes, until the tomatoes have softened and are lightly browned here and there. Tear the leaves from the basil and scatter them over the tomatoes, then place the sliced cheeses on top of the tomatoes. Inevitably some won't be covered, but it doesn't really matter.

Return to the oven for five minutes or so, until the cheese melts and some of it runs into the oil. Serve immediately, with hunks of crusty bread – a baguette or ficelle would be ideal – to spread the molten cheese and tomatoes on.

Enough for 2 as a substantial lunch

**July 27
A supper
of summer
greens**

The organic bag arrives: new potatoes, vine-ripened tomatoes, two heads of tough and stringy celery, a basket of small, deeply flavored blueberries, the inevitable bananas, which I need like a hole in the head, elegant, black-purple beans with green, juicy insides that snap crisply, as if they were picked no more than an hour ago; rose- and cream-colored peaches, which I will ripen with my usual patience, horrid mealy apples (I genuinely don't know why they bother in July), some slender, earthy carrots, a lettuce so pert and fresh I break off some of the leaves and crunch them as I unpack; a couple of onions and a package of rainbow chard with its yellow-veined leaves and stems of pink, orange and yellow as pretty as a sweet shop. I put it all away the moment it arrives. I have been known not to.

Supper is boiled purple beans tossed in olive oil, which turn out to be more interesting raw. Though in fairness I may have overcooked them. Green salad with a dressing of chopped green olives and slices of crisply grilled pancetta, and a mad dash to the shops for a tub of Rocombe Farm vanilla ice-cream.

July 30
Beets, their
greens and a
little tongue

The greengrocer has young beets, with their tops in fine condition. They are not organic, but as fresh as a daisy. We cut off the tops and cook them quickly in boiling water, then drain, chop and drizzle with oil and the merest pinch of toasted caraway seed. The beets themselves get wrapped in foil and roasted. They take a good hour even though they are only the size of a Christmas tree decoration. Unwrapped, they are sliced and eaten with sour cream, watercress, olive oil and slices of tongue from the butcher.

July 31
Filled
flatbread

Hazy morning, the air silent and heavy. The garden is turning from pink to orange, aflame from midday, when the sun comes over the top of the house and floods the garden with burning light. Montbretia, nasturtiums, Indian Prince marigolds, dahlias, zucchini flowers, hot, eye-watering flowers in bright sunlight line the beds. The tomatoes are ripening, a single eggplant is hanging down from the purple-leaved plant in a deep pot on the back steps. The garden is suddenly a vibrant, vulgar, scorching place to eat.

There are three of us for a meal that started out as lunch but is rapidly becoming dinner. It is so hot that I keep putting off lighting the grill. It is one of those rare, high-summer days when you want to drink rosé. Unfortunately there isn't one around, so instead we drink chilled Gamay, which turns out to be just the sort of fruity, easy-drinking wine you want with the pungent flavors of the lamb. There are loud flavors here, with the spice-encrusted meat, garlic-scented yogurt and the hot smokiness of ground paprika.

Lamb-filled flatbread

coriander seeds – 1¼ teaspoons
cumin seeds – 1¼ teaspoons
black peppercorns – 6
garlic – 3 cloves
olive oil – 3 generous tablespoons
a whole fillet of lamb

For the yogurt:
cilantro – a small bunch
mint leaves – a few sprigs
thick yogurt – 7 generous tablespoons
garlic – 2 small cloves

To serve:
arugula or watercress – 4 handfuls
a few whole mint leaves
a lemon
flatbreads – 4, warmed
a little hot smoked paprika

Grind the coriander, cumin and black peppercorns to a rough powder with a mortar and pestle. Peel the garlic and mash it into the spices with the olive oil. Rub this paste all over the lamb fillet and set aside for an hour or two.

Make the yogurt dressing by pulling the leaves from the herbs and chopping them finely. Stir them into the yogurt. Peel and finely chop the garlic and mix it in. Cover tightly and keep refrigerated till the sandwiches are ready.

Get the broiler, barbecue or a ridged cast-iron grill pan hot. Season the lamb with salt, lay it on the grill and leave to brown nicely – a matter of five or six minutes. Turn and cook till the other side, too, is crusty and the inside a rosy pink. Set aside for a full five minutes to rest.

Toss the arugula or watercress and whole mint leaves with lemon juice. Slice the lamb thickly, then place two or three slices on a piece of warm flatbread, together with a handful of salad and a large spoonful of yogurt. Dust with a shake of paprika and roll up.
Makes 4 stuffed flatbreads

august

Bream with lemon and
anchovy potatoes

Baked eggplant with sheep
cheese and mint

A salad of red mullet
with lime and ginger

Roast tomato soup with
basil and olive oil toasts

Grilled monkfish with
rosemary, served
with garlic mayo

Orange yogurt water ice

Lamb chops with oregano
and tsatziki

Cannellini beans with coppa,
spinach and mustard

Grilled chicken with
lemon and couscous

Grilled zucchini with
basil and lemon

Mozzarella with grilled fennel

Grilled chicken with garlic
and lemon butter

Seared beef with mint
and mustard dressing

Garlic shrimp

Bread and tomato salad

**August 1
Cool
cantaloupe,
roast fish
and ripe
peaches on
a blazing
summer's
day**

There has been a cantaloupe melon in the larder for five days now. Each morning I give it a turn and a sniff, rolling it over and over in my hands. This morning it is as ripe as anyone could wish for. Heavy with juice, it has a dent in one side and won't last another day. There are four of us for lunch, so I pick up some prosciutto to go with the melon. The two ingredients remain my first choice with which to start a summer meal.

Yesterday Steve Hatt had four beautiful bream on his slab, which I got the boys to clean for me, asking for the fish to be left on the bone so I could bake them whole. Then I went in search of a net bag of salad potatoes, which against all culinary laws I intend to bake with the fish. Such tight-textured, waxy potatoes slide to a delightful fudginess in the oven.

The garden is currently full of sweet peas, a tangle of magenta, lilac, white and purple-edged blooms. They look as pretty as a picture in a cream-colored jug. I would never, ever arrange flowers for the table – in fact I sometimes think there should be a law against it – but I do occasionally plonk a bunch unceremoniously in a vase if someone is coming. It is not just a 'guy thing', it is a question of aesthetics. There is nothing pleasing to my eye about a mixture of flowers contorted and contrived into a formal display. But then, I feel much the same about food.

Today there is a jug of sweet peas on the table. This is partly because there will be three garden lovers amongst us, who I know will appreciate their scent, and partly because the more sweet peas you pick, the more seem to appear the next day.

After a bottle of Pinot Grigio (slightly too cold, someone whispers) and some thin slices of fennel-seed-bespeckled salami, one of my guests suggests it is too hot to eat in the sun, so we drag the garden table under the robinia tree. This sends dapples of light over the table, making it look more beautiful than it really is (it is just a piece of wood rescued from a skip), and the meal look cool and romantic.

After the melon and the fish come piles of peaches I bought from the supermarket cosseted in polystyrene. An outrageous waste of packaging but it kept them unbruised, even if I did have to nudge them towards ripeness using the old trick of putting them in a brown paper bag with a ripe banana. Piled high on an oval plate, they look extravagant in the extreme, a glorious celebration of warm, softly fuzzy skin and sweet, amber juice. I didn't tell anyone they had been on special offer.

Bream with lemon and anchovy potatoes

sea bream – 4 whole fish, cleaned but left on the bone
olive oil
a little dried oregano

For the potatoes:
waxy-fleshed potatoes such as Anya or Pink Fir Apple – 2lbs
olive oil – 5 tablespoons
a large lemon
anchovy fillets – 12
vegetable stock – 2 cups

Set the oven to 400°F. Slice each potato three or four times. If you do this lengthways, you will end up with long, elegant pieces. Warm the olive oil in a roasting pan over a moderately hot flame, then put the potatoes in and let them color on both sides. They cook best if you leave them alone for several minutes in between stirring. You want them to be pale gold. Cut the lemon in half, then into thick segments, and add to the potatoes. Add the anchovies, which will appear to dissolve as they cook, and then pour over the stock. Transfer to the oven and bake for fifty minutes, until the potatoes are soft and deep gold.

Lay the fish in a roasting tin and drizzle with a little olive oil, then add the oregano and a mild seasoning of salt and black pepper. Bake in the preheated oven until the flesh will slide easily away from the bone in big, juicy pieces. This will take a matter of fifteen to twenty minutes. Serve with the potatoes.
Enough for 4

August 2

Ruined a perfectly good salad today. It started out as a pleasing jumble of milky buffalo mozzarella, sliced vine tomatoes, basil from the deli in Penton Street whose leaves were as big as lettuce, and some slices of Parma ham. Simple, cool, classic. I should have left it at that. But for some reason I decided to add a bit of blue cheese I had in the fridge (for the record, a few slices of piquant Picos). Don't know what I was thinking of.

A long, blisteringly hot summer's day and frankly I can't be bothered to cook. After ruining my lunch and thanking God that there was only me to eat the result, I spend longer than usual putting together a warm eggplant salad for supper.

Baked eggplant with sheep cheese and mint
I slice a couple of eggplant thickly, brush them with olive oil and season their cut sides with black pepper, crushed garlic and crumbled

dried oregano, then I bake them on a flat baking sheet in a hot oven till tender and soft. A matter of twenty minutes or so. Whilst the eggplant are still warm, I scatter them with crumbled feta from the Turkish shop down the road, toasted pine nuts and some small, fresh mint leaves from the garden, the pointed variety with no hairs. Then I drizzle the result with a little more olive oil. Juicy, silky, nutty and warm, it is good, and enough for supper with some of the flat sesame bread I picked up when I got the feta, but it would have been so much better had I bothered to make some grilled meatballs or lamb burgers to go with it.

August 3
A pink
dinner for
two

The kitchen doors are open wide, large white butterflies chase one another over the fennel, the pyramids of sweet peas, and the oregano that has just come into flower. This is how cooking should always be – a delight for all the senses.

Two of us for supper today and I have very little time to cook. The fish market has small Cornish red mullet, as pretty a fish as you could imagine. I want to do a recipe that usually uses a large mullet per person, so I buy two each and get them filleted. The fish market's boys do it in seconds, perfectly. If I do it, it will look like a kedgeree. Before the fish, a salad of tiny leaves tossed with a little walnut oil, and a scattering of whole, skinned walnut halves, toasted in a dry frying pan until golden. To follow, more meltingly ripe peaches and some decent apricots so ripe they glow like candles.

A salad of red mullet with lime and ginger
A starter should sharpen and excite the appetite. This recipe does exactly that.

white wine vinegar – 4 tablespoons
lime juice – ½ cup (3–4 limes)
lime leaves – 6
a small carrot
a small onion
a small garlic clove
a small fresh red chili pepper, seeded and very finely sliced
palm or brown sugar – 1 teaspoon, more if needed
star anise – 2 whole ones
coriander seeds – 1¼ teaspoons
white peppercorns – 10
black peppercorns – 8
olive oil – 6 tablespoons
red mullet – 2, filleted by the fish market
a small knob of fresh ginger, about ½in long
a little parsley, quite finely chopped

Pour the wine vinegar and lime juice into a stainless steel saucepan. Add the lime leaves, scrunching them slightly to release their fragrance as you go. Scrub the carrot and slice it as finely as paper – you should almost be able to see through it – then peel the onion and slice that similarly. Drop them into the pan together with the garlic, peeled and squashed flat (you just want the merest whiff), the chili, the palm sugar (though you may need to add some more later), the star anise, coriander seeds and white peppercorns. Bring the lot to a boil, add a good pinch of salt and eight black peppercorns, then pour in the olive oil and let the mixture simmer for a minute or two. You want the onion to soften slightly. Heat off, lid on, and leave to settle.

Warm a little olive oil in a non-stick frying pan. Season the red mullet fillets with salt and black pepper and lay them in the hot oil, skin-side down. Cook them lightly on one side – which will mean keeping the heat high and letting them color underneath – then turn them over and let them color on the other side. Lift them from the pan with a spatula and place them in a shallow dish.

Grate the ginger into the marinade and stir in the chopped parsley. Taste it, adding a little more palm sugar if you think it needs it. It should have a kick to it. Spoon it over the fish and leave to cool.

Lift the fish on to plates and spoon over the vegetables and liquor. Serve triangles of rye bread on the side, buttered if you must.

Enough for 2 as a light supper, 4 as a starter

August 7 Smoke, garlic, lemon and salt

My shopping list says 'something for the grill'. Followed by a scribbled note to check I have anchovies, rosemary, garlic, lemons. I don't have any particular meat, fish or vegetable in mind. All that matters are the seasonings, strong, robust, heady. Flavors that, along with the smoke from the grill, give food an unmistakable sense of high summer.

I settle on a fat fillet of monkfish from Rowley Leigh's shop at the top of Kensington Church Street. It costs twenty quid but is meaty and spanking fresh, its pearlized skin glistening on the ice. It will feed four of us.

At home I cut the fish into thick chunks and toss it with lemon and olive oil, anchovies, garlic and needles of rosemary. Covered, it will stay happily in the fridge for two or three hours, maybe longer as the pieces are so big and beefy. On the grill I will let the edges singe, so the flavor of the smoke permeates the fish. Of course, it could have been a fillet of Welsh lamb, a pile of halved eggplant, a bag of long-whiskered shrimp. What matters is the chemistry of fresh air, charcoal smoke, garlic, lemon and salt.

With a tomato soup to start with and a loose, garlicky mayonnaise with the fish, this becomes part of a meal so heady with garlic that they must be able to smell it three gardens away; a hot breeze of August eating.

Roast tomato soup with basil and olive oil toasts

Chilled soups never really do it for me, save for cucumber, which I find elegant, gentle and unmistakably English. But there is no reason why you couldn't serve a robustly flavored tomato soup thoroughly iced on a searing-hot day.

If I am going to serve my soup cold, then I make it early in the day and get it completely chilled. You can never chill a cold soup too much.

deep-flavored tomatoes – 1¾lbs
a red bell pepper
garlic – 2 fat cloves
olive oil – 3 generous tablespoons
vegetable stock – 4–5 cups
basil – a small bunch
French bread for toasting, and some fruity olive oil

Set the oven to 425°F. Cut each tomato into six and put them in a roasting pan. Halve the pepper, pull out the seeds and white core and discard, then cut the pepper into six or so pieces and add to the tomatoes. Peel and roughly chop the garlic, add to the tomatoes and pour over the olive oil. Season generously with salt and black pepper, then roast for forty-five minutes or so, until the tomatoes are soft, their skin lightly blackened in places.

Pour the stock into the roasting pan with the vegetables. Pull the basil leaves from the stems and add them, then bring briefly to a boil on the burner. Remove from the heat and liquidize most, but not quite all, of the mixture in the blender or processor, leaving a good couple of handfuls of tomatoes and pepper behind. Lift out the tomato and pepper and chop finely.

Correct the seasoning of the soup and chill thoroughly. Pile the chopped tomato and pepper in the center of four bowls and ladle the soup around it. Float the toast on top, then drizzle with olive oil.
Enough for 4. Picture on previous page

Grilled monkfish with rosemary, served with garlic mayo

At first I was unsure what I wanted to give everyone with this. Nothing immediately sprang to mind apart from some jelly-ripe tomatoes but we were eating those to begin with. Then I hit on the idea of very lightly cooked samphire, literally one minute in boiling, unsalted water, and lots of lemon juice. I also made a very oily garlic mayonnaise to serve in a big, quivering dollop on each plate.

rosemary – 3 bushy sprigs
anchovy fillets – 4
garlic – 2 large or 4 small cloves
a large lemon
olive oil – 3 generous tablespoons
monkfish fillet – 1¾lbs

Pull the leaves from the rosemary stalks and chop them finely, then tip them into a bowl large enough to take the fish. Rinse the anchovy fillets and smash them to a rough pulp with the flat edge of your chopping knife. Peel the garlic, crush it flat, then smash it to a purée in the same way. Stir together the herb, anchovy and garlic, adding a grinding of black pepper and a little salt. Remember the anchovies are quite salty. Halve the lemon, squeeze it into the other ingredients and slowly blend in the olive oil. You will be left with a green and fragrant slush.

Make certain that the fish market has removed all the pearly membrane from the fish. It is edible, but hardly pretty after cooking. If it wasn't, then peel it away with your fingers. Slice the fish into two long, thick strips, then cut each one into four roughly equal pieces (each person will get two).

Push the fish pieces down into the marinade, turning them over in the oil. It will not cover them. Cover the bowl and leave it in the fridge for a minimum of an hour, maximum of three.

Get the grill hot. Lift the pieces of monkfish from their marinade and set them on the grill. They will take a good five minutes on each side, depending on the heat of your grill, and it is worth checking that they are cooked right through. I am not keen on the fashionable 'raw in the middle' way of cooking fish, but it is up to you.

As the fish comes off the grill, season with more salt and a good squeeze of lemon at the table.
Enough for 4

The garlic mayo:
garlic – 4 plump and juicy cloves
egg yolks – 2 large free-range
olive oil – at least 1¼ cups
the juice of half a lemon

Peel the garlic cloves and put them in a mortar with a large pinch of sea salt. Crush them to a paste, then stir in the egg yolks. You will have a sticky, shiny cream. Now pour in the olive oil, very, very slowly at first, almost drop by drop, stirring as you do, until the mixture starts to thicken. If you get impatient and add the oil too quickly you will never get it to thicken. Believe me.

Once you have a small amount of thickening mayonnaise, you can

turn up the speed a little, adding the oil in a long, thin trickle, stirring all the time. Stop when you have a thick mayonnaise. It need not be so thick you could cut it with a knife, but it should be well on the way.

Squeeze the lemon juice in at the end, still stirring. The color will fade slightly, but the emulsion should be almost crocus yellow.

Orange yogurt water ice

Pale, gentle, refreshing – an antidote to two loud courses. The late-season Valencia oranges are fine for this deeply refreshing ice. It complements any summer fruit, but especially lusciously ripe peaches and apricots. Perhaps the prettiest way to serve it is as I did, the pale orange water ice surrounded by handfuls of the last of the dark red cherries from Kent, still attached to their stalks.

water – 1½ cups
superfine sugar – 1 cup
very finely grated zest of 2 large unwaxed oranges
the juice of 4 medium oranges
the juice of 2 lemons
thick plain yogurt, preferably sheep – ¾ cup

Bring the water and sugar to a boil in a stainless steel saucepan. The sugar only has to dissolve, so remove it from the heat as soon as you can no longer see the grains of sugar when you (gently) stir it. Mix in the grated orange zest and set aside to cool.

Mix the juices together. In a large mixing bowl, stir a little of the juice into the yogurt to loosen it, then add the cooled sugar syrup and the rest of the juice and mix thoroughly. I use a whisk for this.

Pour into your ice-cream churn and freeze according to the manufacturer's instructions. Alternatively, pour the mixture into a freezer box and place in the freezer. Remove after two hours and whisk the mixture firmly with a balloon whisk or electric hand mixer, bringing the frozen edges into the middle. Now return it to the freezer for a further two hours, then repeat the whisking and freeze again. When it is well on the way to freezing, after about a further two hours – beat the mixture one last time, then freeze again.
Enough for 4

**August 9
Fried
potatoes
and the rest
of the
mayonnaise**

The sun is so hot I cannot cross the stone slabs of the terrace in bare feet. I have absolutely no intention of cooking anything much in this heat. Instead I boil some new potatoes in their skins, drain them and cut them in half. I fry them cut-side down in olive oil in a shallow pan till their surfaces are crisp, golden and encrusted, then I drain them on paper towels and serve them with the remains of yesterday's garlic mayonnaise and a couple of bottles of very cold beer.

Oregano always does well in this garden, and it's in flower now. Tall stems that sway in the wind and tangle themselves amongst the deep red French roses, Louis XIV, recommended to me by the photographer Howard Sooley. There are two varieties of oregano here: a pinky-purple-flowered pot marjoram (*Origanum onites*), which flowers profusely and has a good, strong aromatic flavor, reminding me of the scent of grilled meats in the Greek Islands. It is a smell you associate with parched hillsides, sun-bleached rocks and fish cooked over charcoal. The other is a rich, royal purple with a softer, almost delicate flavor and scent. I keep that for the flowers, which I scatter over pale leafy salads of Boston lettuce or mâche, not so much for its taste, but for the shock of seeing acid green leaves and deepest purple flowers, a combination I have always loved in the garden. I see no reason not to bring it to the table.

Lamb chops with oregano and tsatziki

olive oil – 2 generous tablespoons
fresh oregano – a tablespoon or so
lamb steaks or large chops – 4

For the tsatziki:
half a cucumber
thick, plain yogurt – 1 cup
scallions – 2
mint leaves – a handful

Grate the cucumber into a sieve or colander, sprinkle it lightly with sea salt and leave in the sink for half an hour.

Tip the yogurt into a bowl. Finely chop the scallions, roughly chop the mint leaves and stir them both into the yogurt. Squeeze any excess moisture out of the cucumber with your hands, then stir the cucumber into the yogurt. Keep the tsatziki cool until you need it.

Get the grill hot. In a small bowl, mix the olive oil with the oregano and a seasoning of salt and black pepper, then rub or brush it over the meat. Cook the lamb over a hot grill or in a griddle pan. Ideally the outside should be dark brown and sizzling, the fat crisp and the inside of the meat a deep, juicy rose pink. Serve the lamb with the tsatziki.
Enough for 4

It is too hot to eat in the sun, so I drag the garden table under the fig tree. The branches hang low, making little room for more than two to spread out their knives and forks. This coming winter I will prune the oldest branches so that the tree grows up into the air rather than horizontally across the terrace.

There is no breeze. Not even the nasturtiums are swaying on their thin stems. The air is still except for the lazy buzz of fat bees in the zucchini flowers, the last of the roses and the aptly named bee (lemon) balm with its crown of mauve spikes. With the cats sprawled out under the trees, you could be in Tuscany.

Cannellini beans with coppa, spinach and mustard

dried cannellini beans – ¾ cup, soaked overnight in cold water
small, tender spinach (or watercress) leaves – 4 handfuls
thinly sliced coppa or other cured meat – 3oz
basil leaves, the thicker and more pungent the better – a loose handful

For the olives:
extra virgin olive oil – 6 tablespoons
red wine vinegar – a generous tablespoon
smooth Dijon mustard – a generous tablespoon
fresh thyme leaves – a generous tablespoon, chopped
black olives – 4oz

Drain the beans, then cook them to tenderness in a large, deep pot of unsalted boiling water. They will take anything from twenty-five to sixty minutes, depending on their age and size. They are ready as soon as you can easily crush them between finger and thumb.

Whilst the beans are cooking, mix the olive oil, vinegar and mustard with a fork in a small bowl, then whisk in the chopped thyme and some salt and pepper. The dressing will be thick and creamy. Pit the olives, dropping each one into the mustard dressing as you go. When the beans are ready, drain and toss them with the dressing. Set aside for an hour or so for the flavors to marry.

When you are ready to eat, rinse the spinach in cold water and shake it dry, removing all but the very finest stems. Put it into a large serving dish. Peel any shreds of skin from the outside of the coppa, then shred the meat into ribbons the width of thick matchsticks. Put them in with the spinach, separating the strips as you go. Tear the basil into small pieces, scattering it into the dish. Tip the beans, olives and dressing over, fold the ingredients gently together then serve.
Enough for 2 as a light lunch with bread

August 13
White cheese, white bread, olive oil

I break my glasses, lose my watch at the gym and realize that the ripe tomatoes I intended to pick for supper have been sucked to a pulp by the snails. The day ends with me slicing a ball of mozzarella into four, trickling olive oil over it and adding some small thyme leaves in lieu of basil. Ciabatta soaks up the milky, olive-oily juices from the plate. A delight, but it does not quite soak up the whole bottle of wine.

**August 14
Salty
lemons,
children
and charred
chicken**

Kids love to be put in charge of an outdoor grill. Once you have explained the horrors that lie in wait for those who treat hot coals and scorching grill bars with disrespect, they know that they cannot fool around. They seem, or at least the ones I know do, to enjoy being responsible for part of everyone's meal. All you have to do is make sure they don't move the food around too much on the grill, to give it time to take up the flavors of smoke and charcoal. Teaching kids to cook and respect heat is one thing, expecting them to be patient is sometimes another thing altogether.

At this point in the year anything with telltale blackened edges from the grill seems more welcome than something steamed, poached or stewed. Anything in broth is unthinkable. Salt, perhaps because of our instinctive summer yearning for the seaside, also figures more than it does in cold weather. Lemony tastes beckon, too. Salt, lemon, smoke. Summer cooking at its most delectably base.

I have one adult and two kids for an early supper today. The kids are put in charge of the chicken. We make the spicy couscous. I love the way children will eat spicy food nowadays; adventurous, eager, responsible. I am not sure I was ever like that.

I have done a couple of versions of this lemon-scented salad this summer. This one is a quicker, milder, nuttier version, and herby rather than spicy. It's a texture thing: the warm grains, the chargrilled chicken and the little nibs of preserved lemon make it sing in the mouth.

Grilled chicken with lemon and couscous

couscous – 1 cup
stock (vegetable stock is fine) – about 2½ cups
olive oil for brushing
chicken breasts – 2 large, boned
a large eggplant
mint – a large handful
cilantro – a large handful
a lemon
preserved lemons – 2
scallions – 4

Put the couscous in a mixing bowl. Bring the stock to a boil and pour it over the couscous. It should cover the grains by an inch or so. Leave until the couscous has absorbed the liquid.

Oil and season the chicken and grill it on both sides until golden. It should still be tender inside. I like to do this either on a ridged grill pan or over the bars of a grill, but it is good enough cooked under the broiler if that is what you have. Set the chicken on one side to rest.

Slice the eggplant thinly and grill it on both sides. Remove from the heat and dress it immediately with olive oil.

Remove the mint leaves from their stems and chop them roughly, then do the same with the cilantro. Fold them into the couscous with the juice of the lemon. Cut the preserved lemons in half and remove the seeds, then chop the flesh into small dice and mix it into the couscous. Finely slice the white of the scallions and add it to the grain, together with the slices of grilled eggplant and a generous grinding of salt and black pepper.

Divide the couscous between two plates or shallow dishes. Slice each breast into about five thick pieces and lay them on top of the couscous. Enough for 2

The zucchini on the kitchen steps are ripening as fast as I can pick them. I ignore all the crucial information about balanced eating and have nothing other than the vegetables from my little vegetable patch.

August 15
A garden
salad

Grilled zucchini with basil and lemon

The flavors are pure summer, and work splendidly with cold roast meats, grilled fish (especially bream and halibut) and mild, milky cheeses. A splendid antipasto, too.

zucchini – 4 medium
the grated zest and juice of a lemon
olive oil – 3 generous tablespoons
basil leaves – a small bunch

Wipe the zucchini and slice them thinly along their length. Each slice should be no thicker than $\frac{1}{8}$in. Put the slices on the grill and let them brown in stripes on the underside. Turn them over and brown the other side.

Meanwhile, make the dressing. Grate the lemon into a mixing bowl. Do this finely and lightly; any white pith will make the dressing bitter. Beat the olive oil into the lemon juice and zest, then add salt and black pepper. Roughly tear the basil leaves, depending on their size – I tend to leave small ones intact but lightly crushed in the hand to release the oils – then add them to the dressing.

As each slice of zucchini becomes ready, drop it into the dressing and mix gently so that the slices become completely soaked. Set aside for ten minutes for the flavors to marry and the vegetables to soften. Enough for 2

It is as impossible to think of deepest summer without mozzarella as it is to imagine Christmas without plum pudding. But there is mozzarella and there is mozzarella. At the top of the tree is mozzarella di bufala, or

August 16
Mozzarella
days

buffalo milk mozzarella, distinguishable from the pedestrian cow's milk version by its loose, open texture, which seems to quiver like a giant poached egg. As you break open the white ball of curd, its interior falls away in thin strings and pools of milk and whey. It will be as white as a baby's first teeth.

A ball of mozzarella di bufala is unmistakably milky, grassy even. It is said to be at its best in spring and summer; at its freshest it barely deserves to be called cheese. This is its charm when eaten raw (on a plain white plate, please), with perhaps a drizzle of olive oil and a gentle grinding of black pepper. Like doughy English muffins, balls of mozzarella look much more interesting when they are split by hand rather than sliced. The rough edges you get are more pleasing in the mouth.

In my house, this cheese cannot become a fridge basic like the everlasting plastic-wrapped feta that so regularly gets me out of a supper crisis (mash the sharp sheep cheese with olive oil, black pepper, chopped tomatoes and basil leaves and you have an emergency lubricant for pasta). The best mozzarella will only keep for a few days.

After you have released it from the fridge, it is best to let your cheese come to room temperature, when its flavor – that of cool milk, a little salt and a slight lactic acidity – is at its best. Simplicity is essential here. *Insalata caprese,* the classic salad of tomatoes, basil, mozzarella and olive oil, is about as complex as we should probably get.

Mozzarella with grilled fennel

I love this salad for the contrast of the slightly charred grilled fennel and milky, cool mozzarella. I don't even think of buying anything but the very best here. For something so essential to my summer, I go for broke.

medium-sized heads of fennel – 2
olive oil – 5 tablespoons
black olives – 24
flat-leafed parsley – a small bunch
buffalo mozzarella – 2 balls

Get the grill or a griddle pan hot. Slice the stalks and fronds from the fennel bulbs, retaining the fronds (you could add the stalks to stock). Cut the bulbs into thin slices, no thicker than 1/8in. Lay the fennel on the grill, letting it color first on one side then the other. Depending on the heat of your grill, this could take anything up to ten minutes.

Pour the olive oil into a bowl and add the olives. Chop the parsley roughly and add it to the olive oil with a seasoning of salt and black pepper.

Lift the fennel off the grill and drop it into the dressing. Toss gently. Divide the salad between four plates.

Slice the mozzarella thickly, or split it by hand, then lay the pieces on top of the salad. Drizzle over any remaining dressing or add a little more olive oil.

Enough for 4

To follow: a bowl of blackberries and raspberries. No cream, no yogurt, just jewel-like fruits in a pretty bowl.

It is not unusual for the little stone terrace outside my kitchen doors to have a pall of smoke over it at supper time. Sometimes it is smoke from my own grill, other days it is that of my neighbors. Smoke imbued with thyme, garlic and rosemary that wafts around the ripening tomato plants and pots of geraniums. Last year, when the summer was as long and hot as I ever remember it, the aromatic smoke seemed to permeate every stone flag and even the wooden planks of the garden table.

There are four of us tonight. I buy four fat poussins. I have a lemon and some chilis and there is some thyme growing up between the cracks in the stone pavers. There are also some peaches that need eating.

Grilled chicken with garlic and lemon butter

Ask the butcher to spatchcock the chickens for you. He will split them down the middle and flatten them out so that they resemble road-kill. Butchered this way, they can be grilled rather than roasted.

chubby poussin – 4
olive oil
a large lemon
small red or orange chilis – 3–4
garlic – 4 large cloves

For the butter:
young garlic – 2 or 3 cloves
butter – 10 tablespoons, softened
fresh thyme – a small handful
the grated zest of a lemon

Get the butcher to slit the poussins down the backbone and open the birds out flat. Sometimes I do it myself. You just need a large, heavy knife. Lay them in a shallow dish and pour a good three or four tablespoons of olive oil over them, then squeeze the lemon over. Chop the chilis finely, discarding the seeds, then peel and finely chop the garlic. Tip them in with the chicken and season generously with black pepper.

Toss the chicken round in its dish, rubbing the oil and seasonings into the skin. Cover with a plate or plastic wrap and set aside somewhere cool for at least a couple of hours.

To make the herb butter, peel the garlic and chop it very finely, then add it to the butter. Chop the thyme and mash it with the butter, lemon zest, garlic and some sea salt, then set aside. It is best to use it at room temperature rather than straight from the fridge.

Get the grill hot. Whether you are cooking the chicken over or under the heat, you will need the temperature set quite low so that the birds cook right through to the bones before the skin browns too much. Flattened, a healthy poussin should take about twenty to thirty minutes, depending on the heat of your grill. Turn it halfway through. Get a salad ready to go with the birds, preferably one with a good blob of mustard in the dressing.
Enough for 4

We end the meal with Italian peaches that I slice and dampen slightly with lemon juice, which makes their vermilion flesh sing.

August 19
Beer and a
new pizza
place

We try a new pizza delivery place today, whose leaflet has been dropped through the letterbox despite the notice that requests them not to. (An unkind friend once suggested that if someone understands what 'no circulars' means, they are unlikely to be pushing leaflets through doors for a living.) Anyway, a phone call and thirty minutes later sees the delivery of four vast rounds of dough, light, thin and charred in big fat yeasty blisters, with toppings of molten mozzarella, anchovies and hot, deep-red chilis. We drink bottles of ice-cold Peroni round the garden table and do our best to catch every long string of hot cheese as we tear our great pizzas apart.

Later I phone to tell them how good the pizzas were. The woman at the other end sounds so chuffed that someone liked them enough to phone, I half expect her to climb down the phone and hug me.

August 20
Hazelnuts

The greengrocer has the first hazelnuts. Pale, pistachio-coloured leaves hide smooth, faintly furry shells of the softest green-white, so tender you can crack them with your back teeth. The diminutive nuts have a milky sweetness and the smell of a young sapling in spring. I eat about twelve of the little pairs of nuts, then shell the rest for a salad of thinly sliced celery and wafer-thin shavings of chalk-white Ticklemore cheese from Neal's Yard. A picture: cream, white and palest green.

August 22
The first
cooking
apples

One of the flower stalls at the farmers' market has a wicker tray of rare cooking apples hidden amongst the deep black buddleja plants and bunches of red zinnias. Emneth Early, a child of Lord Grosvenor and Keswick Codlin, is a big teapot of an apple, a matte pale green, and appears when nothing is further from your mind than a baked apple. Three of them go in the bag along with the day's baby leeks, Gertrude Jekyll roses, tiny strawberries, eggplant, small, egg-shaped tomatoes and the last of the blackcurrants. In truth, they have seen better days but the currant season is so short you have to make the most of them. There are round squash, zinnias and Czar plums but I resist, pushing away the unstoppable onset of autumn for another week. The bag I take home, with its basil, mint and raspberries, is still very much a portrait of summer. Autumn can wait.

Lunch is a vast salad in the largest of the white bowls. Little Gem, baby chard and something unidentified and frilly which I fear is lollo bianco, tossed with cherry tomatoes, blanched green beans and some late peas. The long, thin beans are the point of it really but I put in some nasturtium flowers too and some torn lumps of white bread fried in olive oil and rolled in salt. A big, bright salad, dressed with olive oil and red wine vinegar for a big, bright day.

We finish with the apples, which have blown up in the oven, their skins split and their flesh like melting snow. As we eat, some drizzling over rivulets of cream straight from the pot, I notice just how many yellow leaves are flying off the robinia tree in the breeze, and suddenly spot that the elderberries overhanging the dahlias are starting to ripen. I still insist on holding on to summer.

August 24 An extravagant supper of rare beef, red salad and cheeses

I am not a fillet kind of guy. Onglet, rump and occasionally sirloin, but never fillet. To my mind, fillet lacks the intense, savory succulence of the other cuts. I never smack my lips after fillet the way I do with a cheaper cut.

But the people coming to dinner tonight are fillet people. I see no reason to push my bourgeois tastes on them, so beef fillet it is. I present it whole, with some majesty, on a long wooden board. Not being used to this sort of thing, I don't have a board long enough, so some of the great piece of meat hangs off the end. I am slicing it thinly, spooning over a creamy dressing flecked with mint and mustard as I go. The accompanying salad is of red leaves – baby chard, red chicory and oak leaf – and I must admit the whole thing is quite sensational. A dish of knobbly salad potatoes, boiled earlier in the day, then sliced and fried till crisp and golden, adds much to the meal. Extravagant in the extreme, but a memorable enough meal with chilled Gamay and some chewy bread. The evening rounded off with a plate of cheeses that I laid out on leaves from the grapevine. I had expected it to look precious and a little too considered. In truth it looks beautiful, especially as the light fades and the garden candles come out.

Seared beef with mint and mustard dressing

black peppercorns – a generous tablespoon
Maldon sea salt – 1 tablespoon
beef fillet (thick end) – 1lb
olive oil
lemon, to serve

For the dressing:
grain mustard – a generous tablespoon
the juice of half a lemon
mint – a small handful (about 20 leaves)
egg yolks – 2
olive oil – about 4–5 tablespoons

Set the oven to 425°F. Crush the peppercorns roughly with a mortar and pestle and mix them with the salt. Rub the beef with a little olive oil, then roll it in the seasoning, pressing down so that most of the salt and pepper sticks to the meat. Warm 2 generous tablespoons of olive oil in a roasting pan placed over the heat. When the oil starts to sizzle, add the meat and brown it quickly on all sides, then roast in the oven for ten minutes only. Remove from the oven and leave to cool.

To make the dressing, put the mustard, lemon juice, mint leaves and egg yolks in a blender and process for a few seconds. Pour in the oil slowly, stopping when you have a dressing the consistency of heavy cream. Slice the beef very thinly, then spoon over the dressing at the table. Pass a cut lemon round for anyone who wants it.
Enough for 4. Picture on previous page

A peaceful and solitary supper of the remaining few slices of last night's rare beef, some of the creamy mint dressing and a couple of orange-skinned tomatoes from the garden. I crumble over a snowstorm of sea salt, which always brings cold meat to life. My hands have the warm, herbal smell of the tomato stems, and as I wipe the dressing off my plate with a piece of not terribly fresh bread I think how much more enjoyable leftovers often are than the real thing.

August 25
Remains
of the day

Six for lunch outside and I want everyone to eat with their hands. Which is my way of saying I want little or no washing up. I buy whole, shell-on shrimp from Mr Hatt, which I will grill and put in the middle of the table with a bowl of butter and some cut lemons. They cost a small fortune. The 'main' dish is cheap belly pork roasted with aromatics, sliced as thin as parchment, then stuffed into soft rolls. It's a hands-on meal, for which I provide finger bowls of warm water with slices of lemon and rose petals in them, and big linen napkins. We drink rosé,

August 27
Six for a
casual lunch
in the sun

lots of it, and some chilled red, and finish up with bowls of warm raspberry and blackcurrant compote. A doddle.

Garlic shrimp

I serve them hot from the grill, heavily seasoned with garlic, with melted butter and salt, piling them in the middle of the table for everyone to help themselves. With everyone tearing off the shells and dipping their shrimp in melted butter and salt, there are few more tactile feasts.

large raw shrimp, shell on – 48
garlic – 5 or 6 large cloves
olive oil
butter – 10 tablespoons
lemons – 2

Rinse the shrimp and put them in a bowl. Peel and finely crush the garlic, then add it to the shrimp with a slug of olive oil. Toss the shrimp to coat them in seasoned oil.

Cook them over the grill or in the broiler till their shells have turned a soft, patchily orange pink. Meanwhile, melt the butter in a small pan. Serve the hot shrimp with the lemons, melted butter and salt.
Enough for 6

To finish, I pile raspberries and blackcurrants into a stainless steel saucepan. Add a sprinkling of sugar and a very little water. Bring them to a boil, then let them simmer till the currants pop. This will keep warm for a good half hour and will also reheat nicely.

August 29 Finnish fungi and simple halibut

My neighbors bring back chanterelles from the market in Helsinki. I cook them in a shallow pan in a little olive oil, salt and a small squashed clove of garlic still in its skin. It gives just the merest breath of itself. The mushrooms are the color of apricots and taste of warm woods and bracken. We eat them with a thick slice of halibut baked with olive oil, lemon and a bay leaf in a very, very hot oven, and some scarlet runners that came in the organic bag and are as crisp as ice. Dessert is apricots, halved, stoned and tossed with slices of watermelon and late strawberries.

August 29 Blazing sun and a tomato salad

There has been much rain over the last few days, floods too, but when it stops and the sun shines, the heat comes in deep, blazing rays. The sort of sunshine that blinds you if you look up, but it also warms your soul. The sort of sun that gives tomatoes the intensity of flavor you find in knobbly, outdoor-grown fruit in Italy. Tomatoes to make your heart sing, vivid red and orange, their flavor sweet-sharp and so juicy the seeds spurt out as you bite.

Bread and tomato salad

Well made, this is a salad of bright flavors, of tomatoes, raw young garlic, basil, olives and anchovy, a jumble of lusciously soft vegetables and crisp, open-textured bread. Few salads are as colorful or as full of flavor – this is a meal for the brightest summer's day. This is not a recipe to get sloppy with: underripe tomatoes, wimpish basil and second-rate oil will end in disappointment. Timing is important here too; this is not something to leave hanging around.

open-textured bread, such as ciabatta – ½lb
tomatoes, ripe and juicy – 1½lbs
a small cucumber
garlic – a fresh, new clove
red or yellow bell pepper – 1
basil – a large bunch
olives – a handful
anchovy fillets – 8
olive oil, something green and peppery – about ½ cup
red wine vinegar – a tablespoon

Set the oven to 350°F. Slice the bread thickly – the pieces should be about ½in thick – and lay them on a baking sheet. Sprinkle each piece very lightly with olive oil and bake for about fifteen minutes, till they are lightly crisp.

Slice the tomatoes, but don't be tempted to peel or seed them. Put them in a large serving bowl. Peel and seed the cucumber and cut it into rough chunks, then add to the tomato. Finely chop the garlic, cut the pepper into small dice and add both to the tomatoes. Tear the basil leaves from their stalks and add them, with the olives, to the bowl. Rinse the anchovies, then mix them in with the salad.

Put the oil and vinegar into a small dish and season with salt – I think you can be quite generous here – and some black pepper. Toss the dressing, bread and salad gently together. Eat before the bread gets too soggy.

Enough for 4

september

A squid in the fryer

A wonderfully moist,
fresh plum cake

Baked mushrooms with
tarragon mustard butter

Grilled squid with
lime and thyme

An almond and
greengage crumble

Mushroom pappardelle

Baked lamb with
tomatoes and rosemary

Roast pork sandwiches

Plum crisp

Zucchini and Lancashire
cheese crumble

A tomato curry

Fresh borlotti with
olive oil and focaccia

September 3
A tomato
for lunch

One of the great joys of this little garden is to walk round in September and pick a handful of raspberries, or snap a green bean and crunch it raw as I walk. Yet nothing quite matches picking a tomato and eating it like an apple. I do this twice today. The first time at about 9.30; the second just before lunch when I bring a large and knobbly Costoluto Fiorentino inside and slice it thinly. No pepper, no oil, a very little salt. No bread either, just a great, fat, gloriously ripe tomato. If only lunch could always be as simple as this.

September 4
A squid in
the fryer

The rule in our house is usually 'bright sunshine – cold food'. Unless it's deep-fried calamari, which for some reason only really works when the sun is in your eyes and you have sand caught between your toes. Otherwise it just tastes like deep-fried rubber bands. I suspect calamari always tastes like deep-fried rubber bands, but the salty sea air and gritty sand season it better than any cook ever could.

I simply slice the cleaned squid into rings the width of a pencil, toss them in flour, then throw them into a little hot oil for a minute. I drain the hot fish and toss it in finely shredded red chili peppers, scallions, cilantro, sea salt flakes and black pepper. We eat it with a crunchy salad of cucumber dressed with soy and sesame oil.

September 5
Corn cobs at
dusk

The corn cobs are piled three feet high at the Sunday-morning market tucked behind Marylebone's main shopping street. Their leaves stick out at right angles, pert and proud, each one sporting a kiss-curl of golden silks peeping out from the green husk. Tug back a leaf or two and there are fat cobs packed tight with plump little kernels of corn. There is little that gladdens the heart of a cook like finding a vegetable in such fine fettle. I buy five for a couple of quid.

In the early evening, I pull back the green leaves of each explicitly firm cob, then pull out the fine corn silks that hide underneath. I then fold back the husk of leaves and wet them under the tap.

They take about twelve minutes apiece on the grill, the canary-colored sweet corn turning deep, buttercup yellow as its protective coat first dries over the coals, then turns black and (annoyingly) flakes all over the place. We eat them, a little too soon to avoid burning our lips, with nothing but salt and the merest amount of black pepper. Even the thinnest smear of butter would seem disrespectful to a supper in such rude health.

Grilling intensifies not the sweetness but the flavor of this vegetable. To me this is important. The new varieties of corn are bred more for their sugar content than for their depth of flavor. So a while over the coals is my preferred way with what could otherwise be a simple sugar-fest.

A feast of plums

It is impossible to remain unmoved by the sight of the local farmers' markets at harvest time. As you approach, shoppers totter towards you hugging their brown paper bags of ripe plums and ears of sweet corn, their faces obscured by bunches of giant sunflowers on long stalks. If you are early, tables are piled high with blackberries, wild mushrooms and yellow squash. There will be bags of scarlet runners and baskets of late strawberries. If you are lucky, you might catch Beth pears barely bigger than crystallized figs (they are grown mostly as pollinators), or greengages on their brief journey from green to amber.

The cherries and gooseberries may be long gone, but there are crates of plums to be had. The Victorias are prolific this year, and I refuse to knock them, as is currently so fashionable, just because they are ubiquitous. Czar (a nineteenth-century cross between Early Rivers and Prince Englebert) is a dark blue plum, better for crumbles than for eating as a dessert fruit. Last weekend I stewed mine with just a modicum of sugar and a few drops of water. We ate the result chilled, with light cream and a slice of toasted panettone. The most luscious fruits I have eaten this year were Macauley plums from Brogdale, the color of honey with a red blush to their cheeks. But then I always find golden or red plums a sweeter eat than the purple varieties, though I wouldn't throw any of them out of bed.

It would be a travesty to leave the market without at least enough fruit for a crumble. As it is, I have bought a basket each of Czar and black and yellow-flushed Opal. Then on my way out, I fall for another of pale greengages and another of Victorias, so richly flavored when left to ripen properly.

The Opals are for dessert – a small, oval plum that eats similarly to a true gage, with the transparent, warmly sweet flesh that you might expect. The Czars and Victorias are for the kitchen: a cake, an almondy tart, a jammy sauce for a slice of shop-bought pecan pie. Hell, I might even make jam. But each needs a couple of days on a sunny windowsill first. A plum is rarely worth eating until you have to shoo the wasps away with a dish towel.

A wonderfully moist, fresh plum cake

butter – 10 tablespoons
superfine sugar – ½ cup plus 1 tablespoon
plums – 16
eggs – 3 large
all-purpose flour – ¾ cup
baking powder – 1¾ teaspoons
ground almonds – ⅔ cup
shelled walnuts – ½ cup

Set the oven to 350°F. Line the base of a square 8-in cake pan, about 2½in deep, with a piece of baking parchment.

Beat the butter and sugar until pale and fluffy. A food mixer will do this far more efficiently than you ever could by hand. I stop only when the mixture is light, soft and the color of vanilla ice-cream. Whilst this is happening, halve the plums, remove the stones and cut each half in two.

Break the eggs, beat them lightly with a fork, then add them bit by bit to the butter and sugar. Sift the flour and baking powder together and fold them gently into the mixture. I do this with a large metal spoon rather than the food mixer. Fold in the ground almonds. Chop the walnuts so they are the size of small gravel and fold them in too.

Scrape the mixture into the lined cake pan. Place the quartered plums on the cake mixture. There is no point in doing this with any real precision as they will sink into the cake as they cook. Bake for forty to forty-five minutes, then test for doneness with a skewer. If it comes out clean, without any wet cake mixture sticking to it, then the cake is ready. Remove the cake from the oven and leave to cool in the pan for fifteen minutes before turning out.
Enough for 12

September 8
A vegetable casserole from the fridge

Did one of those mixed vegetable casseroles tonight that is really a glorified way of cleaning the fridge out. Leeks, peppers, eggplant, tomatoes, zucchini sautéed in that order, seasoned with garlic and thyme, then moistened with tomato passata and cooked slowly with the lid almost on for a good forty minutes. It was okay, but not the supper of my dreams. But it did make me feel better about the vegetables that had collected in the fridge.

September 9
Some great field mushrooms and a waning tarragon plant

There are field mushrooms at the greengrocer's this morning the size of your hand. They are perfect, without tear or blemish, and quite irresistible. I buy four, then look round for something to go with them. I must have lost a dozen or more tarragon plants over the years; each spring I put in another, hoping that this will be the one that lasts forever. Today I notice the leaves curling up in that sad way that says the end is near. It is just what I need for the mushrooms.

Baked mushrooms with tarragon mustard butter

butter – 10 tablespoons
smooth Dijon mustard – 2 generous tablespoons
tarragon – leaves pulled from 8 or 9 stems and roughly chopped
the juice of half a lemon
large field mushrooms – 4
olive oil

Set the oven to 400°F. Cut the butter into cubes and mash it in a small bowl with a wooden spoon. You could use a food processor but I am not sure you really need to. Add the mustard, the roughly chopped tarragon leaves, a few grinds of salt and pepper and the lemon juice, then mix to a thick paste.

Lay the mushrooms in a roasting pan; they can be snug but only barely overlapping. Trim the stalks if they are woody, or even remove them entirely, then fill their hollows with the butter, dividing it more or less equally. Drizzle with olive oil.

Cover the pan with foil or baking parchment and bake in the oven, basting the mushrooms from time to time with the melted butter and pan juices. When they are tender and sodden right through with juice – a matter of twenty-five to thirty minutes or so, depending on their thickness – serve with rice, toast, or sandwiched between two soft buns. Take care not to waste any of the hot herb butter.

Enough for 2

September 11
A squid on the grill

It is not often Mr Hatt fails to have a box of glistening squid on his ice-strewn counter. Invariably at least one will have its long, white tentacles hanging over the side to smear squid-dribble on your coat as you stand in the queue.

Squid's squeaky-clean white flesh, so dull when badly cooked, comes alive when it is grilled and seasoned with sea salt. I have always seasoned grilled fish with either thyme and lemon juice or cilantro and lime. Sometimes rules are for breaking, and today is one instance where I find myself breaking my own. We eat this as a light supper, with bread to mop up the juices from our plates. It is good as a light meal like this, but I could have done with some fried potatoes, too.

Grilled squid with lime and thyme

a large, juicy garlic clove
thyme sprigs – a handful
olive oil – 2 generous tablespoons
cleaned squid (body sacs and tentacles) – 1lb
Maldon sea salt flakes

For the dressing:
the juice of 2 limes
olive oil – 2 generous tablespoons
fresh thyme – the leaves from a couple of sprigs

Peel the garlic and crush it to a paste with a mortar and pestle. Strip the leaves from the thyme and mash them into the garlic with the olive oil to give a smoothish marinade.

Give the squid a good once-over, removing any stray bits of gut or slime the fish man has left behind, and rinse it thoroughly. Shake it dry, then cut each sac down one side so that it opens out flat. Take a very sharp knife and score the flesh on one side in a criss-cross fashion, but not so deep that you cut all the way through. Turn the squid in the marinade and set aside for a good thirty minutes, longer if you can.

Make the dressing in a small bowl or a jar with a screw-top lid by mixing the lime juice, olive oil and thyme leaves together.

Get the grill or a ridged griddle hot. Lay the pieces of squid on the ridges and let it grill for a few seconds on each side. It will probably roll itself up into beautiful white curls. Remove it as soon as it is lightly colored here and there from the grill bars (a matter of just a minute or two). Divide between two plates, tip over the dressing and sprinkle lightly with flakes of sea salt. Eat whilst all is hot and sizzling.
Enough for 2

The greengages seem to be going on forever this year. They arrive with green-gold skins and honey-colored flesh, only to turn almost jelly-like as they ripen. They make one of the juiciest crumbles of all.

An almond and greengage crumble
I know it's a drag stoning plums but I really think you have to here. There is nothing quite so boring as continually having to spit the stones out when you are eating. This isn't cherry pie.

plums, greengages or a mixture – 2lbs
superfine sugar – 3–4 tablespoons, depending on how sweet your fruit is

For the almond crumble:
all-purpose flour – 1¼ cups
butter – 7 tablespoons, cut into cubes
superfine sugar – 5 tablespoons
ground almonds – 5 tablespoons

Set the oven to 350°F. Rinse and stone the plums, removing any stalks as you go. Toss the fruit with the sugar in a deep baking dish.

Process the flour and butter in a food processor until the mixture resembles fine, fresh breadcrumbs, then add the sugar and almonds. Tip on top of the fruit and bake till the fruit is bubbling under the pale, golden crumble – about forty to forty-five minutes.
Enough for 4–6

September 13
An autumnal
pasta supper

Some nights it just has to be pasta. Not out of sloth, but because tender yet substantial ribbons of starch will hit the spot like nothing else. This is one of those nights. A fine autumn day has turned to a chill evening, where the dry leaves are being blown against the windows, whirling and crackling in sudden gusts.

Mushroom pappardelle

I sometimes think I could measure my life in pasta suppers, but the fact is that no other food fits the bill quite so successfully for a weekday supper. Lovely autumnal flavors here, if you let the mushrooms cook until they are nut brown and stickily tender.

portobello mushrooms – ¾lb
butter – 6 tablespoons
olive oil – 2 generous tablespoons
garlic – 2 cloves
dried pappardelle – about ½–¾lb
parsley – 5 bushy sprigs
Parmesan cheese, grated – ½ cup

Slice the mushrooms thinly. Melt the butter in a shallow pan, then add the olive oil and mushrooms. Leave to cook on a moderate heat.

Peel and finely slice the garlic, then add it to the pan with a few grinds of salt and black pepper. Stir the mushrooms from time to time, but it is important to let them color so that all their sweet nuttiness comes out.

Put a deep pot of water on for the pasta. Bring it to a boil, then salt it generously. Toss in the pasta and leave to cook until it is tender but still has a bit of bite to it. This will take about seven to nine minutes, so test it from time to time.

When the pasta is ready, drain it and tip it into the cooked mushrooms. Throw in the chopped parsley and grated Parmesan, continue cooking briefly, then tip into warm bowls.
Enough for 2

Much modern cooking is so exquisitely contrived that the chunky, 'rustic-looking' dish, inelegant and apparently thrown together, is something of a rare treat. This is the food I long for whenever I am presented with a fashionable chef's twee plateful of contorted food drizzled with a ring of 'jus'. The main culprits are hotel chefs, who seem oblivious to the fact that most people who dine out now want proper cooking. Cooking with a heart and soul.

**September 16
A chunky,
inelegant
dish of
baked lamb**

Having suffered a particularly precious hotel dinner last night, I need to be brought back to earth with a robust, loud-flavored plate of food. On the face of it, the dish appears awkward, chucked together even, and in a way I suppose it is. But it is none the worse for all that, and just the sort of casual, hearty food to restore your faith in the pleasures of plain, simple eating.

Baked lamb with tomatoes and rosemary

small potatoes – about 8
plum tomatoes – 4
a large eggplant
onions – 2 medium
garlic – 6 large cloves
olive oil – about 6 tablespoons
rosemary – at least 4 bushy sprigs
lamb – 4 really thick neck chops, at least ½lb each

Set the oven to 400°F. Scrub the potatoes and slice them in half length-ways, then drop them into a shallow oven-safe dish or roasting pan. Halve the tomatoes, again lengthways, and cut the eggplant into short, thick chunks, then add them to the potatoes. Peel the onions and slice them thickly. Peel the garlic but leave it whole. Add the onions and garlic to the potatoes with the olive oil and a good grinding of salt and black pepper. Toss everything together, so that all the vegetables are covered with seasoned oil. Tuck the rosemary, still in large sprigs, amongst the vegetables and bake, uncovered, for thirty minutes.

Rub the lamb chops with a little olive oil and season them thoroughly with salt and pepper. Remove the roasting vegetables from the oven, toss them gently and put the chops on top. Turn the oven up to 425°F and return the dish to the oven for thirty minutes. Test a piece of the lamb; it should be golden brown outside and slightly pink inside.
Enough for 4

Summer seemed to slip into autumn last night and today the garden has a woodsy, almost fungal smell to it. There are six of us for lunch and it's warm enough to eat out of doors if you sit with your back to the glowing autumn sunshine. It's a laid-back sort of affair, the leaves falling on the table as we eat, and the smell of wood smoke drifting across the gardens. There is no starter; we just go straight to the main course of thin slices of roast pork stuffed into soft bread. If I'd used a suckling pig instead of a shoulder, then you could have called it porchetta, but I can't handle cooking a piglet.

Omnivore I may be, but I draw the line at suckling pig. I guess I'm just squeamish about the thought of taking a whole baby animal, complete with ears and wiggly tail, from the oven, even if it probably does have the crunchiest skin and most melting flesh. But the idea of some sort of roast pork stuffed into soft, country bread is altogether too good to miss, so I wimp out and cook a large joint instead.

I used Pugliese, a soft, lightly crusted Italian country bread, this time, though everything from pita to ciabatta would be fine for these pork buns, the soft, floury bread perfect for holding the hot, herb-scented pork and its juices.

I carve the roasted meat and its amber fat so thinly that you can almost see through it, piling it on to a warmed plate as I go, then put it in the center of the table with a basket of bread, a dish of salt and lots of red wine. Sometimes you expect everyone to dither, no one wanting to be the first to tuck in, but this time they all go for it as if they haven't eaten in a week.

Roast pork sandwiches

a large onion
olive oil – 5 tablespoons
garlic – 4 cloves
rosemary – a couple of bushy sprigs
large, fresh bay leaves – 3
black peppercorns – 18 or so
fennel seeds – 2½ teaspoons
a lemon
a piece of belly pork with plenty of fat, scored by the butcher – 2lbs
bitter salad leaves
soft rolls for 6

Heat the oven to 350°F. Peel the onion, then halve and slice it thinly. Soften it in the olive oil over a moderately high heat. Peel and finely chop the garlic, then stir it into the onions.

Pull the rosemary leaves from their branches and chop them finely; you should have a good tablespoon. Stir this into the onions, then finely chop the bay leaves and add them too. Crush the peppercorns, stir them in with the fennel seeds and a grinding of salt and let everything cook until it is pale gold and fragrant. Squeeze in the lemon juice. It will dissolve any gooey pan-stickings into the mixture.

Salt and pepper the pork and lay it skin-side up in a baking dish or small roasting pan, tucking the seasoned onion around it. Bake for a good hour, occasionally stirring any onion that threatens to stick on the pan.

Wash the salad leaves and cut the bread rolls in half. Remove the meat from the oven and let it rest for five minutes, then slice it thinly. Divide the salad between the bread and pile the sliced pork and seasoned onions in place.
Makes 6

Plum crisp
Blink and you will miss the damson season, which seems to get shorter with each passing year. I catch them at the farmers' market, small black

fruit with a blue, powdery bloom and the occasional brown leaf. There is no crumble like a damson crumble, no fruit whose flavor is so piercingly intense, no juice so royally purple. They will stain your shirt, your fingers, your dish towels; the piddling stones are annoying in the mouth (anyone who stones enough damsons for a crumble is quite out of their mind) and they occasionally surprise you with a prune-like flavor. That said, they are my favorite of all cooking fruits, rated in my book above even the apple or the plum.

Roast pork followed by damson crumble could well be my perfect meal, the inherent sharpness of the fruit slicing through the richness of the meat and its joyous fat. It need not be a straightforward crumble. The classic crumble works well with additions of oats and brown sugar, breadcrumbs and melted butter, ground almonds and cinnamon.

After the pork, something less buttery than the usual crumble topping might be a good idea, and with a crisper, less sweet crust. I have made this with apples, plums and damsons – all divine. But I insist on cream or ice-cream with it. That biting coldness is essential with the mouth-scalding hot fruit. If you are using damsons, I suggest you add a tablespoon or so of sugar to the fruit. Oh, and you really do need only the merest whiff of cinnamon.

ripe plums, greengages or damsons – 2lbs
a knife point of ground cinnamon
soft white bread – 5 slices
light brown sugar – $\frac{1}{3}$ cup
butter – 6 tablespoons
vanilla ice cream or heavy cream, to serve

Set the oven to 375°F. Cut the plums in half and remove their stones. Drop the fruit into a buttered pudding bowl or shallow casserole and toss very gently with the ground cinnamon.

Process the bread to rough crumbs in a food processor. You don't want them to be too fine – more of a soft rubble than a fine sand. Mix the breadcrumbs and sugar and cover the plums loosely with the mixture. Melt the butter in a small pan, then pour it over the crumbs, making certain to soak them all. Bake for thirty-five minutes, till the plums are soft and melting and the crumbs on top are golden and crisp.
Enough for 6

There are zucchini in the garden the size of baguettes. I ignore them and pick the smaller ones for what I plan to be a quick supper of zucchini stuffed with ricotta. As the day goes on and the wind sends leaves bobbing and swirling through the air, I decide on something altogether more substantial. By the time I hear the kids kicking conkers through the leaves outside, my idea of stuffed zucchini has changed to

**September 23
A hearty
vegetable
supper for
a windy
evening**

one where the vegetables are matched with potatoes and warming rose-mary under a blanket of cheesy crumble. This is, after all, the month of the crumble.

Zucchini and Lancashire cheese crumble

I am aware that this sounds like 1970s vegetarian restaurant fodder but make no apologies for it. With a juicy filling of zucchini and rosemary and a crisp cheese and walnut crust, it is a sound and somewhat frugal lunch or supper for an autumn day. I make it in a cast-iron casserole dish, about 10in in diameter, so that I need use only one pan through-out.

a large onion
butter – a thick slice (about 3 tablespoons)
rosemary sprigs
small potatoes – 4 (about ¾lb)
zucchini – 2 large (about 1lb)
vegetable stock – ⅔ cup (from powder or a cube)
Lancashire cheese – 2oz

For the crumble:
fresh white bread – 4 slices
walnut pieces – ¾ cup
rosemary
Lancashire cheese – 2½oz

Make a fragrant, savory base for the filling by peeling the onion, chop-ping it roughly and leaving it to cook slowly with the butter in a heavy casserole over a moderate heat. Pull the rosemary needles from their stems; you will need about a tablespoonful of them. Chop them finely and stir them into the onion. Scrub the potatoes but don't peel them. Cut them into large dice and, once the onion is pale gold and glossy, stir them in. Cover with a lid and leave to color for ten minutes, stir-ring them after seven or eight.

Chop the zucchini into the same-sized dice as the potatoes and add them to the pan along with a seasoning of salt and black pepper. Cover once more and leave to cook for a few minutes. Pour in the stock, let it bubble and steam briefly (you don't want it to evaporate). Set the oven to 350°F.

Make the crumble by reducing the bread to crumbs in a food processor, adding the walnuts, then a little rosemary – a tablespoonful will do – and adding the 2½oz cheese in small pieces. You should end up with a savory crumble flecked with bits of chopped rosemary.

Remove the lid from the filling, turn off the heat and crumble the 2oz of cheese over the top. Tip the crumble on top of that, transfer to

the oven and bake for thirty-five to forty minutes, till the top is crisp. Enough for 4

I have a knee-jerk reaction to tomatoes that means they invariably appear on my table in some sort of Italian way. It is partly, I suppose, a lack of imagination, but they somehow just seem comfortable with garlic, basil, olive oil, mozzarella, Parmesan or olives, and I see no reason to stray. The fact that the most successful tomatoes I grow in the garden are an Italian variety only seems to justify my habit.

Right now there is a pile of fruit that needs using. There is no question of a tomato salad; the day is windy, turning over the pots of rosemary, eggplant and tomatoes on the garden table, and rain is lashing at the kitchen skylights. I have a craving for a curry.

Tomatoes seem strangely alien to the world of cumin, ginger and turmeric. That said, their sweet-sharpness is uplifting in a curry, bringing freshness and vitality to the deep warmth of the gravy.

A tomato curry

onions – 2 medium
peanut oil – 3 generous tablespoons
garlic – 4 juicy cloves
a hot red chili pepper
brown mustard seeds – $1\frac{1}{4}$ teaspoons
ground turmeric – $2\frac{1}{2}$ teaspoons
cumin seeds – $2\frac{1}{2}$ teaspoons
a 'thumb' of fresh ginger
crushed canned tomatoes – 14oz
tomatoes – 8–12 (large, but not quite beefsteak)
thick yogurt – $\frac{1}{2}$ cup

Peel the onions and chop them roughly, then let them cook slowly in the peanut oil over a low to moderate heat. Peel the garlic, slice it thinly and add it to the onions. Chop the chili finely, then add it, with its seeds, to the onions. Stir in the mustard seeds, turmeric and cumin seeds and continue cooking. Peel the ginger and cut it into matchstick-sized shreds. Add it to the pan and let it cook briefly, then add the canned tomatoes, $1\frac{3}{4}$ cups of water and a grinding of black pepper and salt. Turn up the heat and bring to a boil, then add the whole tomatoes.

Turn the heat down to a gentle simmer and leave to cook, covered with a lid, for twenty-five to thirty-five minutes, turning the tomatoes once or twice during cooking. You want them to soften but not totally collapse. Add a little more water should the mixture thicken too quickly.

Push the tomatoes to one side, then stir in the yogurt. Let the sauce heat through, stirring gently, but without letting it come to a boil. Serve with rice or warm naan.
Enough for 4. Picture overleaf

There is a chill to the house, and sweaters all round. Supper is risotto, the first of the season. I insist this warming, gooey rice dish has a season, just as porridge does. This is a Gorgonzola risotto. It's just butter, a little finely chopped onion, rice, stock and blue cheese. This time I add the cheese just before we eat, when the rice is tender and each grain has a glistening coat of thickened stock. I pull the pan off the heat just as the pieces of cheese become liquid, before they dissolve completely. The way to catch them is to watch closely, and serve the rice just as each piece of cheese starts to lose its shape.

September 25
A risotto
caught at the
point of
perfection

The farmers' market had a mellow note today and everywhere the heavy scent of ripeness. Much is still in fine fettle: the last of the plums, purple-red Marjorie's Seedling and deepest red-flushed-blue Alex; nut-brown Kent cobs, their frilly leaves now crisp as old brown paper; deep claret-colored raspberries; zucchini, eggplant and oval Roma tomatoes for a garlicky bowl of ratatouille; red peppers and chilis turning the color of a Thai sunset. On one of the smaller trestle tables stacked with purple basil and long red chilis is a loose pile of cream and pink borlotti beans. Three years running I have tried and failed to grow these exquisitely mottled legumes, a rare find in the shops and often too expensive to make sense. I buy five great fistfuls. These are the beans I wait for all year, in their own way as enchanting as the tiny fava beans I found in May or that first crisp snap of the summer scarlet runners. I stagger home stacked up with ears of sweet corn, beets and beans, a loaf of focaccia with rosemary needles embedded in its crust, and waving a bunch of long-stemmed gladioli.

September 26
Autumn
beans and a
frugal lunch

Fresh borlotti with olive oil and focaccia
Lunch is boiled beans, nutty, warm and firm, with garlic, arugula leaves and thick, emerald-green olive oil. A salad with all the scent of Italy to it.

borlotti beans – 9oz (shelled weight)
bay leaves – 2
garlic – 2 cloves
olive oil
arugula leaves – a handful

Bring a large pot of water to a boil. Shell the beans and add them to the boiling water with the bay leaves, but avoid any temptation to add

salt. Cook them for about forty minutes, until they are tender but still have a bit of bite to them. Drain and season with salt, then drizzle with a little olive oil.

Peel and slice the garlic and warm gently, without coloring, in a good four or five tablespoons of olive oil in a shallow pan. Toss the beans in with the olive oil, stir gently, then tip them into a bowl with the rinsed arugula leaves. Eat with the foccacia, whilst the beans are still warm.

Enough for 2

october

Pork ribs with
honey and anise

Roast haddock with
bacon and parsley

Fennel, watercress
and pear salad

Macaroni with Fontina
and mustard

English apple cake

Pot-roasted pigeon with
luganega sausage

A carrot salad

Roast pork with grapes,
juniper and Vin Santo

Haddock with breadcrumbs
and tarragon

Roast partridge

Raspberry vanilla
ice-cream cake

Ham and butter beans

Roast eggplant with tahini

Sweet and sticky
chicken wings

Pan-fried sausages with
cream and mustard mashed
potatoes

My very good chocolate
brownie recipe

**October 1
English
apples and
a fat pig**

October days can be warm enough to eat outside, yet some carry a chill that will slice through the thickest fleece. This year it is simply damp. There are still tomatoes on the vines outside the back door, and raspberries the color of blood from a deep cut still hang on their wizened canes. As early as the first week of the month, there is a heavy, fungal smell to the garden, a scent of mushrooms and tobacco that I usually associate with Halloween. Already, the farmers' market is aglow with the amber and jade of early pumpkins and cooking apples.

The first two trees I planted in this garden were apples: a Blenheim Orange, the apple of the Benedictine monasteries, for cooking, and a Discovery for its copious blossom and the scent of its small, flat fruit, which reminds me of the apple trees we had when I was a child. Neither has fruited well this year, and what fruit there was has been eagerly scrumped by the squirrels. So the fruit in the market, tumbled into brown wooden crates, is more tempting than ever. It is the smell that gets me first, the pear-drop notes of the honey-skinned Russets, others still with hints of raspberry, banana or green hazelnuts. I am a crunch fanatic, choosing apples so crisp they make your gums ache. Ribston Pippin, Jupiter and the Pearmains are sure to be a cracking eat this early in the season, though I have been known to pick up early Coxes too, before they soften and their flesh sweetens.

This is also the season of the pig. My appetite for pork is what stops me being a vegetarian, and now, with the damp turn in the weather, I want it even more than usual. Next to the farmers' market is a butcher's shop where, depending on the day, you may find meat from Tamworth and Gloucester Old Spot pigs. It has a thick coat of dense, white fat, which is what gives it its succulence. I buy ribs with more fat and bone than flesh to them – perfect for Chinese cooking, when the fat softens to a quivering morsel, a sweet nugget of silky savoriness that quivers on your chopsticks.

**October 2
Pork ribs
with honey
and anise**

A truly sticky ribs recipe this one, but without the ubiquitous black molasses and tomato purée. Sweet, slightly hot and absurdly sticky, they will fill the kitchen with that warm, aniseed smell you so often encounter in Chinese restaurants.

thickish honey – 7 generous tablespoons
oyster sauce – 3 heaped tablespoons
garlic – 4 cloves
dried chili flakes – 1¼ teaspoons
whole star anise – 4
salt flakes – ½ teaspoon
black peppercorns – ½ teaspoon
meaty pork ribs – 3½lbs

To make the marinade, spoon the honey and oyster sauce into a roasting tin or baking dish. Peel and chop the garlic and add it to the dish with the chili flakes, star anise and salt. Grind the peppercorns roughly and add them to the marinade.

Toss the ribs in the marinade, then set aside for an hour or so. It won't hurt if they stay there overnight.

Roast the ribs at 350°F for an hour and fifteen minutes, turning them in their sauce from time to time. Keep an eye on them, as sometimes they tend to burn easily. They are ready when the meat is tender, though far from falling off the bone, and the ribs are glossy with sauce.

Serve with rice, spooning over the sauce from the pan.
Enough for 2–3

October 4 White fish, smoked bacon

I am mindful of the fish we should not use; those species that have been over-fished to the point where conservationists fear for their existence. That said, I do buy the odd piece of cod, haddock or monkfish, when it becomes a treat more precious to me than truffles. I dare say you could use any other white fish here. Haddock fits perfectly – its flavor is not so delicate as to be pushed into submission by the bacon, and it is currently a good price. It would be well worth trying it with hake, too. If you can't find a lightly smoked bacon, then use unsmoked bacon instead. Oh, and it needs a salad, by the way, something sweet and crisp like fennel, watercress and pear.

Roast haddock with bacon and parsley

olive oil or butter
haddock fillet – 14oz
smoked back bacon – 7oz
parsley – a small bunch (a handful)

Get the oven hot. It should be at about 425°F. Pour a couple of tablespoons of olive oil (or a thick slice of butter) into a shallow oven-safe pan that doesn't stick. Put it over a high heat, then when it starts to shimmer, season the fish on both sides with salt and black pepper and add it to the pan, skin-side up. Fry for a minute or so, until the flesh underneath has turned a light, gold color.

Turn the fish over and put the pan in the oven. Remove the rind from the bacon and cut each slice into short, finger-thick strips. Warm three tablespoons of olive oil in a shallow pan, add the bacon and leave to sizzle for about five minutes, until golden and lightly crisp. Chop the parsley leaves.

Test the haddock. It is done when a single flake of fish will come away from the skin with one light tug. This should take about seven to

ten minutes in the oven, depending on thickness. Transfer the fish to warm plates. Chuck the parsley into the bacon, stir, then tip parsley, bacon and oil over the plated fish.
Enough for 2

Fennel, watercress and pear salad
No pears? Then use a crisp, slightly tart apple instead. This is a salad that I sometimes eat as a main course, adding shavings of firm British cheese such as nutty Wensleydale, Appleby's Cheshire or a mild and crumbly Caerphilly.

watercress – a bunch (about 2oz leaves)
a large, crisp pear
fennel – a medium-sized bulb (about 5oz)

For the dressing:
the juice of a lime
light olive oil – 3 generous tablespoons

Trim the watercress and pinch it into bite-sized sprigs (it is almost impossible to eat a salad containing long pieces of watercress politely). Wash thoroughly.
   Make the dressing in a salad bowl. Whisk the lime juice and olive oil together with a grinding of salt and black pepper. Wash the pear but don't peel it. Cut it into quarters, remove the core and then slice the flesh thickly. Drop the pieces into the dressing, toss gently, then add the watercress.
   Trim the fennel, cut it into thin slices and toss gently with the watercress and pear. Serve with, or after, the fish.
Enough for 2

Back from a week in the States with two traditional American tart pans (shallow aluminum with holes in the base to keep the crust crisp) and the recipe for the best supper I ate there – a warming bowl of macaroni with a thick sauce of mustard and cheese. In New York, my steaming bowl of rib-sticking pasta had truffle oil shaken over it, which I think did nothing for it. I make it without.

**October 12
A souvenir
from
America**

Macaroni with Fontina and mustard
A rich and nannying version of the classic nursery supper. We follow this with a spinach salad and, for dessert, a plate of new season's Conference pears, chilled for an hour so they are thoroughly cold and juicy.

small macaroni, penne or other short, hollow dried pasta – ¾lb
half-and-half – 5 cups
a small onion, peeled and halved
a bay leaf or two
butter – 5 tablespoons
all-purpose flour – ½ cup
white peppercorns – 10
Fontina cheese – 5oz
smooth Dijon mustard – 1¼ teaspoons
grain mustard – 2½ teaspoons
fresh white breadcrumbs – 1½ cups
grated pecorino cheese – 5 tablespoons

Set the oven to 400°F. Cook the pasta in plenty of boiling salted water
till it is virtually tender. This should take about eight minutes, but will
depend on which brand and shape you are using. Drain the pasta as it
becomes ready.

Meanwhile, warm the milk in a saucepan with the onion and
bay leaves. As it comes to a boil, turn it off. Melt the butter in another
pan, add the flour and stir over a moderate heat until you have a
pale biscuit-colored paste. Gradually pour in the milk and whisk till
there are no lumps, then leave to simmer over a very low heat till the
sauce is the consistency of heavy cream, stirring regularly so it does
not stick.

Crush the white peppercorns and season the sauce with both the
white pepper, a good grinding of black and a very little salt. Cut the
Fontina into large dice. Fold the drained pasta, the Fontina and
the mustard into the sauce, then taste for seasoning.

Tip the mixture into a gratin dish. Avoid the temptation to smooth
the top. Toss the breadcrumbs with the grated pecorino and scatter
over the top. Bake for about thirty-five to forty minutes.
Enough for 4

The best, possibly the only, places to get crisp apples with any true
depth of flavor are the farmers' markets and farm shops. Greengrocers
no doubt do their best, but when did you last see a Michaelmas Red or
a Peasgood Nonesuch at your local shop? I walk thirty minutes every
Sunday to get a decent apple. Today there are strawberry-scented
Worcester Pearmains, small, striped Ellison's Orange, maroon-flashed
Laxton's and orange and rust Egremont Pippins. I avoid the Cox's
Orange Pippins, knowing they will be better after a few weeks in storage. I come home with a mixed woven basket that looks like something
from a medieval country fair; certainly nothing like the blue polystyrene trays and plastic wrap so typical of the supermarkets. I put it
on the kitchen counter for all to admire.

**October 13
A basket
of apples**

The cooking-apple label has always seemed inappropriate. You can cook almost any apple; even the Russets will fluff up in a hot oven, though the complexities of their flavor may dim with the heat and the essential drizzle of cream. If it's the majesty and froth of a baked apple I am after, then it's Peasgood Nonesuch by choice, followed by a fat organic Bramley. Today I make a cake, a shallow square with an open crumb and chunks of sweet apple. I use a mixture of apples – not that it will be any better that way but I can't make up my mind which one to use. We eat it warm, with thick, yellow pouring cream.

English apple cake

A slim, moist cake, best served warm, that will keep for a day or two wrapped in foil.

butter – 1 cup plus 2 tablespoons
superfine sugar – ½ cup plus 1 tablespoon
'eating' apples – 3
the juice of half a lemon
ground cinnamon – ¾ teaspoon
light brown sugar – 2 generous tablespoons
eggs – 2 large
flour – 130g
baking powder – 1¼ teaspoons
fresh white breadcrumbs – 4 tablespoons
a little extra sugar

Set the oven to 350°F. Line the base of a square 9-in cake pan, about 2in deep, with a piece of baking parchment. I do this with one sheet of paper cut to the exact size of the base of the tin but long enough to come right up the sides. That way you can just lift the paper to remove the cake.

Put the butter and superfine sugar into a food mixer and beat till light and fluffy. Whilst this is happening, cut the apples into small chunks, removing the cores as you go and dropping the fruit into a bowl with the juice of the half lemon. Toss the apples with the cinnamon and brown sugar.

Break the eggs, beat them with a fork, then gradually add them to the butter and sugar. Sift the flour and baking powder together and fold them gently into the mixture. Scrape into the lined cake pan. Put the spiced apples on top of the cake mixture, then scatter with the breadcrumbs and, if you wish, a little more brown sugar.

Bake for fifty-five minutes to an hour. The edges should be browning nicely and the center firm. Leave to cool for ten minutes or so before turning out. Eat warm.
Enough for 8

I am not one to get fancy with mushrooms. My inclination is to cook all of them in much the same way, be they expensive, apricot-colored chanterelles or everyday field mushrooms. That is, in a shallow pan with butter, some garlic and a handful of chopped parsley. Aside from the addition of sea salt and black pepper, the only real trick is to be gentle with the garlic, generous with the butter and to keep the parsley roughly chopped. A last-minute squeeze of lemon will make the earthy flavors sing.

I pile tonight's fried mushrooms on to buttered rounds of thick sourdough toast, then lay thin slices of Bayonne ham on top. As TV suppers go, this is as good as it gets.

A cold, wet autumn begs for game birds, roasted and served up with mash (potato, celeriac and potato, pumpkin, parsnip), if for no other reason than they feel right. Imagine a roast partridge, its skin crisp, its flesh the rose side of bloody, with a mound of nutty-tasting celeriac and potato mash; a grouse with a pool of hot bread sauce and a couple of roast parsnips; or pigeon, as bloody as you like, with a mash of buttered, peppered turnip.

I roasted a partridge the other night. Spread with butter and crushed juniper berries, it took only thirty minutes at 375°F. As it hissed and crackled in the oven, I steamed some thick slices of pumpkin over hot water, then beat them to a fluff with some butter and a scraping of nutmeg. As a weekday supper, it seemed extravagant, yet was less trouble than, say, pasta alla carbonara. Tonight it's the turn of pigeon, pot roasted with thin Italian sausages and a pile of mashed potato for the gravy.

Pot-roasted pigeon with luganega sausage

Luganega sausage, also spelled luganiga or lucanica, is a thin variety sold by the meter in Italy. Elsewhere it tends to come pre-packed but is hardly the worse for that. If this mildly spicy and relatively coarse sausage evades you, then try a well-flavored butcher's sausage or, more appropriately, good, herby chipolatas.

luganega sausage – 9oz
a large onion
sage leaves – 4
bay leaves – 3
plump young pigeons – 2
stock (vegetable bouillon will do) – 2 cups

Put the oven on to 400°F. Cut the sausage into short lengths, about the size of a wine cork, then let them cook in a deep, heavy, oven-safe pan over a low heat. Some of the fat should leak out as they color. While they are cooking, peel and roughly chop the onion. When the sausages are pale gold on all sides, add the onion to the pan and continue cooking until it is soft and translucent. Stir in the sage and bay leaves, then push all to one side of the pan, turn up the heat a little and put in the pigeons. Lightly brown the birds on all sides.

Pour in the stock and bring to a boil, then season with a little salt (the sausage can be quite salty, so I go easy here) and some black pepper. Cover with a lid and put in the oven for twenty-five to thirty minutes, then remove the lid and cook for a further five minutes to brown the pigeon. Lift the birds out and keep them warm (I do this in a warmed Pyrex bowl with a plate on top), then put the sauce over a moderate heat and let it reduce by a third, until it is glossy but not especially thick.

Place the birds on warm plates, beside greens or potatoes, and spoon over the hot sausage sauce.

Enough for 2 with steamed greens or mashed potato

**October 16
A carrot
salad**

Root vegetables seem to be breeding in the veg rack. The best of the carrots get scrubbed and grated this evening, then tossed into a salad bowl with peanuts that I have toasted in a dry frying pan, then dressed with lemon juice, a very little walnut oil and great handfuls of watercress. The less interesting vegetables, and those carrots that fail to snap crisply, will be used for soup. Tomorrow, or maybe the next day.

**October 17
A sweet
pork roast**

Autumn grapes, sweetly honeyed and with their distinct whiff of Muscat wine (or, to some, cat pee) are clearly the fruit of the moment. On a single shopping trip I find dusky-bloomed Fragola grapes at the cheese shop, softly flushed Muscats at a supermarket in Marylebone, and even decent Italia grapes at the greengrocer's. The Italias are almost yellow and virtually translucent, though knowing the greengrocer this is probably more by luck than good judgement. They taste of honey and elderflowers. A bunch goes in minutes, with the guilt of gluttony being forgotten in the knowledge that this is fruit and therefore 'a good thing'. The dark Fragola grapes have curiously loose skin and the faintest flavor of hazelnuts and strawberries. They are as addictive as M&Ms. Their season will be over within the next couple of weeks, so again greed can be forgiven.

Those that aren't eaten straight from the bag or put in a bowl on my desk to be eaten as I type are used in the kitchen, adding sweetness to the gravy for roast pork. Any sweet grape will do here.

Roast pork with grapes, juniper and Vin Santo
Get the butcher to score the fat, so that it crisps nicely into crackling. Make sure that the pork fat is dry when you season it. I find it best to leave it in the fridge, completely uncovered, overnight. That way the

skin has a chance to dry out a bit. Wet fat rarely crisps up properly in the oven.

boned pork loin, scored – 4lbs
olive oil
sea salt flakes – 1¼ teaspoons
black peppercorns – 1¼ teaspoons
juniper berries – a generous tablespoon
garlic – 8 cloves
Fragola or Muscat grapes – a large bunch
bay leaves – 3
Vin Santo (or dry Marsala) – 3 glasses
medium-sized potatoes – 6

Preheat the oven to 425°F. Rub the pork all over with a little olive oil. Crush the salt, peppercorns and juniper berries in a mortar and pestle. You want a rough spice mixture; the berries and peppercorns need crushing only lightly. Sit the pork in a roasting pan and rub in the spice mixture. Inevitably some will fall off into the pan but pat it down on to the meat as best you can. Press down on each of the garlic cloves with the flat of a large knife blade so they are squashed, then peel off the skins and put the cloves around the roast. Pull the grapes from their stems and put them in the pan with the bay leaves and two glasses of Vin Santo. Put the meat in the oven, roast for ten minutes, then turn the heat down to 400°F and continue roasting for fifty to sixty minutes, until the juices run clear when the flesh is pierced with a metal skewer. If they are pink, put the meat back for a bit longer.

While the pork is cooking, peel the potatoes and cut them into halves or quarters. Bring a pot of water to a boil, salt it, then lower in the potatoes. Let them boil for twelve minutes, then drain and shake them about a little in the pan, so the edges 'bruise' – this will make sure they crisp nicely. Warm a little olive oil in a roasting pan or cast iron baking dish, add the potatoes and put them in the oven, on a lower shelf than the pork.

When the pork is done, lift it out on to a carving board and keep warm. I cover mine with an upturned mixing bowl. Let it rest for fifteen minutes; it will be juicier that way. Bring the potatoes up a shelf in the oven, turning the heat up a notch if they look as if they need a bit of help.

Put the roasting pan over a moderate flame and stir the pan juices. With a draining spoon, crush the grapes and garlic into the juices, then pour in the last glass of wine and simmer until reduced to a thin gravy. Taste, season, then pour through a sieve. It should be slightly sweet from the wine, slightly bitter from the juniper. Carve the meat thinly

and serve with the potatoes, the pumpkin on page 328, and the hot 'gravy'.
Enough for 6, or 4 with seconds

Still haven't made the vegetable soup I promised to make almost a week ago to clear out the vegetable rack. And now, when there is every opportunity to make a pan of creamy parsnip and carrot soup, I am distracted by half a dozen of the most meltingly ripe tomatoes on the vine, their skins ready to burst with juice. I slice them thickly, then toss them with black olives and pieces of thick toast torn into chunks and drizzled with unfiltered olive oil. No basil, no garlic, no seasoning; just the peppery rush of thick, green oil, ripe tomatoes and black-edged toast.

My local cheese shop has an entire shelf of blue cheeses: bleu de Gex, Fourme d'Ambert, two types of Gorgonzola, Colston Bassett Stilton, Cashel Blue, Picos, Beenleigh Blue and three types of Roquefort. I decide on a thick piece of Roquefort *biologique*. Later, three of us settle down to a salad of raw apple, spinach leaves, toasted walnuts and crumbled Roquefort. The dressing is little more than olive oil, walnut oil and lemon juice. We make it more substantial by putting long, thin slices of toasted baguette on the side, each one, as it came from the toaster, drizzled with some of the salad dressing.

   Afterwards we eat crumble made with some late, dark red plums. For a change I put coarsely ground hazelnuts in the crumble and chopped ones on top.

A sweet salad dressing sometimes hits the spot when there is an autumnal dampness in the air. To a standard olive oil and lemon dressing, I add a little grain mustard and some runny honey. Even a fairly basic green salad can take on a pleasing smoothness here. But when you use such a dressing on the leaves of bitter radicchio, frisée, watercress or arugula, the whole thing really comes to life. Add a few large chunks of grilled bread and some walnut oil and you have a feast.

The tarragon plant has finally given up the ghost. Since I am unable to keep a plant for more than a single season, the harvesting of the last stems of curling leaves has become an annual event. This year they will be roughly chopped and used to flavor a crumb coating for pearlized flakes of haddock. Few fillets are as moist or meaty. We eat this with piles of lightly steamed rainbow chard, the leaves added to the pot only when the stalks have reached tenderness.

Haddock with breadcrumbs and tarragon

haddock – two 7-oz pieces of fillet
fresh (ish) white bread – 5 slices
anchovy fillets – 8
tarragon – a small bunch
an egg
a little flour
peanut oil and a thin slice of butter for frying

Skin the fish. Tear the bread into chunks and reduce it to fine, soft crumbs in a food processor. Failing that, you could always grate the bread on the coarse blade of a grater. Rinse and pat dry the anchovies, then chop them finely. Pull the leaves from the tarragon stalks and stir them into the breadcrumbs with the chopped anchovies and a grinding of salt and black pepper.

Crack the egg into a shallow bowl or deep plate and beat it lightly with a fork. Put a thick layer of flour in another bowl, then put the seasoned breadcrumbs in a third. Dip the fish first into the flour, then the egg and finally the breadcrumbs. Pat the crumbs on both sides of the fish until each fillet is coated with a deep layer of herbed crumbs.

Warm the oil and butter in a shallow pan. May I suggest you make it a non-stick one? When the oil starts to sizzle, lower in the fish, leaving it to cook at an enthusiastic bubble till the underside is golden. Turn the fish and cook the other side. It will need about three or four minutes per side, depending on the thickness. Test it by gently breaking off a piece. Drain the fish on kitchen paper briefly before serving. Enough for 2

October 23
A bowl of pure delight

Miso soup presses all the right buttons for me, being at once light, easy to make and deeply, deeply savory. I generally do two tablespoons of yellow miso paste to 5 cups of boiling water. This time I stir in some shredded scallions, a tablespoon of fish sauce and some crisp green beans. Okay, I could put in a skein of cooked noodles too, and maybe even a grilled chicken breast cut into slices, but right now all I want is to sip the clear, umami-rich depths of the amber soup.

October 24

Yesterday produced a white cabbage and apple salad that was no nicer than it sounds and an orange-rinded French cheese whose flavor was too strong. Even the wine, an organic red from Argentina, did little to help its appeal. I wish I had had fish sticks and french fries. Today is a day of golden, autumn light, the garden awash with yellow and russet leaves. I pick Autumn Bliss raspberries for an ice-cream cake and cook some simple roast partridges that the shop had 'reduced to clear'. They worked out to be about the same price as lamb chops.

Roast partridge

I pepper and salt the four plump little partridges, smear them with butter inside and out, then put a sprig of thyme up them. I am not sure the thyme does a fat lot, but it makes them look the part. I place two slices of the Ginger Pig's fat bacon over their breasts and roast them for twenty-five minutes at 425°F. We eat them with nothing but home-made bread sauce and a thin gravy made by pouring a glass of Madeira into the roasting pan and letting it bubble for a few minutes.

Raspberry vanilla ice-cream cake

You could, of course, make your own sponge cake for this simple ice-cream dessert. But then, if you are going to that much trouble you might as well make your own ice-cream, too. Some major food shops sell really buttery plain sponge cakes, and if they have ground almonds in, then all the better, or you could use a brioche loaf or a plain panettone instead. It is essential to bring the cake out of the freezer a good half hour before you intend to eat. I know this seems like a long time, but trust me, it takes that long to soften enough to cut.

plain sponge cake – ¾lb
vanilla ice-cream – 2 pints
raspberries – 1lb
confectioners' sugar – 2 generous tablespoons

You will need a cake pan, approximately 9in square, lined with plastic wrap or wax paper.

Slice the sponge thinly and use half of it to line the bottom of the tin. Leave enough to put a layer on top later. Patch it where you must, but try to keep the slices as large as possible.

Let the ice-cream soften slightly in its container, but it must not melt. Scatter half of the raspberries over the cake, then spoon the ice-cream on top, pushing it right into the corners. Smooth the top, then cover with the remaining raspberries. Cover with the reserved slices of sponge cake. Press down firmly to compress the fruit and ice-cream.

Cover tightly with plastic wrap, then freeze for a good hour (it can stay frozen for several days if tightly wrapped). Bring the cake out of the freezer a good thirty minutes before you need it, to let the sponge soften. Remove the cake from the pan and dust with the confectioners' sugar before slicing with a large, heavy knife.
Enough for 8. Picture overleaf

**October 25
The knee-
jerk lentil
supper**

Once again there are small green lentils bubbling in a pot of water on the stove that need nothing more than draining, then tossing immediately with red wine vinegar, olive oil and lots of parsley, to be eaten with slices cut from a log of chalky, ash-rolled goat cheese. This is the

supper I make when we really don't know what to have; a supper of knobbly, fudgy textures and milky, nutty flavors that works on every level. It's cheap, too. Love it.

The last fat, yellow leaves fell off the fig tree this morning, leaving next year's buds at the tip of each gray branch and forty green fruits that will never ripen. You approach the tree with caution, each piece of stone around its base splattered with potentially lethal squashed figs, hoping for just one edible fruit. But there is no such thing, and the tree that promised so much in May has failed to deliver. We have been grateful for the shade of its leaves though, keeping the sun off the butter and the wine, and protecting our necks as we ate our tomato lunches under its boughs. The figs we eat today are those sent by a kind reader, and we gorge on their melting flesh like lushes.

October 26
Spanish ham and the last of the tomatoes

There are still tomatoes on the plants by the back door, their leaves crisping nicely in the autumn sun, the fruits taking on an intense sweetness as their skin wrinkles and cracks. They offer warmth and richness and not a little sharpness still, which works well with the Spanish ham and coarse chorizo from the Brindisa shop in Exmouth Market. Three slices of ham and half a dozen small tomatoes apiece.

October 27
An altogether different ham

The last week of October has brought a gentle shift of gears in the kitchen. The garden door is still open as I cook – I have had lunch outside twice this week, but on both occasions I had to put on a sweater halfway through. When someone started burning leaves, the smell of wood smoke wafting across the back gardens made our lunch of roast tomatoes and mozzarella seem insubstantial and wanting.

I have held on to summer for as long as I can but, as each day now ends with a chill breeze, I want smokier, more earthy flavors: ham cut thicker and of a deeper, more herbal cure; rust-red chorizo rather than mild saucisson; gold vegetables, not green. Last night I moved the jars of dried beans to the front of the cupboard.

My cooking slows down at this time of year, and weekend lunches are cooked in a succession of much-loved casseroles: an old earthenware dish, a deeper one of heavy cast iron, and my ancient and ridiculously cheap Chinese pot, which does for anything in which star anise or ginger is involved. Beautiful, useful kitchenware that is patiently growing older with me.

Since slow cooking became fashionable again, there has been a plethora of 'chuck-it-in-the-oven-and-forget-it' recipes. I wallow in this sort of cooking, letting the meaty, mushroomy smells fill the house and tantalize us all for hours before we finally sit down to eat. Absurdly, this 'slow food' that is so precious to foodies who take themselves seriously is, in practice, less trouble than the fast food they are often so quick to condemn.

Fat, bones and succulence

Cooking food slowly on a low heat, covered with a lid, gives time for the ingredients to come together, for the flavors to mellow and soften and become as one. This gentle style of cooking in liquid has an hour or more to draw the marrow from the bones, which, together with the fat, deeply enriches the cooking juices. You effortlessly create a softly burbling pot of succulence and savor.

Everything hinges on the bones and fat. I pick out cuts of meat that have the thickest bone or a visible layer of fat – shanks, middle neck and shin – and ask for birds that are older, stronger and have had the chance to run around outside. Traditional breeds given free range.

As the weather turns to autumn, then winter, there are half a dozen recipes that crop up time and again in this kitchen. Today it's a ham and bean casserole the color of rusting iron; another week it was a gently braised duck, whose warm, spicy smell filled the whole house. Tender meat and rich gravy for cold days.

Ham and butter beans

Certain recipes are inextricably linked with falling leaves and the damp, fungal scent of autumn. This casserole of mildly spicy, deeply smoky flavors is such a meal. I think of it as principally a Saturday lunch dish, so I try to remember to soak the beans on a Friday night. Last night I forgot, so this time my ruddy stew will end up as dinner instead.

dried butter beans – 2½ cups
a little olive oil
thyme – a few sprigs
a piece of boiled ham – about 2½lbs
onions – 2
garlic – 4 large cloves
carrots – 2
canned chopped tomatoes – 2 14-oz cans
smoked paprika
chorizo sausage – 2 (about 9oz in total)

Soak the beans for at least eight hours in deep, cold water. Drain, then boil them in unsalted water for about an hour, till they start to show signs of tenderness. Turn off the heat. Set the oven to 350°F.

Warm a couple of tablespoons of olive oil with one or two sprigs of thyme in a deep casserole. Cut the fat from the ham in one thick piece and let the fat colour briefly on both sides in the oil. This lends a little of the pork flavor to the oil. As it cooks, peel the onions and chop them roughly. Lift out the piece of fat and set it aside.

Soften the onions in the flavored oil, letting them color lightly as you go. Meanwhile, peel the garlic cloves and add them whole to the pot. Scrub and roughly chop the carrots. Stir them through the onions and garlic, then tuck in a good three or four sprigs of thyme.

Add the drained, cooked beans (keep the cooking liquid) and the chopped tomatoes and gently mix them with the onions. Season with black pepper, a very little salt and a teaspoon, no more, of smoked paprika, then tuck in the chorizo sausages and the piece of fat to enrich the sauce. Lower the ham on top of the sausages, pushing it down into the sauce as best you can. Pour in enough of the bean cooking liquid almost to cover the meat.

Bring to a boil, cover and bake for about an hour and a half, till all is meltingly tender. Serve in thick slices with a wedge of sausage, plenty of the beany sauce and a piece of the fat for those who want it.
Enough for 4. Pictures on page 308 and previous page

**October 28
An Eastern
eggplant
roast**

The leaves are piling up under the chestnut trees opposite the house and I spend most of the morning shoveling them into bags and lugging them through the house to the compost heap. In such an urban situation, I feel as if I have found gold. Late in the afternoon, and having spent the entire day tying up the sagging dahlias and the flopping sweet peas and tugging hard at the climbing nasturtiums that threaten to strangle the remaining tomato plants, I realize how hungry I am. I want something richly warming to sit on top of a soft mound of rice. What transpires is a meal of nutty eggplant and brown rice, followed by a clean-tasting dish of stewed apples, made as usual but flavored with a few drops of rosewater. The scent of toasted pine nuts, brown rice and rosewater in my little kitchen makes me wish I were somewhere altogether more warm and mysterious.

Roast eggplant with tahini

eggplant – 2 medium
olive oil – ½ cup
ground cardamom
pine nuts, toasted – ¼ cup

For the dressing:
plain yogurt – 2 generous tablespoons
tahini paste – a generous tablespoon
olive oil – a generous tablespoon
fresh thyme leaves – 1¼ teaspoons
lemon juice to taste

Set the oven to 400°F. Remove the leaves from the top of each egg-plant, then cut it into four from stem to tip. Cut each piece into three short, fat lengths. Toss the eggplant with the olive oil and tip it into a roasting dish. Season with salt, black pepper and a little freshly ground cardamom. Roast for forty to forty-five minutes, until the eggplant are soft and toasted.

Make the dressing by mixing the yogurt, tahini paste and olive oil in a blender or with a small whisk. Season with salt and black pepper and most of the thyme leaves, then check the flavor. You may want to add a squeeze of lemon juice.

Tip the warm eggplant into the dressing and toss gently until lightly coated. Spoon on to a serving plate and scatter with the toasted pine nuts and the reserved thyme leaves.
Enough for 4 as a side dish or 2 as a main dish served with steamed brown basmati rice

This is the time of year I want sticky food. Not the crisp, clean-tasting flavors of spring and summer but the sort of robust food that makes you lick your fingers. I wouldn't even attempt to eat these sweet and sticky bits of chicken with a knife and fork. They are strictly meant for picking up in your fingers, preferably whilst curled up on the sofa in front of the television. Although the mustard brings with it a certain amount of deep warmth, these are not at all spicy, and are for those who revel in an occasional sweet and extremely tactile supper. You will need some sort of salad with them – perhaps something crunchy and cooling with bean sprouts and cucumber in it.

October 29 Sweet and sticky chicken wings

chicken wings   12 (about 1¼lbs)
grain mustard – 2 heaped tablespoons
runny honey – a heaped tablespoon
lemon – a large, juicy one
garlic – 3 large cloves

Set the oven to 425°F. Carefully check the chicken wings for stray feathers (they are often the least scrupulously plucked bit of the bird), then put them in a roasting pan.

Mix the mustard and honey with the juice from the lemon. You should get about 6 tablespoons from a large fruit. Peel the garlic, crush it and add it to the honey mixture with a grinding of pepper and salt.

Toss the wings in the honey mixture and roast for forty minutes, by which time they will be a healthy color. Turn them over and continue cooking for ten minutes. They will now be intensely dark and sticky.
Enough for 2–3, depending on the size of your wings. Picture overleaf

Hallowe'en is far from my favorite night of the year, and I would happily see the intrusion of trick or treating outlawed, but the food is another matter altogether. Like Guy Fawkes' Night, this is the moment for piping-

October 31 Sausage and brownies

hot casseroles and deep pots of beans, for sausages and steaming piles of potato and, in our house at least, for dense, chocolatey cakes.

Pan-fried sausages with cream and mustard mashed potatoes

plump, herby butcher's sausages – 6
peanut oil – a very little

For the potatoes:
mealy potatoes – 4 medium (about 1¼lbs)
parsley – a few bushy sprigs
butter – a thick slice
light cream – 1 cup
smooth Dijon mustard – a generous tablespoon
grain mustard – a generous tablespoon

Peel the potatoes, cut them in half and bring them to a boil in salted water. Turn down the heat to an enthusiastic simmer and leave for fifteen to twenty minutes, till tender.

Meanwhile, put the sausages into a shallow pan with a little peanut oil and leave to cook over a low to moderate heat, turning each one over as it colors. They are ready after about twenty to twenty-five minutes of slow cooking, their skin a deep, burnished golden brown.

Chop the parsley for the mashed potatoes, but not too finely. When the potatoes are tender to the point of a knife, drain them, let them dry briefly over a low heat, then tip them into the bowl of a food mixer. Beat them with the butter, chopped parsley and a generous seasoning of pepper and salt until smooth and fluffy.

Bring the cream and mustard to a boil in a small pot, stirring as you go, then tip them into the potato. Check the seasoning and serve with the sausages.
Enough for 2, with seconds

My very good chocolate brownie recipe
No nuts, no flavorings, just a 24-karat brownie, as dense and fudgy as Glastonbury Festival mud. Whatever else you add is up to you.

superfine sugar – 1⅓ cups
butter – ½lb plus 2 tablespoons
chocolate (70% cocoa solids) – 9oz
eggs – 3 large, plus 1 extra yolk
all-purpose flour – ½ cup plus 2 tablespoons
finest-quality cocoa powder – ½ cup plus 2 tablespoons
baking powder – ¾ teaspoon

You will need a baking pan, about 9in square, preferably non-stick, or a small roasting pan.

Set the oven to 350°F. Line the bottom of the baking pan with baking parchment. Put the sugar and butter into the bowl of a food mixer and beat for several minutes, till white and fluffy. You can do this by hand if you have to, but you need to keep going until the mixture is really soft and creamy.

Meanwhile, break the chocolate into pieces, set 2oz of it aside and melt the rest in a bowl suspended over, but not touching, a pan of simmering water. As soon as the chocolate is completely melted, remove it from the heat. Chop the remaining 2oz into gravel-sized pieces.

Break the eggs into a small bowl and beat them lightly with a fork. Sift together the flour, cocoa and baking powder and mix in a pinch of salt. With the machine running slowly, introduce the beaten egg a little at a time, speeding up between additions. Remove the bowl from the mixer to the work surface and mix in the melted and the chopped chocolate with a large metal spoon. Lastly fold in the flour and cocoa mixture, gently, firmly, without knocking any of the air out.

Scrape the mixture into the prepared cake pan, smooth the top and bake for thirty minutes. The top will have risen slightly and the cake will appear slightly softer in the middle than around the edges. Pierce the center of the cake with a fork; it should come out sticky but not with raw mixture attached to it. If it does, then return the brownie to the oven for three more minutes. It is worth remembering that it will solidify a little on cooling, so if it appears a bit wet, don't worry. Leave to cool for at least an hour before cutting into squares.
Enough for 12

november

Roast squash with thyme

Raspberry ricotta pancakes

Pumpkin and tomato laksa

Poached pears with ice cream
and chocolate sauce

Baked onions with
Parmesan and cream

Roast chicken with cheese
mash and garlic gravy

A crisp salad for a cold day

Blackberry and apple pie

Slow-cooked duck with
star anise and ginger

Mushroom lasagne
with basil and cream

Hot and sticky roast quail

Stilton, onion and potato pie

Celeriac and walnut
rcmoulade

Coffee and walnut cake

**November 2
Sweet,
golden
pumpkins
and sticky
sausages**

I have never enjoyed shopping for my supper more than in the last few weeks. The air is crisp. The market stalls are groaning with fat roots, purple cabbage and wacky mushrooms. The new apples spurt with juice and the Conference pears are still hard enough to hurt your gums. There are pomegranates, quinces and fat figs. Partridge is there too, with plump, wet scallops and diminutive beets complete with their bloodshot plume of leaves. Above it all, someone, somewhere, is roasting chestnuts. It is the squashes that steal the show, tiny crinkle-edged patty pans, long-necked butternuts and others as fat and round as a football. I tend to prefer moderately sized fruit, squashes whose skins are thin enough to cut without resorting to the axe and small enough to bake within an hour. I do nothing with them other than soup, often with the addition of strips of crisp bacon or cubes of Gruyère introduced at the table, or I simply roast them with butter and thyme.

A roast pumpkin is a side order rather than a main dish, though I do occasionally eat it for supper with brown rice and a thick tomato sauce. What really works for me is roast pumpkin and sausages. A plate of sweet, caramelized flavors for a cold night.

Roast squash with thyme

small to medium squash – 4
butter – 2 tablespoons
a generous tablespoon of olive oil
fresh thyme leaves

Set the oven to 350°F. Cut the squashes in half and scoop out the pulp and seeds from the center. Lay the squashes cut-side up on a baking sheet. Cut the butter into thin slices and put a slice in the center of each squash, together with a little olive oil, a good pinch of thyme leaves, a grinding of salt and plenty of black pepper.

Roast for an hour, checking them occasionally to see how they are doing. You want them to be sweet smelling and the flesh to be totally tender when you pierce it with a knife.
Enough for 4

Raspberry ricotta pancakes
Thick, soft pancakes about the size of a silver dollar and mottled with the juice of the late-autumn raspberries. An autumnal version of the orange ones I made in May.

ricotta cheese – ½lb
superfine sugar – 5 tablespoons
eggs – 3, separated

finely grated zest of an orange
melted butter – 2 generous tablespoons (plus a little for cooking)
all-purpse flour – ½ cup
raspberries – 1 cup

In a large bowl, mix the ricotta, sugar and egg yolks. Grate the orange zest into the bowl and stir it in gently with the melted butter. Sift in the flour and tenderly fold in. In a large bowl, beat the egg whites with a balloon whisk till stiff, then fold them lightly into the ricotta. It is important not to knock the air out. Carefully fold in the raspberries.

Warm a non-stick frying pan over a moderate heat and brush it with a little butter. Place a heaped tablespoon of mixture in the pan, then another two or three depending on the size of your pan. Let them cook for a minute or two, till they have risen somewhat and the underside has colored appetizingly, then, using a spatula, flip them over to cook the other side. Do this as if you mean it, otherwise they will collapse as you turn them. A further couple of minutes' cooking, then serve immediately, hot from the pan.
Makes 8

No party this year, just four of us for Bonfire Night, and there are only sparklers, fireworks being just too traumatic for the cats. Supper is as informal as it comes: a bowl of big soup, a dish of poached pears with chocolate sauce and then another batch of the gungy brownies I made last week.

**November 5
Spiced soup
and poached
pears**

Pumpkin and tomato laksa

pumpkin – 9oz unpeeled weight
small, red bird's eye chilis – 5
garlic   4 cloves
a lump of ginger the size of your thumb
lemongrass – 2 plump stalks
lime leaves – 6
cilantro roots – 5 or 6
cilantro – a large handful
a little vegetable oil
chicken or vegetable stock – 2 cups
coconut milk – 1¾ cups
cherry tomatoes – 24
nam pla (Thai fish sauce) – 2 generous tablespoons
the juice of half a lemon
dried noodles – ¼lb, cooked as it says on the packet
mint leaves – a large handful

Cut the pumpkin into large chunks and place in the top of a steamer (alternatively, steam them in a colander balanced over a pan of boiling water). The pumpkin should be tender in twelve to fifteen minutes. Remove from the heat.

Chop the chilis, removing the seeds first if you wish, peel the garlic and ginger and chop roughly. Put them all into a food processor. Discard the outer leaves of the lemongrass and roughly chop the inner leaves, shred the lime leaves, then add them to the chilis. Scrub the cilantro roots and add them to the chilis, along with half the cilantro leaves and stems. Process them to a pulp, adding a little vegetable oil if the mixture needs it to go round.

Place a fairly deep pot over a moderate heat, add half the spice paste (keep the other half in the fridge for tomorrow) and fry it, moving it round the pot so it does not scorch. Do this for a minute or two, then pour in the stock and coconut milk and bring to a boil.

Cut the tomatoes in half and add them to the soup with the *nam pla* and lemon juice. They will take seven to ten minutes to cook. Add the chunks of pumpkin and continue cooking for a minute or two. Place a swirl of cooked noodles in each of four bowls, pour over the laksa and add the mint and the remaining cilantro.
Enough for 4

November 6 A warm salad for supper comprising roast eggplant and zucchini slices and some small tomatoes, left in the oven till their skin blackens, tossed with olive oil, basil leaves and halves of baby mozzarella. Afterwards a slice or two of shop-bought fig and almond tart.

November 7 The chestnuts that are cooked over coals in the street are not living up to the promise of their nutty, charcoal-edged aroma. At home, they are worth taking trouble with, by which I mean soaking in boiling water, peeling and scrupulously de-fuzzing. It takes an age, but the canned varieties lack the sweet nuttiness of the fresh (the delectable and hideously expensive *marrons glacés* are a different matter altogether). I roast my peeled nuts in a dry frying pan, letting them color deeply before salting gingerly and offering them warm, with pre-dinner drinks. The wonderful thing is that everyone thinks you have gone to so much trouble. The truth is that you have.

The Italia grapes in the greengrocer's today are irresistible. They have the sweetness and flavor of Beaumes de Venise and should, I think, be served very cold, so that they burst juicily in the mouth. I have taken to eating them after supper with the new walnuts, which if you catch them young are pale and supple. I don't eat the grapes too soon. They are worth keeping until they reach an almost transparent golden-green, when their sweetness will be at its most noticeably honeyed.

The Turkish figs, plump, purple and tender as a bruise, make up for autumn's lack of peaches and apricots. What they miss in flavor they make up for in sheer sensuality. Unless you are going to bake them, they must be wantonly ripe. Look for a bead or two of nectar around the base. A ripe autumn fig is gagging to be eaten.

With last week's purchase of Comice pears edging their way towards perfection on the kitchen windowsill, it seems right and fitting to get the most suitable cheese to go with them. With their cold flesh as soft and clear as a fruit sorbet, you could take a salty or nutty cheese – either will work. Nuggets of old, craggy parmigiano reggiano fit like a dream with a ripe pear, but so do the milder English cheeses, such as the floral, buttery Mrs Kirkham's Lancashire. The best cheese I have picked up this month has to be the Ticklemore from Neal's Yard in Borough Market. Its crust the beige and white of a field mushroom, this is a nutty, firm-fleshed goat cheese whose milk-and-green-hazelnuts flavor seems more pronounced than I have ever known it. The cheese is there for those who want it; for those who don't, there's a dish of poached pears and dark chocolate sauce.

Before the pears a pan-toasted sandwich of sliced preserved artichokes in oil from the deli counter and thin slices of Gruyère. The cheese melts slowly over the artichokes and oozes out slightly from the edges of the sandwich.

Poached pears with ice cream and chocolate sauce

superfine sugar – 2 generous tablespoons
a vanilla pod
the juice of half a lemon
pears – 4
praline ice cream
fine, dark chocolate – 7oz

Pour 5 cups of water into a deep, wide pan, then add the sugar, vanilla pod and lemon juice and bring to a boil. Peel the pears and tug out their stalks, then halve the fruit and scoop out their cores with a teaspoon. Drop the fruit into the sugar syrup and let them simmer for ten to fifteen minutes, till they are translucent and tender. Leave them in the syrup to cool. During this time they will become silkily soft and soaked through with syrup.

Get the ice cream out of the freezer. Chop the chocolate. Bring ¾ cup water to a boil, then whisk in the chocolate, removing from the heat as soon as it has melted – a matter of seconds. Place two pear halves on each of four dishes, add the praline ice cream – one ball per person should be ample – and pour over the warm chocolate sauce. Enough for 4

**November 8
Slow-roast
chicken and
creamy
onions**

We must cook, rather than graze, if we are to survive the cold and the wet. Those allergic to cooking may need to bite the bullet and get the casserole down from its shelf if they are not to short-change the family dinner table. No supermarket dinner-in-a-dish will hit the spot now. Only onions, starch and meat juices can get through to our marrow when everyone comes home soaked to the skin. Herbivores might like to try boiling onions in their jackets, then lifting them into a roasting dish with butter, salt and black pepper, letting them bake sweetly till their flesh is as soft as silk.

Baked onions with Parmesan and cream

I normally eat these deeply savory baked onions as a side-dish to cold roast beef, and that is probably when they are at their best. But today I have them with a plainly roasted chicken (butter, salt and pepper and a few herbs tucked inside, roasted at 350°F for sixty minutes till juicy and golden) and it is quite one of the most splendid meals I can remember. Frugal, too, as there is cold chicken left for tomorrow.

onions – 4 medium to large
whipping or heavy cream – 1¼ cups
grated Parmesan – a good handful

Set the oven to 350°F. Peel the onions and bring them to a boil in a deep pot of water. Leave them at a bright simmer for about twenty-five minutes, until tender. Lift them out with a draining spoon.

Slice the onions in half from root to tip and put them cut-side down in an oven-safe dish. Tip the cream over the onions. Season with salt, pepper and the grated cheese and bake for twenty-five to thirty minutes, till golden and bubbling.
Enough for 4

**November 9
A chicken
dinner in
two parts**

The 'meat and two veg' meal rings no bells for me. The sight of a piled-high plate of Sunday lunch tends to sap my appetite rather than excite it. I prefer to go back for seconds than to plow my way through a dog's dinner of a meal. I generally serve the meat first, with a little gravy and maybe a roast potato or two, then have the greens with some of the roasting juices as a separate plate afterwards. Today, there are four of us to lunch and I am doing a variation on my usual. This time, a plate of the roast meat with a little of the pan juices and some roast potatoes, followed by a plate of fluffy mashed potato beaten with milk and grated cheese and a pool of hot thyme- and garlic-scented gravy. I chose an English cheese, but the only real prerequisite is that it needs to have a bit of clout to it. There will be no proper dessert, but a green salad (Little Gem lettuce, watercress and parsley) followed by pears and walnuts.

Roast chicken with cheese mashed potatoes and garlic gravy

a large chicken, with giblets – about 3½lbs
butter
thyme – 4 or 5 bushy sprigs
garlic – 2 whole heads
potatoes – 2 medium to large ones

For the gravy:
a small onion, halved
a carrot
a couple of bay leaves
white wine – ⅔ cup

For the cheese mashed potatoes:
mealy potatoes – 5 large ones
butter – 4 tablespoons
hot milk – ½ cup
mature cheese such as Wensleydale, Lancashire, Cheddar – 5oz, grated

Set the oven to 400°F. Remove the giblets from the chicken and rub the bird all over with salt, pepper, butter and thyme leaves, pushing a couple of sprigs of thyme inside the cavity. Place upside down in a roasting pan. Cut the heads of garlic in half horizontally and tuck them beside the bird. Put the bird into the oven to roast.

Meanwhile, peel the potatoes, cut each one into about six (you alone know exactly how big you like your roast potatoes to be) and bring them to a boil in deep, salted water. Cook until they are almost tender, a matter of twelve minutes or so, then drain them.

After forty-five minutes' cooking, turn the chicken the right way up, add the potatoes to the pan, rolling them over in the fat, then let the chicken roast for a further thirty to forty-five minutes.

While the chicken continues to roast, make the gravy and the cheese mashed potatoes. Put the chicken giblets in a pan with the onion, carrot and bay leaves and about 1½ cups water. Bring to a boil and simmer for twenty minutes. Meanwhile, peel the potatoes, cut them into large pieces and bring them to boil in deep, salted water. Once they have boiled, turn them down to an enthusiastic simmer till they are tender to the point of a knife, a matter of twelve to fifteen minutes or so.

Remove the chicken and potatoes from the roasting pan, together with some of the roasting juices, and keep them warm whilst you finish the gravy. Put the roasting pan over a moderate heat. Pour in the wine and ⅔ cup of the giblet stock. Bring to a boil, pressing the garlic cloves with a wooden spoon to squash them, then season.

Drain the potatoes and beat them with the butter and hot milk. I do this in a food mixer but you could do it with a potato masher if you prefer. Stir in the grated cheese. Cover with buttered foil and place in the switched-off oven.

To serve: carve the now rested chicken and serve it with the roast potatoes and the small quantity of roasting juices that have collected in the dish. Once you have eaten, bring the gravy to a boil and check the seasoning. Serve the mashed potatoes on the same plates, spooning over the gravy and holding back the thyme and garlic as you go.
Enough for 4

I open the fridge and there are the remains of yesterday's chicken winking at me. Today it looks full of opportunities and promise; by tomorrow it will begin to depress me. So I spend a good ten minutes stripping the meat from the carcass, then toss it into a crisp salad of small, spiky green and red leaves and mix it with a slightly spicy chili sauce dressing.

November 10
A crisp salad for a cold day

mixed salad leaves – 4 large handfuls
cilantro – a handful
cherry tomatoes – 12, cut in half
a large carrot
cucumber – a 2-in length
leftover roast chicken – 4 good handfuls

For the dressing:
ginger – a thumb-sized knob
a shallot, finely chopped
rice vinegar – a generous tablespoon
sweet chili sauce – a generous tablespoon
water – 3 generous tablespoons

Peel and grate the ginger. Make the dressing by shaking all the ingredients together in a screw-top jar. Put the washed and dried salad leaves in a bowl together with the cilantro and the halved tomatoes. Peel the carrot and cut it into matchsticks, then do the same with the cucumber, removing the seeds as you go (otherwise the salad will be too wet). Cut the chicken into long strips and toss all the ingredients together, seasoning with a little salt.

Blackberry and apple pie
You will need a traditional shallow metal pie dish with a rim, about 9in in diameter.

Bramley apples – 5 good-sized ones (about 3½lbs)
blackberries – 2 cups
superfine sugar – 5 tablespoons
a little milk and sugar, to glaze
heavy cream, to serve

For the pastry:
all-purpose flour – 2½ cups
butter, cold from the fridge – 6 tablespoons
lard, cold from the fridge – 6 tablespoons
ice-cold water

Put the flour into a large mixing bowl with a small pinch of salt. Cut the butter and lard into small chunks and rub them into the flour with your thumbs and fingertips. You could do it in a food mixer but I can't really see why. It only takes a minute by hand. What is more, you will miss the tactile joys of pastry making. To bring the mixture to a rollable dough, add a little ice-cold water. Start with a tablespoonful, adding it gingerly (too much is difficult to correct) and drawing the dough in from the sides to form a ball. You may need a couple of tablespoons. You are looking for a dough that is firm enough to roll but soft enough to demand careful lifting. Set aside in the fridge, covered with a dish towel, for thirty minutes.

Set the oven to 400°F. Peel, quarter and core the apples, then slice them very thinly. Put them in a bowl with the blackberries and toss with the sugar.

Cut the chilled pastry in half and roll half of it out, then use it to line the pie dish. You need enough extra pastry around the edge to be able to cut off and cover the rim of the dish (plus a few scraps to make some leaves, if you like that sort of thing). Put both pie shell and spare pastry in the fridge.

Put a cookie sheet in the oven to heat up. Roll out the second piece of pastry. Fill the empty pastry shell with the apples and blackberries, layering the apples tightly as you go. Wet the edge of the pastry rim. Place the second piece of pastry over the pie and trim the edges. Press the edges firmly down to seal. Crimp them with your thumb and first finger or by pressing down with the prongs of a fork. Decorate with pastry leaves or not as the mood takes you. Brush with a little milk and sprinkle with sugar. Cut two or three short slits in the top of the pastry to let out the steam.

Bake for fifty to fifty-five minutes on the hot baking sheet, turning the heat down to 375°F after ten minutes, until the pastry is crisp and pale gold. Dust with more sugar. Leave to cool for fifteen minutes, before cutting and serving with cream.
Enough for 6

I return from another trip to the U.S. This time to New York, San Francisco and Los Angeles. After an initial and deeply disappointing peep in the fridge (it just stared back and seemed to say, 'Well, what exactly did you expect?'), I phone out for pizza and beer. Tomorrow I will go to Chinatown to stock up.

I visit Chinatown once a week, usually on a Friday, for plastic bags of greens – bok choi, yellow-flowered choy sum, lanky Chinese broccoli – and for papayas, net bags of lychees and cheap bunches of cilantro. I pick up ginger if I need it but only if it is truly plump and smells faintly of lemon when you scratch the skin with your nail. Sometimes there is heavier shopping: bottles of salty oyster sauce and light soy, packets of noodles, or a duck for roasting. I am always tempted by the fresh pork buns, which I take home to steam and then remember how they are somehow never the same as when you have them in a restaurant.

Occasionally, the streets there seem intimidating. Trolleys bite at your ankles. The back doorways smell of pee. The shopkeepers rarely crack a smile. But there is a buzz too, especially in the mornings when the lorries are unloading their wicker baskets of greens and polystyrene boxes of small blue crabs and live gray shrimp. There is nowhere more exciting to shop.

Today I have brought a duck home with me. I mean a dead one rather than one as a pet. The up side of cooking a duck in a casserole is that the flesh stays moist and juicy. The down side is the lack of crisp skin. Cooked in a stew of ginger, star anise and rice wine, the meat takes on the heavenly flavors and smells that greet you when you walk into a first-rate Chinese restaurant. I make deep bowls of snowy white rice to soak up the scented liquor from the pot. Best of all is to make the stew today for eating tomorrow. That way, the excess fat will solidify in the fridge and you can scrape it off effortlessly.

Slow-cooked duck with star anise and ginger

peanut oil – 2 generous tablespoons
duck pieces on the bone (legs, breast etc) – 8
onions – 2
garlic – 6 large, juicy cloves
fresh ginger – about 8 'coins'
scallions – 6
palm or brown sugar – $2\frac{1}{2}$ teaspoons
chicken stock – 2 cups
rice wine – $\frac{1}{2}$ cup
star anise – 3 whole flowers

Set the oven to 350°F. On the burner, warm the oil in a heavy casserole to which you have a lid, then lightly brown the duck pieces in it. Peel and roughly chop the onions. Lift the browned duck out on to a plate. Add the onions to the pan, turn the heat down a little and let them cook, with only the occasional stir, until they are soft and sweet.

Peel the garlic and slice each clove thinly, then stir it into the onion as it cooks. Cut the ginger into matchsticks, stir them in, then cut the scallions into short lengths and add them to the pot. Leave everything to soften for a few minutes, then stir in the palm sugar, chicken stock, rice wine and star anise. Season with black pepper and salt and bring to a boil. Let the mixture boil for a good minute, then return the meat to the pot, together with any juices that may have escaped. Cover with a lid and transfer to the oven, setting the timer for an hour and fifteen minutes.

Check the duck for tenderness. It should be soft but far from falling off the bone. Season the stew with a little salt. Scoop off as much of the liquid fat from the top as you can – there will be lots – then either lift the pieces of duck on to shallow bowls of rice and spoon over the juices, or let everything cool, then refrigerate overnight. If you take the latter option, the next day scrape off the white fat that has settled on top, reheat the stew and serve with rice.
Enough for 3–4

November 20

A big salad of roast cherry tomatoes, black olives, both arugula and the heart-leaves of Little Gem lettuce, basil leaves, finely sliced rounds of coppa with its marbling of aromatic white fat, wide, thin shavings of pecorino and a dressing of olive oil, salt and black pepper. I could have used Parmesan but the pecorino was pleasingly crumbly and had a dry, almost lemony flavor in the mouth.

November 21

Lunch today consists of a dish of roasted tomatoes crushed to a pulp with the potato masher, then let down to a soupy consistency with vegetable stock, poured over pieces of toasted stale bread drizzled with olive oil and a shake of chili sauce. A warming little number after a morning in the garden.

November 22
A big pie
for six

I have hardly cooked on the stove this month. Pasta, of course – once, that chewy, corkscrew-shaped stuff with black olive paste and tomato (horrid, I cannot imagine what I was thinking of), and another day some gossamer-thin ravioli filled with ricotta and spinach. It was like eating the softest silk cushions, a dribble of creamy olive oil over them and just a scattering of crunchy, toasted pine nuts. There has been a stir-fry, too – of squid again, this time with noodles and some Vietnamese chili sauce. Garlic goes in first, frying with chopped scallion in just a little smoking-hot peanut oil, then the squid, cut into rings, then, just seconds later, when all is popping and banging in the wok, some tiny bird's eye chilis, the ripe red ones, and then the boiled noodles and a shot (several, actually) of hot Vietnamese chili sauce. What I ended up with was a fast, mouth-stinging bowl of food for a frosty midweek supper.

Today there are six for lunch and I know that at least half of them don't eat meat. The main course must be warming and slightly luxurious. There are big pouches of basil leaves at the deli so I buy two and make a whole mess of pesto, which I layer between lasagne, mushrooms and cream. I could have used ready-made pesto sauce, but it lacks the peppery greenness of fresh basil to me, though I did buy the béchamel.

Mushroom lasagne with basil and cream

onions – 2
garlic – 3 small cloves
a thick slice of butter
dried porcini mushrooms – a ½oz packet
portobello mushrooms – 1¾lbs
chopped parsley – a good handful
freshly grated Parmesan – 5 or 6 tablespoons, plus 4 for later
heavy cream – ½ cup
béchamel sauce – 3 cups (ready-made is fine for this)
dried lasagne – ½lb (or, better, ¾lb fresh lasagne)

For the basil sauce:
pine nuts – ½ cup
basil leaves – ½ cup
garlic – 2 cloves
enough olive oil to make a thick, spoonable paste
grated Parmesan – 5 tablespoons

Peel and roughly chop the onions, peel and thinly slice the garlic, then set them to cook in a deep-sided frying pan with the butter. Cover the dried porcini with warm water – barely ½ cup – and leave to soak. Cut the fresh mushrooms into thick slices. After twenty minutes' cooking, the onions and garlic will have softened and taken on an almost translucent quality.

Meanwhile, either process the pine nuts, basil, garlic, olive oil and Parmesan in a food processor or do it the hard way by pounding the garlic with a little salt in a mortar, then mashing in the basil, pine nuts, cheese and olive oil to make a rough and slightly sloppy paste.

Stir the sliced mushrooms into the onions and garlic and partially cover with a lid. The mushrooms should color and soften. Add the

reconstituted porcini and their soaking water, then the parsley, 4 or 5 tablespoons of Parmesan and the cream. Season with salt and ground black pepper and simmer and stir until the cream has thickened somewhat.

Spread a few spoonfuls of the béchamel sauce over the bottom of a large dish (I used a 16-in oval baking dish), then cover with a single layer of the pasta. Spoon on half of the mushroom filling, cover with another layer of pasta, then a second layer of mushrooms. Top with a third single layer of pasta. Spread the basil sauce over the pasta, then smooth the last of the béchamel sauce over and cover with the remaining Parmesan. Bake at 350°F for fifty minutes or until golden and bubbling.

Enough for 6

After spending far too long making the lasagne, I refuse to do anything much for dessert, so I pass round a plate of pineapple, dripping with juice and cut into fat wedges like a melon. It goes down well, though I suspect a few of them expected a proper dessert.

November 23
A bowl of
pure, white
rice

Ate too much yesterday. Eat steamed basmati rice, into which I stir chopped mint and basil leaves and several twists of black pepper, followed by a ripe papaya.

I have something of a personal ritual when cooking rice. The rice is tipped into a bowl and covered with warm water, I swoosh it about a bit and pour off the water, then repeat. Twice. The final time, the rice is left covered in warm water for a full twenty minutes, then drained and cooked with a shallow covering of fresh water and a tight lid. I tuck a clove of garlic in, a few green cardamom pods, half a cinnamon stick and sometimes a clove or two. It is ready when the water has evaporated and several deep holes have formed in the rice. I leave it, still covered, for a further ten minutes, then run the tines of a fork gently through it. A fragrant meal of peace and purity.

November 24
Little birds,
Indian style

Supper was going to be either sausage and french fries or pickled herrings from a jar with boiled potatoes in their skins and a chucked-together salad of apples, celery and walnuts. It all sounded great, but then I saw a box of fat little quail on one of my very rare trips to the supermarket. I only went in for blueberries and trash bags but came out with mangoes, two beautiful avocados and a large carton of passion fruit smoothie. That's another reason I hate supermarkets: stuff jumps into your basket when you're not looking. Tonight, as I walk home, I notice just how much autumn is already nudging its way into winter.

Hot and sticky roast quail

Sticky little birds, these. A spot of plain brown rice would go well here. If you don't fancy or cannot find quail, then chicken thighs would work too. They will need a bit longer in the oven, at a slightly lower temperature.

garlic – 4 plump and juicy cloves
peanut oil – a generous tablespoon
ground cayenne – $1\frac{1}{4}$ teaspoons
the juice of half a lemon
light soy sauce – 2 generous tablespoons
salt – $\frac{3}{4}$ teaspoon
grainy mustard – 5 teaspoons
oven-ready quail – 4

Preheat the oven to 425°F. Peel and crush the garlic, then mix with the oil, cayenne, lemon juice, soy, salt and mustard. Place the quail in a small roasting pan – they should not touch. Pour over the basting mixture so that the birds are soaked in it and some of it drizzles into the pan.

Roast the quail for twenty to twenty-five minutes, basting once. They should go rather sticky. Eat while they are hot, nibbling the bones and tearing them to pieces as you go.
Enough for 2. Picture on previous page

Just a slithery, cold noodle salad today, the drained skinny noodles tossed with strips of cucumber, shreds of carrot, toasted sesame seeds and a little sesame oil.

November 25

Sometimes you just need comfort food of the highest order. This 'pie', with its mashed potatoes, onions and cheese, is what I want when I come home cold and wet from a long winter walk. The peeling of the potatoes and slow cooking of the onions take a good hour, so it's not something to throw together for a midweek supper. This is what I call weekend food. The slow cooking of the onions is essential, so they turn soft and sweet and 'melt' with the cheese. Expect this to take a good twenty to twenty-five minutes over a low heat.

November 27
A cheesy pie to warm the soul

All this molten cheese and mashed potato needs something contrasting. I usually serve lots of vivid green spinach or frills of kale with it, though this time it got frozen peas because I came back from the shops without any. Either way, they need no butter.

Stilton, onion and potato pie

mealy potatoes – 3½lbs
onions – 4 medium
butter – 7 tablespoons
milk – ½ cup
Stilton – ½lb
grated Parmesan – ¼ cup

Put a large pot of water on to boil. Peel the potatoes and cut them into halves or quarters, then add them to the boiling water. When it comes back to a boil, add a little salt and turn down to a lively simmer. Check the potatoes now and again; they should be tender in fifteen minutes or so.

Whilst the potatoes cook, peel the onions and cut them in half, then cut each into five or six segments. Put them into a heavy-based frying pan with 3 tablespoons of the butter and let them cook over a moderate to low heat, stirring from time to time. They will need twenty to twenty-five minutes to become thoroughly soft and sticky.

Bring the milk to a boil and turn off the heat. Drain the potatoes, then tip them into the bowl of a food mixer fitted with a beater attachment. Mix as you slowly add the milk and the remaining butter. Beat to a smooth mash, stopping well before it becomes gluey.

Set the oven to 400°F. Butter the base and sides of a heavy 11-in frying pan with a metal handle or a similar diameter baking dish – I use a black, cast-iron frying pan. Spoon in half the mashed potato, smooth the potato a little, then add the onions and a grinding of black pepper. Crumble the Stilton over the onions. Pile the rest of the mashed potato over the top and smooth lightly with the back of the spoon or a rubber spatula.

Dust over the grated Parmesan, then bake for twenty-five to thirty minutes, by which time the top will be pale gold and the filling will be bubbling up around the edges.

Enough for 6 as a main dish with greens. Picture on previous page

**November 28
A Sunday
lunch in
honor of
the pig**

Late autumn, with the air on the slide from cool to cold, was the time many families used to kill their pig. The offal, which could not be cured or dried or made into a fat-covered confit for keeping, would be the *après*-slaughter feast. The blood that was saved was made into blood sausage. This cold November Sunday seems as good a time as any to raise a glass to the pig.

To the farmers' market in Marylebone with no shopping list, just a vague idea I want something to go with some paper-thin slices of French ham I bought yesterday and some greens for later in the week. One of the stalls has a pile of ivory-colored celery root, complete with its topknot of fresh, green leaves. The time-honored treatment is to grate the woody lump coarsely and stir it into a mustard mayonnaise to make celeriac remoulade, but with a bit of tweaking you can eat it hot, too. I give it much the same treatment, just changing the oily mayonnaise to sharp crème fraîche and adding a shake from the wine vinegar bottle. The mustard is what makes it, so I don't go overboard; I don't want to cancel out this root's deep mineral flavor.

Celeriac and walnut remoulade

crème fraîche – 1 cup
the juice of half a lemon
grain mustard – 2 generous tablespoons
shelled walnuts – a handful
a large celeriac – about 1¼lb
Bayonne ham – about 16 slices

Mix the crème fraîche, lemon juice and mustard together, then stir in a little salt and black pepper. Roughly chop the walnuts and stir them in.

Peel the celeriac and cut into large chunks, then either shred very coarsely on a grater or cut into long, matchstick-width pieces. Put them in with the dressing.

Divide the ham between four plates and add a spoonful of celeriac remoulade to the center of each plate.
Enough for 4

Lunch continues in a porky manner with slices of grilled blood sausage cut thick and pan-fried slices of apple with triangles of crisply fried bread. This is put on large plates with a simple salad of frisée with a lemon and oil dressing. It looks surprisingly beautiful, and eats well, the slices of sausage crumbling delectably amongst the spiky leaves and golden apples. We finish with an old-fashioned cake.

Coffee and walnut cake
Made with unsalted butter, unrefined sugar and organic eggs, this will give you something infinitely superior to any shop-bought cake. It will take about an hour from start to finish.

butter – 12 tablespoons
superfine sugar – ¾ cup
large eggs – 3
self-rising flour – 1¾ cups
baking powder – 1¼ teaspoons
instant coffee granules – 2½ teaspoons
walnut pieces – ½ cup

For the butter cream:
butter – ½lb
confectioners' sugar – 3 cups
instant coffee granules – 2½ teaspoons
walnut pieces – ½ cup

You will need two 8-in loose-bottomed cake pans.

Set the oven to 350°F. Line the base of the cake pans with baking parchment. Beat the butter and sugar till light, pale and fluffy. You could do this by hand but it is far easier and, frankly, better with an electric mixer. Crack the eggs into a bowl, break them up with a fork, then add them a little at a time to the butter and sugar, beating well after each addition.

Mix the flour and baking powder together and gently mix into the butter and sugar, either with the mixer on a slow speed or by hand, with a large metal spoon. Dissolve the coffee granules in a tablespoon of boiling water, then stir into the mixture. Chop the walnuts and fold them in gently.

Divide the cake mixture between the two pans, smooth the top lightly and bake for twenty to twenty-five minutes. I have noticed mine are pretty much consistently done after twenty-three minutes. Remove from the oven and leave to cool.

To make the butter cream, beat the butter with an electric beater till soft and pale, then add the confectioner's sugar and beat till smooth and creamy. Stir a tablespoon of boiling water into the coffee granules, then mix it into the butter cream. Fold in the walnut pieces.

As soon as the cake is cool, turn one half of it upside down on a plate or board, spread it with a good third of the butter cream, then place the second cake half on top. Spread the remaining butter cream on top and round the sides.
Enough for 8–10

I make a bowl of miso broth (2 tablespoons of yellow miso paste to 5 cups of water, a tablespoon of fish sauce and a few shakes of dark soy) and bring it to a boil. I then steam some little shrimp dumplings that I picked up frozen at the Chinese supermarket and drop them into the miso broth. A small handful of cilantro, a shredded scallion and that is it. A rather curious meal, and frankly just the sort of hybrid I usually disapprove of, yet two of us got through the whole pot of soup and twelve little dumplings apiece.

November 30

december

Nigel's Christmas pudding

Christmas cake

Taleggio and parsley cakes

Sautéed chicken with spices, fennel and cream

Marinated feta and artichoke salad

Baked red mullet with pine nut stuffing

Roast duck with pancetta and potatoes

Lemon ice-cream tart

Potatoes with duck fat and garlic

Bean sprout salad with cilantro and mint

Walnut and candied peel tartlets

Grilled pork steaks with vermouth and fennel

Roast leg of pork with onion and Marsala gravy

Cabbage with orange and juniper

Roast goose, juniper sauce and apple and lemon purée

Passion fruit roulade

Cheese bubble and squeak

**December 1
Yet another
quick pasta
supper**

It's the lights that get me in the end. The candlelight bouncing off the oh-so-carefully polished glasses on the table; the dim, amber glow from the oven that silhouettes the golden skin of the roasting bird; the shimmering string of lanterns I weave through the branches of The Tree. That, and the carols that float from the radio or those I catch as I pass by the open doors of St Saviour's. The food's good too, of course, especially Boxing Day lunch, the bread sauce, the mince pies and the pudding, but doesn't it all taste so much better when you put a taper to the candles?

Some food looks better than others in candlelight: a bowl of shining consommé, the crisp skin of a roast goose, a slick of ruby-colored cranberry sauce, a jelly mold studded with citrus fruit, all look quite magnificent when there are tea lights on the table. Call me sentimental, but I light the candles when we eat Christmas lunch, even if it is the brightest day of winter.

But there is much to be done before that. There is a good three weeks of everyday eating before we roast the goose and pull the crackers. It is simply that the older I get, the more I love Christmas. Just writing the word December gets me going.

Supper tonight is a tossed-together pasta affair. Flat ribbons of pappardelle, sliced globe artichokes in oil from the deli, torn flat-leaf parsley, peppery olive oil and the juice of a lemon. It's nice enough. Then I toast some thin slices of ciabatta, drizzle them with olive oil and grate over a bit of Parmesan before returning them to the broiler till the little strands of cheese melt. A few capers in the pasta and the whole thing comes alive. We drink cold Gamay and finish with sticky dates from the fridge. An unexpected delight.

**December 2
Stirring the
pudding**

The day I make the Christmas puddings, stirring the fruit and sugar, tucking in the old-fashioned silver coins, sealing the china bowls with paper and string, then boiling them for several hours, is the cooking day I look forward to almost more than any other. The rich, heavy scent of dried fruits and brandy on a winter's day has much to do with it, and the sharp note of citrus peel amid the flat, bland smell of boiling puddings. This is not a day to rush, but one to savor.

The new heatproof plastic pudding bowls with their clip-on lids make good sense, cutting out much fiddle. Yet I still do it the traditional way, wrapping old china bowls in greaseproof, white muslin and string. At least I do this year. Next time I'll invest in the modern alternative.

This pudding is lighter and a little less sweet than most. It has the seedy crunch of dried figs, a sparkle from hand-cut peel and a slight tartness from the apricots and orange zest. I don't go in for brandy butter, or even home-made custard, much preferring the silky contrast of organic heavy cream.

Nigel's Christmas pudding

golden raisins – 2⅓ cups
raisins or currants – 2⅓ cups
dried figs – 1 cup, chopped
candied peel – 1⅔ cups, chopped
dried apricots – ⅔ cup, chopped
dark glacé cherries – ½ cup, halved
brandy – ⅔ cup, plus some for flaming
apples or, better still, quinces – 2, grated
the juice and zest of 2 oranges
large eggs – 6
shredded suet – 2 cups
brown sugar – 1¾ cups
fresh breadcrumbs – 5 cups
self-rising flour – 1¾ cups
pumpkin pie spice – 1¼ teaspoons

You will need two 8-cup plastic pudding bowls and lids, buttered, two old sixpences or two pound coins, scrupulously scrubbed, two circles of parchment paper, buttered, large enough to cover the top of each pudding, with a single pleat folded down the center of each.

Soak the golden raisins, raisins or currants, figs, candied peel, apricots and cherries in the brandy overnight. The liquid won't cover the fruit but no matter; just give it a good stir now and again.

Mix the grated apples, orange juice and zest, beaten eggs, suet, sugar, crumbs and flour in a very large mixing bowl, then stir in the soaked fruit and the spice. Divide the mixture between the buttered pudding bowls, tucking the coins in as you go. Cover with the parchment paper, folded with a pleat in the center. Pop the lids on and steam for three and a half hours. Allow the puddings to cool, then remove the parchment paper, cover tightly with plastic wrap and the plastic lid and store in a cool, dry place till Christmas.

To reheat: steam the puddings for a further three and a half hours. Turn out and flame with brandy.
Each pudding is enough for at least 8. Picture overleaf

**December 3
Fridge rice,
Spanish-
style**

There is some cooked rice in a cracked earthenware dish in the fridge. It will make a supper for two, just. I fry off some chopped scallion and a chopped clove of garlic in a shallow pan with a glug of olive oil, then chuck in some chopped celery, several slices of brick-red Spanish chorizo and a couple of pieces of blood sausage too. When all is sizzling and the smell of warm sausage comes up from the pan, I stir in the rice, gently teasing the grains apart. We eat the result, which whilst being utterly delicious looks a bit of a mess, with bottles of cold beer.

I am extraordinarily fond of making the Christmas cake and look
forward to it for weeks. Not even a baking loaf makes the house smell
so welcoming. I try to make the cake at the beginning of the month,
then feed it every week or so with brandy, so that by Christmas Day it
is thoroughly moist, but a few times I have left it to the last minute and
it is almost as good. Over the years I have probably been asked for this
recipe more than any other. Sometimes I ice it, sometimes I don't.
My own cake is the one that appears in *Appetite*, which is a good large
size, capable of feeding sixteen or more. Each year I get asked for
a scaled-down version for those who don't want to be eating Christmas
cake till February. This year my recipe feeds just twelve, though somewhat generously.

Christmas cake

butter – ½lb plus 2 tablespoons
light brown sugar – ½ cup plus 2 tablespoons
dark brown sugar – ½ cup plus 2 tablespoons
dried fruits – prunes, apricots, figs, candied peel, glacé cherries,
4½ cups in total
large free-range eggs – 3
ground almonds – ½ cup
shelled hazelnuts – ⅔ cup
raisins, currants, cranberries – 2⅓ cups in total
brandy – 4 tablespoons, plus extra to 'feed' the cake
the zest and juice of an orange
the zest of a lemon
baking powder – ¾ teaspoon
all-purpose flour – 2½ cups

You will need a deep 8-in cake pan with a removable base, fully lined
with a double layer of lightly buttered baking parchment, which should
come at least 2in above the top of the tin.

Set the oven to 325°F. Beat the butter and sugars till light and fluffy.
I needn't tell you this is much easier with an electric mixer, though I
have done it by hand. Don't forget to push the mixture down the sides
of the bowl from time to time with a spatula.

While the butter and sugars are beating to a cappuccino-colored
fluff, cut the dried fruits into small pieces, removing the hard stalks
from the figs. Add the eggs to the mixture one at a time – it will curdle
but don't worry – then slowly mix in the ground almonds, hazelnuts,
all the dried fruit, the brandy and the citrus zest and juice. Now mix
the baking powder and flour together and fold them lightly into
the mix. Scrape the mixture into the prepared pan, smoothing the top
gently, and put it in the oven. Leave it for an hour, then, without open-

ing the oven door, turn the heat down to 300°F and continue cooking for one and a half hours.

Check whether the cake is done by inserting a skewer – a knitting needle will do – into the center. It should come out with just a few crumbs attached but no trace of raw cake mixture. Take the cake out of the oven and leave to cool before removing it from the pan.

Feed the cake by pouring brandy into it every week until Christmas. Pierce the cake with a skewer and drizzle in some brandy. Cover tightly and leave in a cake pan till needed. It will keep for several weeks.

Almond paste

To cover this size of cake you will need 1¾lbs marzipan. I have always made my own until this year, when I found a brand of organic almond paste in my local healthfood shop. It was fine, if not as yellow as most brands of the commercial stuff, and perfectly pleasant if you like that sort of thing. I brush the cake with apricot jam or marmalade to help the almond paste stick to it. To ice the cake, see December 22nd.

December 7 There is the most stunning nutmeg in the shops. Not the usual beige nut but a glossy brown shell with the nut rattling inside it. It takes a pair of crackers to gain entry. I have seen fresh nutmeg, with its lacy shell of mace, growing in the foothills of Sri Lanka but it is rare to see spice of such quality here. We crack one open to grate on to a dish of potato Dauphinoise for supper. For once I put cheese in too, layering grated Gruyère in amongst the thin slices of potato and cream. With a nutmeg in the house this good, I get the urge to make the slitheriest, most quivering of egg custard tarts, with pastry as fine and crumbly as old parchment. Needless to say, I don't.

December 8
A frugal
supper
I am not a great fan of leftover cookery, generally finding that a discreet binning might have been a more fitting end. Leftover risotto is another matter. Squashed into balls and loosely flattened, yesterday's risotto reheats enticingly in butter, forming a crisp golden crust outside whilst staying soft and creamy within. A cube of Taleggio cheese tucked inside as you shape the balls (just a thought and by no means essential) will ooze out softly as you cut into them. This is my standard way of clearing up leftover rice, and I half wonder if yesterday I deliberately made too much just so I could have these little cakes today. While the cakes are frying, I make a crisp salad of Barolo-veined Trevise, sharpened with lemon and more parsley.

Taleggio and parsley cakes

leftover risotto – about 2 cups
parsley – a small bunch

grated Parmesan – 2 heaped tablespoons
Taleggio – 5oz
a little butter and olive oil for frying

Leave the risotto to go cold and stiffen up. If it's yesterday's, then all to the good. Remove the leaves from the parsley and chop them roughly (or at least not too finely). Stir them into the rice with the grated Parmesan and a grinding of black pepper.

Cut the Taleggio cheese into cubes, discarding the rind. Take a tablespoon of the rice and press a cube of cheese into it, then press more risotto on top to cover the cheese, squeezing the rice into a rough ball as you go. Set aside and continue with the rest. You will probably make four or five decent-sized balls.

Warm a large knob of butter and olive oil in a non-stick frying pan. Flatten the rice balls a little and lay them in the hot fat. Let them color on one side, then turn and lightly brown the other. Press the rice down with a spatula so you end up with a thick patty. They are ready when a golden crust has formed on both sides and the melting cheese is trying to escape. Slide on to warm plates.

Enough for 2. Picture overleaf

There are four of us tonight, for curry and beer. What was planned to be a big bowl of curry to bring us out in a sweat has ended up as something much more refined, passive even. This mildly spiced chicken supper, at once fragrant and creamy, is the result, and despite the dozen ingredients is actually simplicity itself. I serve it with brown rice and some lightly cooked spinach for mopping up the amber sauce.

**December 9
A chicken
supper with
spices and
cream**

Sautéed chicken with spices, fennel and cream

large chicken thighs – 8
peanut oil
fennel – 2 medium-sized heads
heavy cream – 1¼ cups
cilantro – a small handful
brown rice, to serve

For the spice paste:
green cardamom pods – 4
ground turmeric – ¾ teaspoon
ground cumin – a level teaspoon
chili powder – ½ teaspoon
garlic – 2 small cloves
grainy French mustard – a generous tablespoon

Rub the chicken with salt and pepper and fry gently in a tablespoon of the oil till the skin is golden and starting to crisp. Over a low to moderate heat, this will take a good twenty-five minutes, during which time a savory golden sediment will attach itself to the pan. After fifteen minutes' cooking, cut each head of fennel into six long wedges and add to the pan, tucking them around the chicken.

While the chicken is cooking, make the spice paste. First crush the cardamom pods, discarding the green husks and crushing the black seeds to a powder with a mortar and pestle. Add the turmeric, cumin, chili and garlic and continue pounding, mixing in the mustard and a tablespoon or two of peanut oil as you go.

When the fennel is tender and the chicken cooked right through to the bone, lift them out with a slotted spoon and set aside. Pour the oil out of the pan (you could keep it for frying potatoes), then add the spice paste to the pan, scraping at any sticky sediment with a wooden spoon and stirring it in. Leave the paste to cook for a minute or two, taking care it doesn't burn (spice pastes catch in a matter of seconds if the heat is too high), then stir in the cream and immediately return the chicken and fennel to the pan. Leave to bubble for a minute or two, then toss in the cilantro, chopped if they are large. Serve with the brown rice.
Enough for 4

The kitchen is heated by a small and ineffective radiator. Most of the time I don't notice the chill but now, with a wind howling and the threat of frost, I find myself on an unstoppable slide towards winter cooking. I make one last autumnal meal of late artichokes and red mullet before snuggling down to winter food proper. Foodie anniversaries such as Shrove Tuesday, Burns Night and even the first day of the wild salmon season tend to get scant attention in my house. Yet odd days like today, which I have a hunch is to be the very last day of autumn, deserve a little recognition.

Marinated feta and artichoke salad

feta cheese – 14oz
dried mint
dried oregano
fresh mint – a few bushy sprigs, roughly chopped
olive oil – 7 generous tablespoons
grilled artichokes from the deli counter – 8

Break the feta cheese into large, jagged lumps. Add the dried and fresh herbs to the olive oil with a grinding of black pepper. As a rule, I allow about a heaped tablespoon of dried herbs per 7oz cheese. Pour the oil over the cheese and leave to marinate for three or four hours.

Drain the artichokes of their oil, cut them in half if they are whole and crumble the marinated cheese over them. Serve with warm bread.
Enough for 4

Large, juicy flakes of fish are what appeal so much here. I always find you need a large red mullet per person, or two smaller ones. This sounds a lot, I know, but they have quite big bones.

The stuffing is good for other things too – whole squid perhaps, or even partridge. Despite the Mediterranean notes, there are some distinctly Yuletide flavors here. A tomato salad would be good with it, but a French bean one would go well too.

Baked red mullet with pine nut stuffing

large red mullet – 4, cleaned but with the heads left on
a large shallot
olive oil
a clove of garlic, finely chopped
fresh white breadcrumbs – 1 cup
black olives, pitted – 6
pine nuts – $\frac{1}{2}$ cup
the juice and finely grated zest of a lemon
raisins – 2 generous tablespoons
chopped parsley – a small handful
rosemary – the leaves from a couple of bushy sprigs, chopped
capers – $2\frac{1}{2}$ teaspoons

Heat the oven to 350°F. Rinse the mullet, pat them dry with paper towels and lay them snugly in a roasting tin. Peel the shallot and chop it finely, then let it cook slowly with a little olive oil and the garlic in a small pan over a moderate heat until it is soft and translucent. Add the breadcrumbs and let them color slightly. Chop the olives and add them to the crumbs with the pine nuts, lemon zest, raisins, chopped herbs and capers. Season with salt and pepper.

Stuff as much of the filling into the fish as will go comfortably. Any remaining stuffing can be scattered over the fish. Squeeze over the lemon juice, add a drizzle of olive oil and a grinding of salt, then bake for twenty minutes, till the fish is opaque and comes easily from the bone.
Enough for 4

Hot apples, cold ice cream
In this house, you get starter or dessert, rarely both. It is not simply to escape the tyranny of the three-course meal but because I genuinely feel that no one really wants all that food. But even with the rich

stuffing, this is a relatively light meal and a dessert of some sort is called for. There is a vote for baked apples, partly because the oven is on anyway. So four majestic apples, split round the middle, emerge from the oven a good hour later. We eat them with vanilla ice cream simply because I love the teeth-juddering contrast between the rock-hard ice cream and the froth of searing-hot apple. Now, of course, we are all too full to move.

December 11 The smell of white rice cooking, clean, nutty and warm, casts a sense of peace over the house. As if snow has fallen. Seasonings change with the day, but tonight it is green cardamom, black cumin seed, cinnamon and, somewhat unusually, a couple of whole star anise flowers. What was once a distinctly Indian smell is now edged with something faintly Chinese. Fleeting, intriguing, gentle. At the table, I bring to it some steamed Chinese broccoli, complete with its long, tender stalks.

December 12
An early
Christmas
lunch

Christmas is not just one meal but many; a series of mini-feasts for people you won't be seeing on the day itself. To do the full Christmas lunch each time would seem awkward, contrived even, but something mildly festive is called for. Hence this Sunday lunch of roast duck with Italian bacon and a lemon tart.

The duck recipe here is for two (you will find it a useful recipe for other occasions). To feed four or five, simply roast two ducks. You will need a very large roasting pan, about eight to ten potatoes, three onions, the same amount of thyme, and you will need to increase the roasting time by about ten minutes. You will also want an extra half a glass of Marsala in the gravy.

Roast duck with pancetta and potatoes

The point of this recipe is that the potatoes absorb some of the duck fat; you then balance the richness with some peas with lemon and mint. I have been known to offer a watercress and orange salad, too.

The fat that you pour from the duck as it cooks shouldn't go to waste – it is one of the most delicious of all cooking mediums. Put it in the fridge to set, then use it for roasting potatoes.

a large duckling, weighing about 5½lbs
potatoes, such as Maris Piper – 6 medium
pancetta – 5oz
olive oil, mild, not fruity
onions – 2 medium
thyme – 5 or 6 sprigs
bay leaves – a couple
a wine glass of Marsala

Preheat the oven to 400°F. Remove the giblets from the duck, rinse the bird inside and out and pat it dry with paper towel. If you can do this an hour or so before you begin to cook, leaving the duck in a cool place, then all to the good.

Peel the potatoes and cut them into finger-thick slices, dropping them into cold water as you go. Cut the pancetta into cubes, then put it into a large roasting pan with a tablespoon of oil. Warm it over a low heat, letting the pancetta flavor the oil but without letting it color. Introduce the slices of potato, shaken dry, into the fat and let them cook slowly.

Whilst this is going on, peel and cut the onions first in half, then each half into about six. Add them to the potatoes along with the thyme leaves stripped from their stems. Turn everything over gently as it cooks, letting the potatoes and onions color very slightly. Season with salt and black pepper and a couple of bay leaves, then remove from the heat.

Prick the skin of the duck all over with a fork, then season it inside and out with salt. Lay the duck on top of the potatoes, then put it in the oven and roast for an hour to an hour and a half, until the potatoes are soft and both they and the duck are golden. From time to time, push the spuds, particularly those that are browning too quickly, to one side, and spoon a little of the cooking juices over any that appear dry. During the cooking, carefully tip off most of the fat that is pouring out of the duck and that has not been absorbed by the potatoes.

Test to see that the duck is done. There should be no sign of blood in the juices and the skin should be crisp and singing. Remove the potatoes to a warm serving dish.

Turn the oven up to 425°F. Put the duck back in the oven and let it crisp up for five minutes or so, then transfer it to a warm dish. Quickly pour the Marsala into the roasting pan and place it over a moderately high heat (you don't want it to boil away), scraping at any stuck bits in the pan. The idea is to get any pan stickings and sediment to dissolve into the gravy. Whilst the sauce is bubbling, carve the duck and serve it with the potatoes. Check the pan juices for seasoning – they may need a little salt – then spoon them over the duck.
Enough to serve 2 generously

Peas with lemon and mint

I can never think of duck without peas. You could serve plain boiled peas if you like, but these are good too, and have the zing of lemon and mint to balance the richness of the duck. Here, the peas are simmered with very little water, so they partly cook in their own steam.

frozen peas – 1½ cups
olive oil – 2 generous tablespoons

the juice of half a lemon
fresh mint – 3 sprigs

Put the peas, a little salt, olive oil and 8 tablespoons of water into a
small pan. Bring to a boil, then reduce the heat to a fast simmer. Cook,
uncovered, for about 8 minutes. Squeeze the lemon juice over and stir
in the mint.
Enough for 2–3

Lemon ice-cream tart with gingersnap crust

butter – 10 tablespoons
gingersnap – 14oz

For the filling:
white wine – ⅔ cup
brandy or Marsala – 2 generous tablespoons
grated zest and juice of 2 lemons
grated zest of an orange
superfine sugar – 5 tablespoons
heavy cream – 2 cups

You will need a loose-bottomed tart pan with a diameter of about 9in.
Line the base of the tart tin with a single piece of wax paper. Melt the
butter in a small pan. Crush the cookies in a food processor or bash
them in a plastic bag. You want them to be a coarse powder. Stir the
cookies into the butter. Line the base of the tin with the buttered
crumbs, pushing some as far up the sides as you can. It doesn't matter
if the edges are rough. Put the crumb-lined pan in the freezer.

Pour the wine into the bowl of a food mixer. Add the brandy or
Marsala and the grated zest of the lemons and the orange. Squeeze the
lemons and add the juice (reserve the orange juice for another occasion). Add the sugar and cream to the wine and zest mixture, then beat
slowly until thick. The consistency needs to be soft and thick, so that it
lies in voluptuous folds rather than standing in stiff peaks.

Scrape the mixture into the crumb-lined pan and freeze for at least
four hours. Remove from the freezer fifteen to twenty minutes before
you intend to serve it. I find it easier to remove the cake from the tin
while it is still frozen, running a spatula around the edge first.
Enough for 8. Picture overleaf

December 13

I barely eat a thing today; just some of yesterday's roast duck stripped
from the carcass and tossed with slices of orange and grapefruit and
several sprigs of watercress. As salads go, it is a stunning mixture of
fresh, clean, rich and hot. It is enough for me, but there are cries of

hunger from elsewhere. They get cheese on toast, with a layer of sharp, chunky tomato chutney under the cheese. Crunch comes in the way of an apple salad, the fruit cut into thin slices and tossed with cider vinegar, walnut oil and fresh sprouted mung beans. Followed by apple and blueberry crumble. I put slivered almonds and a fine grating of nutmeg in the crumble topping, which seems to go down well. No one seems to notice that both salad and dessert are made with the same fruit.

Nothing will get me to waste the creamy-white fat from the duck. It is the best stuff going in which to fry potatoes, in which case they will end up crisp, rich and deeply savory. I fry them in thin slices, cooked until deep, burnished gold, with an ice-crisp salad of frisée, watercress and chicory on the side.

December 14
Fried
potatoes and
a crisp salad

Potatoes with duck fat and garlic

potatoes – 4 medium
duck fat – 4 tablespoons
thyme leaves – a small palmful
a single clove of garlic, chopped

Peel the potatoes and slice them as thinly as you can. They should be no thicker than $1/8$in. Melt the duck fat in a heavy, shallow pan – I use a cast-iron skillet – and add the potato slices, neatly or hugger-mugger, seasoning them with salt, black pepper, thyme leaves and a little chopped garlic as you go. Cook over a moderate heat for thirty to forty minutes, till golden brown.
Enough for 4

A green and white winter salad
You don't need me to tell you how to make a straightforward salad of white chicory, watercress and frisée, or how to dress it with a classic oil and vinegar dressing. But I feel I should mention that I find the balance best when there are equal amounts of watercress and frisée, with just a few long, thin chicory leaves thrown in for extra crunch.

The Christmas shopping list – there has to be one, no one has a memory *that* good – is the longest of the year, especially if you have left it to the eleventh hour to stir the pudding. If we are to make sense of The Feast and the umpteen 'lesser' meals that surround it, we need to include some dishes that will carry over from one meal to the next. A vast piece of ham, say, served with potato cakes and buttered spinach, only to be brought out the next day, cold but with just as much pride, in thin slices with a dazzling salsa. Consider also a roast guinea fowl or

December 15
The Feast
starts here

pheasant, whose bones can be used later for a parsley-flecked broth for ravioli. A whole salmon, a vast pork pie and a rib of beef are all ingredients that will introduce some sanity into the proceedings, both practically and financially.

Last year I paid a king's ransom for a piece of ham, boned, rolled and scored by the butcher, which I poached in organic, unfiltered apple juice with an onion, a fat carrot, a stick of celery and four flowers of star anise. I let it cool awhile, peeled away the skin, then spread the joint thickly with a hot-sweet mixture of marmalade, seed mustard, the juice and zest of an orange and a handful of fresh white breadcrumbs. I then let it bake to a soft, golden brown glaze. It was a huge success with a mound of braised black-leaf kale and a salt-crusted baked potato. Two days later, the generous remains appeared in sandwiches with watercress and hot onion pickle, some Burt's potato crisps on the side, and then again in paper-thin slices with a salad of raw fennel, green olives and lemon. The first meal took a while to prepare, the second and third almost made themselves.

Over the next week or so, I shall endeavor to sit down and give an hour or so's thought to the Christmas feast – what we shall eat, what we shall drink. I know it all sounds a bit 'good housekeeping', but I really cannot face a last-minute panic on Christmas Eve. Been there, done that.

**December 16
A hot, sweet salad and some cute little pies**

In winter, salads tend to become a little more substantial, their dressings maybe a little richer. Today, a clean, sweet-tasting antidote to the heavier notes of winter cooking. Dessert is sliced papaya and persimmon.

Bean sprout salad with cilantro and mint

superfine sugar – 2 generous tablespoons
white wine vinegar – ⅓ cup
cucumber – half
carrots – 2
scallions – 6
small hot red chili peppers – 2
bean sprouts – 2 large handfuls
sesame seeds – a generous tablespoon
cilantro – a handful
mint leaves – a handful

For the dressing:
light soy sauce – a generous tablespoon
rice vinegar – 2 generous tablespoons
sesame oil – a few shakes

Put the sugar and vinegar into a small pan, bring to a boil and leave to cool.

Peel the cucumber, halve it lengthways and remove the seeds, then cut the flesh into long, matchstick-thick pieces. Put them into a colander in the sink, sprinkle with salt and leave for twenty minutes.

Peel the carrots and cut them into short, matchstick-thick pieces. Shred the scallions, seed and finely shred the chilis, and mix them with the carrots and the bean sprouts. Toss with the cooled sugar and vinegar and leave for fifteen minutes.

Toast the sesame seeds in a dry, non-stick pan. Roughly chop the cilantro and mint leaves. Lift the vegetables from the sweet vinegar dressing and put them in a clean bowl. Rinse the cucumber and pat it dry with kitchen towels. Mix the ingredients for the soy dressing together, then toss it with the vegetables and herbs, scattering the sesame seeds over at the end.

Enough for 2

Walnut and candied peel tartlets

I can't help feeling there is something magical about little tartlets of nuts and spice, the sort of thing they might cook in a fairytale. Fragile though they are, you should be able to get them from their cases without them breaking too much. Serve them warm with ice cream.

golden syrup – ⅔ cup
walnuts – 1 cup
candied orange and lemon peel – 1⅓ cups
a pinch of pumpkin pie spice
butter – 2 tablespoons
soft amaretti – 5 (or 5 tablespoons cake crumbs)
a large egg, lightly beaten

For the pastry:
cold butter – 10 tablespoons
all-purpose flour – 3 cups

You will need twenty-four tartlet or shallow muffin pans, 3in in diameter and ½in deep.

For the pastry, cut the butter into small pieces and rub it into the flour with your fingertips until it resembles fine breadcrumbs. You can add a tiny pinch of salt if you want to. Drizzle in a very small amount of water – I would start with just a teaspoon or two – bringing the mixture together to form a soft, but not sticky, rollable ball.

Pat the pastry into a fat sausage the same diameter as your tart tins, cover with plastic wrap and chill for twenty minutes. This will give the pastry time to rest, making it less likely to shrink when it's in the oven.

Set the oven to 350°F. Warm the syrup in a small pan over a low heat. Add the walnuts, roughly chopped, the finely diced peel, the spice and the butter, then, when the butter has melted, crumble in the amaretti or cake crumbs. Remove the pan from the heat and stir in the beaten egg.

Cut the roll of pastry into 24 thin slices, then use them to line the tart tins. Trim the edges with a small knife. Divide the mixture between the tartlet cases – you don't want to overfill them – then bake until golden and bubbling, about fifteen to twenty minutes.

The finished tarts are very crumbly. Allow them to cool a little before attempting to remove them from their tins. Serve with vanilla ice cream.

Makes 24

December 17   Chicken thighs tonight, roasted with olive oil, a little butter and roughly chopped lemons. They sing and sizzle as they come from the oven, filling the house with the scent of hot, crisp chicken skin with the sharp edge of citrus. Baked potatoes on the side, rolled in sea salt and served with no butter, just the juices from the roast bird.

December 18   **Grilled pork steaks with vermouth and fennel**
Putting a chop on the grill, even one seasoned purely with salt and pepper, will give you a simple supper of juicy flesh and deep, savory pleasure. But we can do better than that. Even the briefest time spent in a marinade of appropriate aromatics – in this case garlic, rosemary and lemon – will add much in terms of flavor. You simply mash the seasonings to a paste with olive oil, then leave the meat in it for an hour or more.

rosemary – leaves from 2 bushy sprigs
garlic – 2 small cloves
black peppercorns – 6
salt – 1½ teaspoons
olive oil – 3 generous tablespoons
the juice of half a lemon
pork steaks – 2
fennel – 2 medium bulbs
butter – a thick slice
white vermouth – a small glass

Strip the rosemary leaves from their stems and chop them finely, then tip them into a mortar. Peel the garlic, chop it roughly and add it to the rosemary, together with the peppercorns and salt. Pound these aromatics in the mortar, mixing in the olive oil slowly, until you have a loose paste, then stir in the lemon juice.

Scrape the marinade into a shallow dish and turn the pork steaks in it until they are covered. Leave them to marinate in a cool place for a good hour, longer if you have it.

Slice the fennel thinly and rinse it under running water. Tip it into a small, deep pan with the butter and let it soften over a moderate flame, stirring from time to time so that it does not burn. After five minutes, pour in the vermouth, then cover with a lid and leave to cook for twenty minutes over a low flame, till soft and lightly caramelized.

Warm the broiler, then cook the chops till they are golden brown on each side, the fat lightly charred a little here and there. Serve them on warm plates with the fennel.

Enough for 2

December 19

A supper of pork meatballs, fries and peas. The favorite brand of meatballs seems to have disappeared, so we settle for what I can get. They are okay, but when you are used to a certain brand nothing ever seems as good. I am happy to change my own recipes on a whim, but I am not sure manufacturers should. There is much comfort in familiar tastes.

December 22
The icing on the cake

Sometimes I ice the cake, sometimes I don't. When I do, I beat the whites of two eggs very lightly with a fork, just until bubbles start to appear. Then I sift in 5 cups golden, unrefined confectioners' sugar in two lots, beating hard with a wooden spoon after the first addition. Whilst I am beating in the second half, I add two teaspoons of lemon juice. I prefer my cake to sport a rough, snowdrift look rather than to have smooth icing, so I simply spread the icing thickly on to the top and sides of the almond-paste-covered cake with a spatula, then make snow peaks with the end of a spoon. Just like my mother did.

December 23
A bit of a pig

I will do anything to avoid a queue. That includes getting up at an ungodly hour, pleading to get something delivered or, in some cases, simply going without. Tomorrow is the Holy Grail of queues, with that of my local butcher, cheese shop and fish market snaking across four or five neighboring shop fronts. The deli has no orderly queue, just a disorganized scrum. I get up early and go to the special Christmas farmers' market for greens (for which, needless to say, I have to stand in line), then to the butcher's (no queue to speak of, though busier than usual for a weekday) and then to the cheese shops (one French, one British). Everything will be fine in the fridge till the 25th, and I cannot help but feel a little smug at having got so much done already, leaving me the possibility of actually enjoying Christmas Eve instead of standing looking at someone's back.

I return home with a vast piece of pork, a bag of fat, herb-flecked sausages, slices of fat bacon, a blood sausage, stock, smoked salmon, fish for Christmas Eve supper, three cheeses, a head of celery complete

with soil and leaves, and a somewhat impromptu purchase of a goose. I already have a squirrel stash of mineral water, Champagne, onions, potatoes, parsnips, oranges, clementines, brandy, pears and passion fruits ripening as I write, Cox's apples, mincemeat, plus all the usual fridge and cupboard stuff such as Parmesan, lemons, olive oil and butter. That leaves only oysters, bread and cream to pick up tomorrow.

I should explain the goose. My plan for Christmas lunch is oysters and Champagne followed by a majestic roast leg of Gloucester Old Spot pork and crackling, pork sausages and blood sausage, onion gravy and roast potatoes with glossy red cabbage. We will then have Mrs Appleby's Cheshire cheese and an oozing Vacherin, followed, some time later, by the Christmas pudding with organic cream or brandy butter. The vegetarians will eat parsnip cakes stuffed with spinach and pine nuts. Not the turkey dinner that has always left me cold, but a sumptuous feast of organic meat and farmhouse cheeses. So far, so glorious. However, I have just discovered that I have to go through the same thing again on Boxing Day. So, unable to face cooking and eating an identical meal for what will be my second Christmas lunch, I will instead offer smoked salmon, which keeps in better nick than oysters, roast goose with juniper sauce and an apple and lemon purée, roast potatoes and red cabbage, followed by Wigmore cheese and pears. Then, much later, a sharp lemon and passion fruit roulade, which although rich, has a bite to it that should offset the inevitable richness of the goose. If there is one thing better than Christmas lunch, it's two Christmas lunches.

Oysters and Champagne

Christmas Day

I don't hold with all the gubbins traditionally served with oysters. Nothing quite takes the salty, iodine tang off a good oyster like the shallot vinegar, Tabasco and lemon. Okay, I might occasionally use the meanest squeeze of lemon but, as far as bells and whistles go, that's it.

I reckon you need six oysters per person, but you could get away with four if there is a really big meal following, such as this one (we still have six).

Roast leg of pork with onion and Marsala gravy

After removing the cooked roast from the roasting tin, I pour the fat off, then warm the gravy in the tin, stirring in the goodness stuck to the tin as I go.

a leg of pork on the bone, 7–10lbs in weight
sea salt

Weigh the pork. You will need to cook it for twenty-five minutes per pound. Get the oven hot. You want to start the pork at 425°F. Check that the butcher has scored the rind. It should have a deep hatching of knife-cuts going across, rather than with, the bone. Each cut should go right down into the fat, but not so far that you get to the flesh beneath.

Season thoroughly with salt, rubbing the flakes into the cut sides of the flesh and into the fat – it will help it crackle. If the salt refuses to adhere, then rub a little oil over the meat first. Put the pork into a roasting pan and leave it in the oven to roast for thirty minutes, then lower the heat to 350°F and continue roasting for twenty-five minutes per pound. You don't really need to baste it, I rarely do, especially if I am trying to get good crackling. The fat itself will keep the meat succulent.

When you think the meat is due to be ready, check its juices by inserting a skewer into the thickest part. They should come out clear or honey colored, not pink.

Remove the pork from the oven and leave it to rest for a good twenty to twenty-five minutes so that the juices can settle throughout the meat. Carve into thin slices and serve with the gravy and stuffing below.
Enough for 6–8, plus lots for eating cold

The gravy:
Like curry, trifle and bean soup, this actually seems to improve if made the day before.

onions – 3 medium
olive oil – 2 generous tablespoons
all-purpose flour – 2 generous tablespoons
dry Marsala – 2 glasses
stock or water – 3 cups
English mustard powder – $1\frac{1}{4}$ teaspoons
grain mustard – a generous tablespoon

Peel the onions, slice them in half and then into thick segments. Leave them to cook with the olive oil in a heavy-based pan over a low heat, giving them the occasional stir so they do not burn. You want to end up with onions that are utterly soft, golden and translucent. Tender enough to squash between finger and thumb. You can expect this to take a good thirty minutes.

Stir in the flour and let it cook for a few minutes. Now pour in the Marsala and the stock or water, stirring into a thin sauce. Season with salt and black pepper and the mustard powder and leave to simmer gently for a good twenty minutes, then stir in the grain mustard and continue simmering for a further five.

Serve or leave to cool and reheat as necessary.

Cabbage with orange and juniper

a medium onion
peanut oil – a tablespoon
a small red cabbage, weighing about 1¾lb
celery stalks – 2
an apple
the juice of an orange
the juice of a lemon
a shot of white wine vinegar
juniper berries – 12

Peel the onion and slice it finely, then let it soften in the oil in a heavy casserole set over a medium heat. Shred the cabbage quite finely; the strips need to be about the width of your little finger. Cut the celery thinly. When the onion has softened, turn the heat up a little, then add the celery and cabbage. Stir. Core and chop the apple and add it to the pan.

Mix the citrus juices together, then add a dash of vinegar. Crush the juniper berries and add them to the juices, then, just as the cabbage is starting to wilt, stir the mixture into the casserole. There should be much sizzling and spluttering. Season the cabbage lightly with salt and cover tightly with a lid. Turn down to a simmer and cook for ten to fifteen minutes, until the cabbage is tender. Check the seasoning and serve.
Enough for 6 as a side dish

Christmas Day 'II'
We start with smoked salmon, which I serve with lemon and thin slices of dark, sticky pumpernickel bread.

Roast goose, juniper sauce and apple and lemon purée
I use yesterday's recipe for cabbage with this.

a goose – approximately 14lbs in weight
the onion gravy on the page opposite, plus 12 juniper berries and 2 generous tablespoons redcurrant jelly

You are going to cook the goose at 425°F for twenty-five minutes, then at 350°F for approximately one and a half hours.

Preheat the oven to 425°F. Pull the excess fat from inside the bird. It will come out in big lumps. Prick the bird all over with a fork, salt it inside and out (but no pepper), then wrap aluminum foil over the legs, which have a tendency to dry out. Put the bird breast-side down in a roasting pan and roast for twenty-five minutes, then turn the oven

down to 350°F. Leave the bird to roast for approximately one and a half to two hours, taking it out halfway through cooking to tip off the fat that has accumulated in the pan, remove the foil from its legs and turn the bird breast-side up. This is also when I add parboiled potatoes to the pan. I do all this with great care, as the fat is copious and blisteringly hot.

To check the bird is cooked, pierce the thighs with a skewer; if the juices that run out are clear, then the bird is ready. Leave to rest for ten minutes before carving, slicing the meat on to warm plates.
Enough for 5–6

The juniper sauce
My goose gravy is the onion gravy on page 382, with twelve lightly crushed juniper berries added with the stock and 2 generous tablespoons of redcurrant jelly stirred in at the end, five minutes or so before serving. Once the goose has been removed to a carving board, I carefully pour off all the fat from the tin and pour the sauce into the roasting pan, bubble, scrape the goodness from the bottom into the sauce with a spatula, and stir.

The apple and lemon purée
At any point during the cooking of the goose, peel, core and chop five dessert apples or three Bramleys and let them cook over a moderate heat with a whole chopped lemon and its juice and $2\frac{1}{2}$ teaspoons of sugar. Once they have fallen to a purée, sweeten to taste and either sieve or whiz briefly in a blender. Keep warm, covered with foil, or reheat just before serving.

Roast potatoes
There have to be roast potatoes and I find it easiest to peel and parboil them while the goose is cooking, then tip them into the roasting pan when I take it out of the oven to pour off the gravy and turn the bird over.

Passion fruit roulade
I don't serve this directly after the cheese course, when it would be too much of a good thing, but about an hour or so later.

large eggs – 6
superfine sugar – $\frac{1}{2}$ cup
lemons – 2
all-purpose flour – 2 heaped tablespoons
confectioners' sugar for dusting

For the filling:
lemon or orange curd – 1 cup
heavy or whipping cream – 1¼ cups
passion fruits, ripe and wrinkled – 12
superfine sugar, to finish

You will need a jelly roll pan measuring approximately 14 x 12in, with shallow sides. It doesn't matter if it is just a few inches out either way.

Set the oven to 400°F. Line the pan with a piece of baking parchment, making sure it comes up the sides.

Separate the eggs, putting the yolks into a food mixer and the whites into a bowl large enough in which to beat them. Add the sugar to the yolks and whisk until thick, pale and creamy.

Grate the zest from both the lemons, taking care not to include the bitter white pith underneath, and squeeze the juice of one of them. Beat the egg whites until they are thick and capable of standing in a soft peak, then fold the juice and zest into the egg yolk and sugar mixture, followed by the sifted flour and then the egg whites. Add the egg whites slowly, firmly but gently, so the air is not knocked out of them as you mix them in. It is crucial not to over-mix. Scoop the mixture into the lined pan, smoothing it gently out to the edges.

Bake for about ten minutes, until the top is very lightly colored and it feels softly set. Let it cool for a few minutes.

Put a piece of wax paper on a work surface, cover lightly with superfine sugar, then turn the roulade out on to it. The cake should be crust side down. I find this easiest to do if you are fairly forthright about it, just tipping the roulade out of its pan in one swift movement. Carefully peel away the paper and cover the roulade with a clean, moist dish towel. It will be fine like this for an hour or two (I have even left them like this overnight and they have come to no harm).

When you are ready to roll the cake, remove the towel and spread the lemon or orange curd over the surface, then whip the cream until it will stand in soft peaks and spread it over the curd. Cut eight of the passion fruits in half and spread the juice and seeds over the cream. Now take one short end of the wax paper and use it to help you roll up the roulade. If the surface cracks, then all to the good. Dust with confectioners' sugar and cut into thick slices, with the remaining passion fruit juice and seeds squeezed over each slice.
Enough for 10. Picture overleaf

**Boxing Day.
The best day
of the year**

I sometimes put in a turkey breast to roast late on Christmas Day, for the Boxing Day sandwiches, which I eat with crisp bacon, spicy chutney and shredded raw vegetables. This year there is no need, there being cold roast pork and goose, both of which make cracking sandwiches if you remember to put enough salt on them. This year there are cries for something hot too, so I end the festivities with a sandwich and a pile of rustling, salty fritters.

I add bacon to my Boxing Day sandwich: unsmoked by choice, crisply fried and present in only slightly smaller quantities than the turkey itself. Chutney, an essential rather than a luxury, could be home-made but is more than likely to be one of the eight jars that will no doubt have turned up under the tree. I vote for a recipe hot enough to clear the sinuses, a pickle that blows away the lethargy that goes hand in hand with Yuletide eating. Then lastly, something crunchy such as sticks of raw carrot or pickled cabbage or even slices shaved from a crisp apple. Sometimes I toast the bread, sometimes I don't. But if I do, then I do it lightly, so that the bread is still softly yielding. Butter or mayonnaise is a no-no unless you forfeit the chutney.

That's my sandwich, and it doesn't have to be goose or pork, or even turkey. The stripped meat from duck, chicken, pheasant or partridge will do too, as will thinly sliced roast pork or beef, in which case I will attempt to unscrew the lid from the pickled walnuts or slather over a spoonful of tomato chutney. The rule with any meat sandwich is to have lashings of meat but sliced as thinly as you can. Few things are less digestible than cold meat cut too thick. If beef is what we have, then I sometimes make a mustardy dressing to drizzle over the slices of meat and salad leaves (olive oil, Dijon mustard, sherry vinegar, grated Parmesan, salt, pepper). Watercress is by far the most suitable leaf here, but keeping it in good nick till Boxing Day is the hardest part. I keep mine in the coldest part of the fridge, upside down in a bowl of ice cubes and water.

You can chuck the horseradish sauce. Let me tell you that the best seasoning for a cold, rare beef sandwich is wasabi mayonnaise. You need quite a bland mayo for this (olive oil is intrusive here), so the bought stuff is fine. Just stir in as much fiery green wasabi paste as you dare, tasting as you go. Remember that your taste buds will become attuned to the increasing heat, so offer the final tasting bit to anyone who passes. When it has enough of a kick to be of interest, add a squeeze more, then spread it thinly over the beef rather than the bread.

Cheese bubble and squeak

equal quantities by volume of boiled potatoes and greens
a handful or two of crumbled cheese
a little chopped thyme
fat or oil for frying

The potatoes will need mashing, but a rough mash is perfectly appropriate here. If you are using cooked greens, they must be lightly

cooked and still with a bit of vigor. If not, cook fresh sprouts, cabbage or broccoli, then drain and roughly chop them. Quantities can be imprecise, but half and half works well. Fold the greens into the mashed potatoes with the cheese, some salt, black pepper and a little chopped thyme if you have some. Squash the mixture together with your hands to form thick patties that will fit into the palm of your hand, with a little flour if you are getting sticky, then fry them in hot, shallow fat or oil till they are crisp on both sides. The best of these I have ever made involved using up a wedge of unexciting supermarket Brie that melted delectably into the potato cakes, putting the cheese successfully out of its plastic-wrapped misery.

Now is also the time to open those jars of pickles, preserves and tracklements you got in your stocking. Otherwise they will only work their way to the back of the cupboard and sleep quietly past their sell-by date. My rule of thumb with the more unusual jars, such as pickled samphire, carrot and onion relish or perhaps someone's home-made piccalilli, is to open them and scatter them around the table to accompany a platter of hot sausages and mash. Even the bizarre seem to find a fan. It is the most successful way I know to rid myself of yet another jar of someone's pickle harvest.

I have mentioned elsewhere my idea of warming yesterday's cold Christmas pudding in a frying pan in a little butter. I stir the disintegrating slices round in a frying pan with some melted butter till they are as hot as I can get them without risk of burning, then pour over a swoosh of cream. It's not a bad way to see off the celebrations.